PRO-CHOICE/PRO-LIFE

Recent Titles in
Bibliographies and Indexes in Sociology

Pacific Island Studies: A Survey of the Literature
Miles M. Jackson, editor

Alcohol and the Family: A Comprehensive Bibliography
Grace M. Barnes and Diane K. Augustino, compilers

Housing and Racial/Ethnic Minority Status in the United States:
An Annotated Bibliography with a Review Essay
Jamshid A. Momeni

Homicide: A Bibliography
Ernest Abel, compiler

Youth Information Sources: An Annotated Guide for Parents, Professionals,
Students, Researchers, and Concerned Citizens
Marda Woodbury, compiler
With a chapter on data bases compiled by Donna L. Richardson

Work and Alcohol Abuse: An Annotated Bibliography
John J. Miletich, compiler

Violence and Terror in the Mass Media: An Annotated Bibliography
Nancy Signorielli and George Gerbner, compilers

Latin America, 1983-1987: A Social Science Bibliography
Robert L. Delorme, compiler

Social Support Networks: A Bibliography, 1983-1987
David E. Biegel, Kathleen J. Farkas, Neil Abell, Jacqueline Goodin, and
Bruce Friedman, compilers

Diffusion of Innovations: A Select Bibliography
Klaus Musmann and William H. Kennedy, compilers

Native American Youth and Alcohol: An Annotated Bibliography
Michael L. Lobb and Thomas D. Watts

The Homosexual and Society: An Annotated Bibliography
Robert B. Marks Ridinger, compiler

PRO-CHOICE/PRO-LIFE

An Annotated, Selected Bibliography (1972–1989)

Compiled by
Richard Fitzsimmons
and
Joan P. Diana

Bibliographies and Indexes in Sociology,
Number 20

Greenwood Press
New York • Westport, Connecticut • London

Library of Congress Cataloging-in-Publication Data

Fitzsimmons, Richard.
    Pro-choice/pro-life : an annotated, selected bibliography
(1972-1989) / compiled by Richard Fitzsimmons and Joan P. Diana.
        p.   cm.—(Bibliographies and indexes in sociology, ISSN
0742-6895 ; no. 20)
    Includes index.
    ISBN 0-313-27579-3 (alk. paper)
        1. Abortion—United States—Bibliography.   2. Pro-choice movement—
United States—Bibliography.   3. Pro-life movement—United States—
Bibliography.   I. Diana, Joan P.   II. Title.   III. Series.
Z6671.2.A2F48   1991
[HQ767.5.U5]
016.3634'6'0973—dc20   91-12625

British Library Cataloguing in Publication Data is available.

Library of Congress Catalog Card Number: 91-12625
ISBN: 0-313-27579-3
ISSN: 0742-6895

First published in 1991

Greenwood Press, 88 Post Road West, Westport, CT   06881
An imprint of Greenwood Publishing Group, Inc.

Printed in the United States of America

The paper used in this book complies with the
Permanent Paper Standard issued by the National
Information Standards Organization (Z39.48-1984).

10 9 8 7 6 5 4 3 2 1

This bibliography is dedicated to all those
inquiring minds seeking information on the
Pro-choice/Pro-life question.

CONTENTS

Preface   ix

Introduction   xi

Bibliography   1

Subject Index   243

PREFACE

The origin of this bibliography comes from the need of students, teachers, lawyers, theologians, researchers, and laymen to have information on the "pro-choice/pro-life" issue, so that they may reach an informed decision on this subject.

It is the purpose of this work to provide access to the literature published in the United States on the pro-choice/pro-life issue, interrelating abortion, birth control, contraception, and family planning.

A work of this scope cannot be successfully undertaken without a great deal of assistance. The compilers specially note the thousands of interlibrary loan requests processed by the University Libraries of Penn State; to a great extent that library system supplied actual copy for review from its own collection; to a lesser degree it supplied library locations nationwide. We acknowledge our Penn State colleagues who worked with us in obtaining resource materials, especially Noelene Martin, Head of Interlibrary Loan Services, Lynn Thornton, Claudia Kwiatek, Marcia Nelson, Judy I. Carr, Janice Lopasky, Barbara Senepedis, and Mary Monahan. In addition, M. Richard Wilt, Natalie Logan, and the late John T. Corrigan provided a variety of indices, and Nancy Kane edited the text. Dr. William Clennell and the staff of the Bodleian Library were most helpful during Fitzsimmons' post-doctoral coursework at Oxford University.

The compilers received Research Development Grants from Penn State for this work. In addition, Fitzsimmons acknowledges a sabbatical leave and faculty stipends from Penn State and a Continuing Education Grant from the Pennsylvania Library Association.

Any errors or omissions in the text are the sole responsibility of the compilers.

INTRODUCTION

The subject of this work deals with the "pro-choice/pro-life" issue in American society.

It is the compilers' intention to provide standard bibliographic access to periodicals and monographs in print and non-print formats addressing this issue which have been published in the United States between January 1972 and December 1989. These dates provide coverage on the subject preceding the Roe v. Wade decision (January 22, 1973), through and following the Webster v. Reproductive Health Services decision (July 3, 1989). The intervening years witnessed further legal decisions and interpretations and unprecedented societal pressures--political, ethical, moral/religious, as well as scientific discovery and the tone set by the Reagan presidency. From each of these influences, contrasting points of view are represented.

The idea for this bibliography resulted from discussions with professional colleagues and students at the higher education and secondary school levels, public library patrons and members of the legal profession.

A review of the literature indicates that for the 1972-1989 period, there is no timely, annotated bibliography providing access to pro-choice/pro-life resource materials. Each item has been personally examined and annotated by the compilers.

It is very important to note that these items are accessible through public, academic, and school libraries. They are not esoteric or privately owned resources. Its timeliness is evident based upon the present judicial review of existing federal and state court decisions, as well as the public's need for a review of pertinent literature on the subject.

Objective, descriptive annotations are supplied by the compilers for each item cited. The annotations have not been written from an evaluative or judgmental basis. That analysis properly resides with the end-user. Further, inasmuch as this publication is not a buyer's guide, information on International Standard Book Numbers (ISBN), International Standard Serial Numbers (ISSN), Library of

Congress Card Numbers (LC), and price of items is not
supplied. This publication is not a publishers' or
producers' record of output. Publications such as
Cumulative Book Index (CBI) and Books in Print (BIP)
should be consulted to satisfy this need.
    The scope of the work is twofold:
1) It is a "selected" bibliography in that the compilers
have conscientiously rejected articles dealing with
other areas of concern on the subject, for example,
contraceptive devices, "how to" methods, abortion clinic
bombings, euthanasia, and solely medical aspects, such
as, articles dealing with the relationship of strokes
and "the pill." Articles that peripherally discuss
abortion among other social policies and concerns,
for example, school prayer and job quotas, are also
excluded.
2) It is a "comprehensive" bibliography in that the compilers have listed all materials fitting the parameters
of the research, namely, ethical, legal, moral/religious,
social, and medical to the extent not excluded above, as
well as items reflecting positions of the Planned Parenthood Federation of America, the Pro-Choice, Pro-Life, and
Right-to-Life/Respect for Life movements.
    This bibliography does not contain newspaper articles
or "letters to the editor" columns included in periodicals.
Items in the bibliography are listed in a single
alphabetical arrangement with the author as the main
entry; if no author is noted, then they are listed by
title. Resources, regardless of medium of publication,
are interfiled in a simple word-by-word sequence, and the
entries are numbered consecutively. All citations are
assigned at least one subject heading, with the Library of
Congress Subject Headings (12th edition) serving as the
authority file.
    Concluding the work is an expanded subject index with
entry numbers in ascending order.
    The comprehensiveness, balance and objectivity of
this compilation, presented in the standard Modern Language Association of America (MLA) bibliographical format,
is advantageous to library researchers. In addition, it
will be a useful reference tool for counselors, social
workers, clerics, legal professionals and laymen.
    To the compilers' knowledge, this is the first time
both sides of this intensely debated question have been
listed bibliographically and fully annotated in the same
publication.

BIBLIOGRAPHY

1. Abas, Bryan. "Right to Life or Right to Lie?" <u>Progressive</u>
    June 1985: 24-25.

    Recounts how right-to-life centers mislead pregnant women in
    order to get them to come to their facilities.

2. Abcede, Jose C. "The Americas: Patterns Are Changing."
    <u>World</u> <u>Health</u> June 1984: 21-23.

    Family planning, encompassing family size, family
    patterns, population, abortion, and pregnancy, is part of
    maternal and child health care and is an essential element
    of primary health care.

3. <u>Abortion</u>. Videocassette. Bill Moyers Journal Series. WNET-
    TV, 1988. 60 min.

    Presents a discussion of the controversies surrounding the
    abortion issue.

4. "Abortion Ads: Fair or Foul?" <u>Advertising</u> <u>Age</u> 17 July 1989:
    20.

    Issue advertising--in which each side can speak to the public
    in words of its own choosing, unfiltered by the news media--can
    play a vital role in defining abortion issues.

5. "Abortion and Fairness." <u>Progressive</u> Sept. 1977: 9.

    Callous and discriminatory actions by the Carter administration,
    the U.S. Supreme Court, and Congress have turned the focus of
    the national debate over abortion from morality to money.

6. "Abortion and the Church." <u>America</u> 10 Feb. 1973: 110-11.

   <u>Roe</u> v. <u>Wade</u> placed the onus and responsibility for choosing
   life or death for the unborn child with the mother. Examines the
   need for new pastoral initiatives, particularly counseling for
   women.

7. "Abortion and the Constitution." <u>America</u> 19-26 July 1980: 24.

   Contends that the Hyde amendment--occasioned by the question of
   public funding for abortions for poor people--should become a
   permanent part of federal and state law.

8. "Abortion and the Court." <u>Christianity Today</u> 16 Feb. 1973:
   32-33.

   The U.S. Supreme Court explicitly allows states to create some
   safeguards for unborn infants regarded as "viable," but in view
   of the Court's overthrow of the abortion statutes of Texas, it
   appears doubtful that unborn infants now enjoy any protection
   prior to the instant of birth anywhere in the United States.

9. "Abortion and the Poor." <u>America</u> 2 Feb. 1980: 73.

   Judge John F. Dooling, Jr., rules that the federal government
   violates the constitutional rights of poor women by excluding
   them from "medically necessary abortions."

10. "Abortion and the Reagan Legacy." <u>New Scientist</u> 6 May 1989:
    20.

    The final irony of the abortion controversy may turn out to be
    in the personal and economic devastation wrought by the
    policies of the Reagan administration.

11. "Abortion and U.S. Protestants." <u>America</u> 24 Feb. 1973: 156-57.

    Underscores similar and divergent opinions of various Protes-
    tant denominations in the United States regarding abortion,
    vis-a-vis the Catholic opinion.

12. "Abortion Anniversary." Editorial. <u>America</u> 3 Feb. 1979: 65.

    An editorial highlighting the increasingly bitter divisions
    among religious communities in the United States in regard to
    the issue of abortion and the law, in the face of the growing
    strength of the anti-abortion movement on the sixth anniversary
    of <u>Roe</u> v. <u>Wade</u>.

13. "Abortion Approved by Governments of East, West Germany."
    Christian Century 15 Mar. 1972: 299-300.

    West Germany approves abortions for medical, ethical, genetic,
    and social reasons. East Germany approves first-trimester
    abortions on demand.

14. "Abortion Around the World." Time 19 Feb. 1973: 76.

    A brief history of countries permitting or forbidding abortion
    for various reasons.

15. "Abortion Battle." Newsweek 4 Feb. 1974: 57.

    A summary article on the status of pro-choice and pro-life
    movements in the first year following Roe v. Wade.

16. "Abortion Bias: How Network Coverage Has Tilted to the Pro-
    Lifers." TV Guide 9 Nov. 1985: 6+.

    Anti-abortion forces acknowledge that the nightly news pays
    more attention to their side of the explosive issue.

17. "Abortion Bombings." Editorial. America 22 Dec. 1984: 413-14.

    Concludes that the bombing of abortion clinics is wrong on
    moral and tactical grounds and should be condemned by anyone
    who is pro-life.

18. Abortion Clinic. Videocassette. Dir. Mark Obenhaus. PBS
    Video, 1983. 52 min.

    Includes the actual abortion process from the counseling
    stage to post-abortion.

19. "Abortion Control Act Struck Down." Origins 25 Jan. 1979:
    497+.

    The U.S. Supreme Court ruled that the Pennsylvania Abortion
    Control Act (1974) is unconstitutional. The Court found the
    law unconstitutionally vague and objected to the use of the
    terminology "may be viable." The majority opinion of the
    Court appears here, followed by the dissenting opinion of
    three Court members.

20. "Abortion Decision." Commonweal 16 Feb. 1973: 435-36.

    The U.S. Supreme Court decision in favor of abortion is a fair
    measure of the growing secularization of American society and
    of the political impotence of the American Catholic church.

21. "Abortion Decision." _Scientific American_ Mar. 1973: 44-45.

    The U.S. Supreme Court's decision in _Roe_ v. _Wade_ relies
    mainly on the right of privacy implied by the Constitution and
    a finding that an unviable fetus is not a person within the
    meaning of the Fourteenth Amendment.

22. "Abortion Decision: A Death Blow?" _Christianity Today_ 16 Feb.
    1973: 48.

    Stresses that the _Roe_ v. _Wade_ decision drastically diminishes
    the constitutional guarantee of the right to life.

23. "Abortion Decision: A Year Later." _America_ 19 Jan. 1974: 22.

    Reflections on the impact and interpretation of _Roe_ v. _Wade_
    and discussion of the "conscience" clause as it developed in 17
    state legislatures.

24. "Abortion Double Standard: Medicaid vs. Health Insurance
    Coverage." _New Republic_ 15 Oct. 1977: 12.

    Federal government employees' health insurance funds virtually
    100 percent of costs for a legal abortion, while the Hyde
    amendment prohibits the use of Medicaid funds for abortions
    for the poor.

25. "Abortion Front: End of the Phony War." _National Review_ 2 Mar.
    1973: 249-50.

    Senator James Buckley says, "The Supreme Court has overturned
    not only a long line of legal precedent in this country, but
    more than two thousand years of humane wisdom."

26. "Abortion Funding." _Christianity Today_ 30 Dec. 1977: 40.

    President Carter signs an appropriation bill funding the
    Department of Labor and Department of Health, Education and
    Welfare (HEW), and establishing new rules for the allocation
    of tax money to end pregnancies.

27. "Abortion Issue: Move to Repeal New York State's Liberalized
    Law." _Time_ 22 May 1972: 23.

    A move to repeal New York State's abortion law draws President
    Nixon, Governor Rockefeller, Cardinal Cooke, and state legis-
    lators into the limelight.

28. "Abortion More Precious than $20 Million Grant: Wattleton."
    Jet 11 May 1987: 36.

Planned Parenthood says conditions to continue receiving $20 million federal grant are unacceptable.

29. "Abortion on Demand." _Time_ 29 Jan. 1973: 46-47.

Recounts the rationale employed by the U.S. Supreme Court in arriving at the _Roe_ v. _Wade_ ruling.

30. "Abortion on the Line." _National Review_ 4 Aug. 1989: 12+.

In _Webster_, the U.S. Supreme Court justices have created a new order with potential pitfalls for both pro-choice and pro-life.

31. "Abortion on Trial: Case of K. C. Edelin." _Newsweek_ 27 Jan. 1975: 55.

Dr. Edelin charged with manslaughter in the abortion of a "well-nourished male fetus."

32. "Abortion Payments Approved." _Christian Century_ 7 Aug. 1974: 767.

The U.S. House of Representatives votes on the Roncallo amendment; rejects the idea of not paying for abortions.

33. "The Abortion Perplex." _New Republic_ 11 July 1983: 7-8.

Poses the question: Are we justified in punishing transgressions against moral standards, even when the behavior involved is not deemed injurious to others?

34. "Abortion Ten Years Later." _Commonweal_ 28 Jan. 1983: 35-37.

We should avoid reducing the abortion dispute to slogans, making our peace with abortion, and putting all our hopes in the law or our energies into politics.

35. "Abortion Time Bomb." _New Republic_ 25 Feb. 1985: 4+.

The future of abortion may depend on developments in neonatology. Advances in medical technology might give a future court just the opportunity it needs to repeal the result of _Roe_ v. _Wade_ without brazenly rejecting its logic.

36. "Abortion Under the Law." _Scientific American_ July 1972: 51.

Presents statistics on abortion from socioeconomic and racial perspectives.

37. "Abortion's Changing Politics Keys House Turnabout." _Congressional Quarterly Weekly Report_ 5 Aug. 1989: 2020-23.

     Rejection of restrictions on District of Columbia funding is the first setback for abortion foes since 1980.

38. "Abortion, Coercion and Anti-Catholicism." _America_ 13 May 1972: 502.

     Pro-abortion groups are openly seeking to revive the latent anti-Catholicism endemic in American society.

39. "Abortion, Deterrence, Facilitation, Resistance." _America_ 2 June 1973: 506-07.

     Discusses three practical problems: 1) What should public policy be in the facilitation of abortion? 2) What should public policy be in applying "conscientious" objections? 3) What should Catholic policy be in resisting the consequences of abortion decisions?

40. "Abortion, Oui!" _Newsweek_ 11 June 1973: 46+.

     The 60-year-old abortion law of France comes under scrutiny.

41. "Abortion, Politics and the Bishops." Editorial. _Commonweal_ 23 Mar. 1984: 163-65.

     Explores the possible proper roles for the Catholic church's hierarchy in seeking social change through political activities and involvement.

42. "Abortion: A Severe Testing." _Commonweal_ 20 Nov. 1981: 643.

     Abortion is a matter that is morally problematic, pastorally delicate, legislatively thorny, constitutionally insecure, ecumenically divisive, medically normless, humanly anguishing, racially provocative, journalistically abused, personally biased, and widely performed.

43. _Abortion: A Woman's Guide_. Planned Parenthood of New York City. New York: Abelard, 1973.

     Discusses how pregnancy occurs, various methods of abortion, and alternative methods of birth control.

44. "Abortion: A Year Later." _Time_ 4 Feb. 1974: 60-61.

     A general report on the first anniversary of _Roe_ v. _Wade_ and an analysis by four regions of the country.

45. "Abortion: An Affirmative Public Good?" <u>Origins</u> 31 Jan. 1980: 534-35.

    The U.S. Supreme Court agrees to hear an appeal of the decision made by a federal district court judge in Chicago who held that the Hyde amendment is unconstitutional.

46. <u>Abortion: Challenges Ahead</u>. New York: Natl. Council of Jewish Women, 1985.

    Proceedings from a roundtable discussion on technology and its impact on abortion availability and policy.

47. "Abortion: Court Decision Removes Legal Uncertainty." <u>Science News</u> 27 Jan. 1973: 54.

    "... as used in the 14th Amendment, does not include the unborn." With these words U.S. Supreme Court Justice Harry A. Blackmun invalidates the anti-abortion laws of 31 states, requires the rewriting of similar statutes in 15 other states, and dashes the legal hopes of the right-to-life and anti-abortion forces.

48. <u>Abortion: Does Anyone Really Care?</u> Videocassette. Prod. Catholic Television Network. Catholic Television Center of Chicago, 1977. 56 min.

    The Reverend John Powell, author and theologian, discusses the issues of abortion and the right-to-life movement.

49. <u>Abortion: For Survival</u>. Videocassette. Dir. Melissa Jo Pettier. Fund for the Feminist Majority, 1989. 30 min.

    Contends that because contraceptives are not fail-safe, abortion remains a needed alternative for many women.

50. "Abortion: Next Round." Editorial. <u>Commonweal</u> 23 Mar. 1973: 51-52.

    Predictable developments following the January 22, 1973, U.S. Supreme Court decision striking down restrictive abortion laws in the United States were juridical problems for medical personnel and institutions with religious and ethical objections to easy and indiscriminate abortions.

51. "Abortion: On Whose Demand?" <u>America</u> 1 Apr. 1972: 335.

    In outlining its logic in proposing liberalized abortion reform, the presidential commission mentions two fundamental developments in our cultural tradition: "a tendency toward... the greater protection of life" and "a deep commitment...to individual freedom and social justice," with emphasis on the latter.

52. Abortion: Personal Portraits--231. Videocassette. Currents-- 1985-86 Season Series. WNET-TV, 1985. 30 min.

Examines the often painful decision of a woman to have an abortion and explores the reasons why that might be the best solution to a difficult situation.

53. Abortion: Right-to-Life vs. Right-to-Choice. Videocassette. Urban Scientific and Educ. Research Inst., 1979. 90 min.

Deals with both sides of the abortion issue through a mix of pretaped segments featuring the activities of two families on opposite sides of the issue and a live discussion with the audience and panelists.

54. "Abortion: The Agonizing Controversy." Senior Scholastic 2 May 1974: 15-16.

A concise statement on how abortion, the "dread secret of our society," came to be a heated debate in society. Cites court cases, key concepts, the "other [religious] views," and related matters.

55. "Abortion: The Debate Continues." Engage/Social Action Mar. 1983: 16-40.

A collection of six articles (pro and con), grouped together in Forum-91 on various aspects of the abortion question.

56. "Abortion: The Debate Goes On: Limiting Medicaid Funds for Abortions." Editorial. America 2 July 1977: 2.

An editorial providing an overview on the question of using federal Medicaid funds for abortions.

57. "Abortion: The Democrats Shift to the Right." Newsweek 25 May 1987: 21.

Democratic contenders for the 1988 presidential election shift to anti-abortion, remembering what happened to Geraldine Ferraro.

58. Abortion: The Divisive Issue. Videocassette. Video Free America, 1975. 28 min.

The pros and cons of abortion are discussed in interviews with leaders from both sides of the issue, including Henry Hyde, the

president of the National Right-to-Life Committee (NRLC), and
Bella Abzug, the president of the National Abortion Rights
Action League (NARAL).

59. "Abortion: The Edelin Shock Wave." Time 3 Mar. 1975: 54-55.

Judge James P. McGuire's decision in the Massachusetts case was
based on the jury's conclusion that Dr. Kenneth Edelin aborted
a living baby.

60. "Abortion: The Role of Public Officials." Origins 26 Apr.
1984: 759-60.

New York's Roman Catholic bishops say that public officeholders
who say they personally oppose abortion but do not wish to
impose their views on others are "radically inconsistent."

61. "Abortion: Women Speak Out." Life Nov. 1981: 45-52.

Yankelovich, Skelly, and White sample a cross section of 1,015
women from all across America. A consensus is strikingly
clear: Despite objections they might have on moral grounds,
not one major grouping believes that a woman should be legally
denied the right to choose to have an abortion if she deter-
mines that the procedure is necessary.

62. "Abortions for the Poor." America 19 Sept. 1981: 134.

In the year after the Hyde amendment went into effect,
Dr. Willard Cates, Jr., found that, nationwide, 94 percent of
the Medicaid-eligible women who wanted an abortion were able
to obtain one. Poor women who want abortions have continued to
have legal and safe abortions, according to a study by the
Center for Disease Control (CDC).

63. ACLU. ACLU Speakers Manual on Abortion. Chicago: Reproduction
Rights Project, Roger Baldwin Foundation of ACLU, 1982.

An American Civil Liberties Union (ACLU) manual intended to
educate the average concerned citizen on the need to speak out
in public on the abortion issue.

64. Adamek, Raymond J. "Abortion: A Pro-Life View." USA Today
May 1984: 98.

Pro-abortionists and pro-lifers agree that society is sometimes
faced with serious problems; pro-lifers do not agree that it is
right to kill to solve those problems.

65. Adler, Jerry. "Chicago's Unsilent Scream." _Newsweek_ 14 Jan. 1985: 25.

    A brief recounting of the motives that led Joseph M. Scheidler to found the Pro-Life Action League (PLAL) and the philosophies that drive him to continue his work.

66. "After the Webster Decision." Editorial. _America_ 29 July 1989: 51.

    Argues that the present abortion controversy may indicate a maturing of the national conscience.

67. "After 'Webster': An Uphill Struggle." _America_ 14 Oct. 1989: 227.

    Turning public sentiment in favor of a pro-life position into effective legislation will be an uphill battle.

68. Ainsworth, Martha. _Family Planning Programs, the Clients' Perspective_. Population and Development Series 1. Washington: World Bank, 1985.

    One in a special series of World Bank Staff Working Papers on population change and development.

69. Alan Guttmacher Institute. _Abortions and the Poor: Private Morality, Public Responsibility_. New York: Guttmacher Inst., 1979.

    A collection of essays on the Hyde amendment and its effect on minqrity women who are more heavily dependent on Medicaid for their medical care.

70. Alexander, Elizabeth, and Maureen Fiedler. "The Equal Rights Amendment and Abortion: Separate and Distinct." _America_ 12 Apr. 1980: 314-18.

    The evidence is clear: the equal rights amendment is not connected with abortion. Congress never intended such a link, and the U.S. Supreme Court has concurred in a long history of precedents basing abortion decisions on "due process" reasoning rather than theories of "equal protection."

71. Alexander, John. "Margaret Sanger: Pioneer of the Future." _Saturday Evening Post_ May-June 1977: 10+.

    A biographical article on Margaret Sanger.

72. Alexander, Shana. "The Politics of Abortion." _Newsweek_ 2 Oct. 1972: 29.

   This year the issue of abortion has been newly politicized. In the platform debates that preceded both political conventions, abortion was acknowledged as the underlying women's issue.

73. _____. "The Politics of Abortion." _Reader's Digest_ Mar. 1973: 69-71.

   In the long and bitter battle over abortion reform, the women of America are coming to realize that they can change their lot through political power.

74. Allen, J. J. "The Abortionist Dictionary: Gilded Words for Guilty Deeds." _Liguorian_ May 1973: 36-37.

   Suggests that to avoid psychic damage, it is important to disguise the facts and use general terms in describing abortion procedures.

75. Allen, James E. _Managing Teenage Pregnancy: Access to Abortion, Contraception, and Sex Education_. New York: Praeger, 1980.

   Provides community leaders and applied researchers with promising approaches for the evaluation of adolescent fertility management practices.

76. Almon, Vera. "Sexual Liberation, V.D. and Our Children." _America_ 24 Sept. 1977: 169-72.

   Family-planning groups have the obligation to think about the epidemic of venereal disease.

77. Alpern, D. M. "Abortion and the Law: Implications of K. C. Edelin's Conviction for Manslaughter in Boston Abortion Trial." _Newsweek_ 3 Mar. 1975: 18+.

   A Boston physician was convicted of a manslaughter charge in an abortion case. The fetus was 20 to 28 weeks old and considered viable by the jury.

78. "AMA Stand on Contraception." _Today's Health_ Feb. 1975: 55.

   A brief historical review of the American Medical Association (AMA) position on contraception, 1935 to date.

79. "America's War on Life." Symposium. _Triumph_ Mar. 1973: 17-32.

Addresses the current state of affairs regarding abortion in America following <u>Roe</u> v. <u>Wade</u>. Discusses the pro-life movement and its strategies, and the position of the Roman Catholic church.

80. Amidei, Nancy. "Get Beyond Labels: Pro-Life and Pro-Family Planning." <u>Commonweal</u> 31 Jan. 1986: 37-38.

The Kemp-Hatch bill would totally gut family planning and thus provide common ground for pro-life and pro-choice supporters to vote down the bill in the United States.

81. Anderson, Joan Wester. "Pro-Life Education: A Practical Parish Plan." <u>Liguorian</u> July 1981: 34-35.

Pro-lifers in a Chicago suburb think they may have found an answer: a simple, one-page fact sheet enclosed in parish Sunday bulletins and read regularly by thousands of families.

82. Anderson, P., et al. "Sexual Behaviour and Contraceptive Practice of Undergraduates at Oxford University." <u>Journal</u> <u>of</u> <u>Biosocial</u> <u>Science</u> 10 (1978): 277-86.

A study at Oxford reveals that the use of contraception increased with the frequency of intercourse and the stability of the relationship.

83. Anderson, Richard. <u>Abortion</u> <u>Pro</u> <u>and</u> <u>Con:</u> <u>Debater's</u> <u>Manual</u>. Los Angeles: Right-to-Life League of Southern California, 1974-82.

A training manual for right-to-life movement volunteers.

84. Anderson, Sharon. "Some Prochoice Advocates Acknowledge Pro-life Impact of Film Depicting an Abortion." <u>Christianity</u> <u>Today</u> 5 Apr. 1985: 46-47.

<u>The</u> <u>Silent</u> <u>Scream</u> film is "the most powerful thing the right-to-life movement has put out to date," says Allan Rosenfield, chairman of the board of the Planned Parenthood Federation of America (PPFA).

85. Andrews, Lori B. "Have You Had Enough Kids?" <u>Parents</u> Apr. 1985: 61+.

One, two, or more? Here's help in making the best decision.

86. Andrusko, Dave, ed. <u>A</u> <u>Passion</u> <u>for</u> <u>Justice:</u> <u>A</u> <u>Pro-Life</u> <u>Review</u> <u>of</u> <u>1987</u> <u>and</u> <u>a</u> <u>Look</u> <u>Ahead</u> <u>to</u> <u>1988</u>. Washington: Natl. Right-to-Life Committee, 1988.

Documents the various activities of the National Right-to-Life
Committee (NRLC) during 1987.

87. _____. The Triumph of Hope: A Pro-Life Review of 1988
and a Look at the Future. Vol. 4. Washington: Natl. Right-
to-Life Committee, 1989.

The fourth volume in a series of essays on the crucial legal
and political developments affecting the abortion controversy.

88. Annas, George J. "Roe v. Wade Reaffirmed." Hastings Center
Report Aug. 1983: 21-22.

The U.S. Supreme Court's message is clear: If states continue to
pass statutes that restrict a woman's access to abortion in
ways not permitted by its 1973 Roe v. Wade decision, the Court
will strike them down.

89. _____. "Webster and the Politics of Abortion." Hastings
Center Report Mar.-Apr. 1989: 36-38.

Reviews the background of the Roe and Webster cases.

90. "Another Double Standard." America 29 Oct. 1977: 274.

The "Call to Concern" campaign of public advertisements
attempts to extend the wall of separation between the religious
and moral commitments on which the United States has been
built, on the one hand, and its social and political processes,
on the other.

91. "Antiabortion Groups Lost a Major Battle Last Month."
Christianity Today 22 Feb. 1980: 49.

Judge John F. Dooling, Jr., rules that federal Medicaid funds
must be allowed for all abortions of "medical" necessity, and
thus overturns the so-called Hyde amendment.

92. "Anti-Abortion Groups Spar over Amendment Tactics."
Christianity Today 6 Feb. 1981: 84.

The National Right-to-Life Committee (NRLC) and the Moral
Majority meet to hammer out common acceptable terminology in
presenting their case to the U.S. Congress.

93. "Anti-Abortion: Not Parochial." Christianity Today 8 Aug.
1975: 22.

The anti-abortion position is not solely a Roman Catholic
issue, and to convince legislators of that, some distinguished

Protestant church figures form the Christian Action Council (CAC). They also claim that persons of other religions or no religion might also be against abortion.

94. Archer, Jules. _Famous Young Rebels_. New York: Messner, 1973.

   Aimed at young adults, this book contains a biographical sketch on Margaret Sanger.

95. "Arguing Life and Death: The Supreme Court Concludes Another Erratic Term--Often Confounding Both the White House and the Justices." _Newsweek_ 18 July 1983: 56.

   A report on the preoccupation of the U.S. Supreme Court in 1982-83 with the question of when life begins.

96. Armstrong, Tory. _Does God Still Bless America?_ El Cajon: Seashell, 1979.

   Attempts to rally Americans to take a stand, to return to Christian ethics, and to support our nation.

97. Arney, William R., and William H. Trescher. "Shifts in Public Opinion toward Abortion." _Intellect_ Jan. 1976: 280.

   Public opposition to abortion has dropped sharply over the past decade, particularly since the U.S. Supreme Court decision of January 1973 striking down restrictive abortion laws.

98. _____. "Trends in Attitudes Toward Abortion, 1972-1975." _Family Planning Perspectives_ May-June 1976: 117-24.   #1.

   Reports on trends and attitudes of American women on abortion, over a four-year period.

99. "As the Abortion Issue Reaches a Political Flashpoint, Two Catholic Experts Clash in Debate." _People Weekly_ 22 Oct. 1984: 93.

   John Willke, a right-to-life advocate, and Daniel Maguire, an

   ex-priest who favors abortion, answer questions from opposing perspectives, with a view to the 1984 presidential election.

100. Aseltine, Gwendolyn, and Ruth Pamenter. "The Planned Parenthood Association of Nashville." Diss. George Peabody College for Teachers, Vanderbilt U, 1977.

   A study of the development of the Planned Parenthood Association (PPA) of Nashville.

101. Ashford, Thomas. "Countdown to an Abortion." _America_ 12 Feb. 1977: 128-30.

A young woman contemplating an abortion receives an unusual offer from a family willing to adopt her child.

102. Ashkinaze, Carole. "The Battle Against Planned Parenthood: Can It Survive?" _Glamour_ Nov. 1984: 85-98.

Details of an agenda by pro-life lobbies and the federal administration to bring pressure on Planned Parenthood.

103. Ashley, Jan L. "The Relationship Between the Level of Moral Development and Birth Control Usage and Pregnancy Among Teenage Girls." Diss. U of Toledo, 1983.

A study that examines the relationship between the level of moral development, teenage pregnancy and birth control usage.

104. Asimov, Isaac. "No More Willing Baby Machines." _Harper's Bazaar_ Aug. 1972: 104-05.

A commentary on the social changes in contemporary times in regard to abortion and family planning.

105. Atkins, Gail. "The Moral Authority of a Natural Right to Life." Diss. U of Nebraska, 1981.

Shows how the shared moral conviction that all human beings have a natural right to life may be analyzed.

106. Atkinson, David John. _Life and Death: Moral Choices at the Beginning and End of Life._ New York: Oxford UP, 1985.

Covers the moral and ethical issues related to the right-to-life controversy.

107. Atkinson, Gary M. "The Morality of Abortion." _International Philosophical Quarterly_ 14 (1974): 347-62.

Says that the arguments commonly given in support of abortion cannot withstand careful scrutiny, either failing to meet the conditions required of a good reason or else serving to justify infanticide and involuntary euthanasia. Maintains that nothing but specious or arbitrary distinctions can be drawn between abortion, infanticide, and euthanasia as moral issues.

108. _____. "Persons in the Whole Sense." _American Journal of Jurisprudence_ 22 (1977): 86-117.

Contends that arguments for the moral justifiability of
abortion or infanticide on the grounds that the unborn or
newborn are not persons are fallacious.

109. Auerbach, Stephanie Kilby, et al. "Impact of Ethnicity."
Society Nov.-Dec. 1985: 38-40.

Not much attention has been given either to cultural determinants of sexual activity or to cultural barriers to contraceptive usage. After a long period of controversy over its
existence, role, and function in society, ethnic background,
as reflective of subcultural distinctions, is reemerging as
an important variable.

110. Axe, Kevin H. "Let's Lower Our Voices About Abortion." U.S.
Catholic June 1976: 14-15.

A Catholic journalist who has not made up his mind on the
abortion question is simply asking for the zealots on both
sides of the controversy to be aware that the undecided
exist; that they do care; that they do take abortion
seriously; that they wish they could come to a firm
decision; that they will continue to read and discuss
the matter.

111. Ayd, F., Jr. "Teenagers and Contraceptives." St. Anthony's
Messenger Feb. 1972: 51.

Discusses the doctor's dilemma: To prescribe a contraceptive
or to counsel chastity as having positive health value.

112. Bachmann, Gloria. "Contraceptive Failure in a College Population." Advances in Planned Parenthood 16 (1981): 34-38.

Evaluates the contraceptive practices of 172 college women who
requested a pregnancy test to rule out an unwanted pregnancy.

113. "Back to the Streets." Time 24 Mar. 1986: 39.

Eleanor Smeal leads a march in Washington, saying, "It's about
time we show our numbers"; claims demonstration meant to
underscore poll results showing a majority of popular support
for freedom of choice.

114. "Backlash on Abortion: Move to Repeal New York State's Liberal
Law." Newsweek 22 May 1972: 32.

New York's conservative legislature debates change in abortion
law, while President Nixon and Terence Cardinal Cooke line up
on opposite sides of the question from Governor Rockefeller.

115. Bader, Diana. "Medical-Moral Committee: Guarding Values in an Ambivalent Society." Hospital Progress Dec. 1982: 80-83.

   The Roe v. Wade decision has made privacy an overriding value by shifting decision-making responsibility from the public to the pregnant woman and her physician, "encapsuling them both within an alleged constitutionally protected 'zone of privacy.'"

116. Baer, Donald. "Now, the Court of Less Resort: Inside the Supreme Court During the Turmoil over Its Abortion Decision." U.S. News and World Report 17 July 1989: 26+.

   Analyzes the possible positions of the U.S. Supreme Court justices regarding the question of abortion.

117. _____. "The Politics of Abortion Takes an Unexpected Turn." U.S. News and World Report 31 July 1989: 26.

   After the U.S. Supreme Court's latest ruling, many politicians have been straddling the abortion controversy.

118. Baird, Robert M., and Stuart E. Rosenbaum, eds. The Ethics of Abortion: Pro-Life vs. Pro-Choice! Contemporary Issues in Philosophy. Buffalo: Prometheus, 1989.

   A compilation of essays on the moral and legal issues surrounding the abortion question.

119. Bajema, Clifford E. Abortion and the Meaning of Personhood. Grand Rapids: Baker, 1974.

   Aims to make a contribution in sensitizing those who read it to the magnitude of the moral issues involved in the abortion decision.

120. Baker, Don. Beyond Choice: The Abortion Story No One Is Telling. Portland: Multnomah, 1985.

   The story of a woman who chose to terminate three pregnancies by abortion.

121. Baker, James N. "The Church Strikes Back." Newsweek 18 Dec. 1989: 28.

   The clergy pressures pro-choice Catholic politicians.

122. Baldwin, Wendy. "Adolescent Pregnancy and Childbearing--An Overview." Seminars in Perinatology Jan. 1981: 1-8.

Statistics for various years through the 1960s and 1970s regarding fertility, birth rates, births by age and race, and births out of wedlock.

123. "Ballot Issues: Abortion and ERA." <u>Ms.</u> Dec. 1984: 76.

A report on various state abortion referenda and equal rights amendment (ERA) votes in the 1984 election.

124. Banks, Bill, and Sue Banks. <u>Ministering to Abortion's Aftermath</u>. Kirkwood: Impact, 1982.

Seeks to assist those women who have already had an abortion and those seeking to minister to them.

125. Banner, Lois W. <u>Women in Modern America: A Brief History</u>. New York: Harcourt, 1974.

In this history of the modern American woman, Margaret Sanger is depicted as a radical feminist.

126. "Baptism of Ire: Morreale Case." <u>Newsweek</u> 2 Sept. 1974: 75.

Recounts the difficulties experienced by a young mother who believed in pro-choice when she attempted to have her baby baptized at a local Catholic church, which refused the sacrament, and tells how the baptism was subsequently performed by an out-of-state Jesuit priest.

127. "Baptist Bombast." <u>Christianity Today</u> 12 Apr. 1974: 31.

Abortion is not just a Roman Catholic issue, despite a resolution from the American Baptist churches which can easily be so interpreted.

128. Barcus, Nancy B. "Thinking Straight About Abortion." <u>Christianity Today</u> 17 Jan. 1975: 8+.

Abortion is undesirable and it must be so considered for soundly stated biblical reasons, reasons that even skeptical readers will say sound clear enough if they have avoided the temptation to dismiss the issue emotionally, and as hastily as possible.

129. Barnes, Fred. "Abortive Issue." <u>New Republic</u> 4 Dec. 1989: 10-11.

Presents the ebbing of pro-life politics.

130. _____. "Tar Baby." New Republic 13 Feb. 1989: 12-13.

   Analyzes the position of the Bush-Quayle administration in
   regard to the pro-life agenda, particularly that of Secretary
   Sullivan.

131. Barr, Samuel J., and Dan Abelow. A Woman's Choice: The Best
   Modern Guide to Unplanned Pregnancy. New York: Rawson, 1977.

   Addresses the social issues related to a woman's decision
   whether or not to continue an unwanted pregnancy.

132. Barry, Robert Laurence. "The Human Life Federalism Amendment:
   A Moral and Critical Analysis." Diss. Washington: Catholic U,
   1984.

   Seeks to determine the moral and jurisprudential character of
   the human life federalism amendment and the influence of the
   amendment on those who endorse the official teachings of the
   Roman Catholic church.

133. Bartleson, Henrietta Lorraine. "The American Birth Control
   Movement: A Study in Collective Behavior with Especial
   Reference to N. Smelser's Model of Norm-Oriented Movements."
   Diss. Syracuse U, 1974.

   Examines and analyzes the birth control movement, emphasizing
   the legislative and judicial processes used.

134. Bartlett, Dewey F. "Abortion." Social Justice Review Feb.
   1974: 357-60.

   A congressional speech by Sen. Dewey Bartlett (Oklahoma) in
   support of the human life amendment, introduced by Sen. James
   Buckley (New York).

135. Baskin, Alex, ed. Woman Rebel. New York: Archives of
   Social Hist., 1976.

   A short biography of Margaret Sanger.

136. Bass, Medora S. "Birth Control Denied to the Mentally
   Retarded." Humanist Mar.-Apr. 1979: 51-52.

   Government regulations are making it almost impossible for the
   mentally retarded to use the two most popular, and among the
   safest, methods of birth control: sterilization and the drug
   depo-provera.

137. Batchelor, Edward, Jr., ed. <u>Abortion: The Moral Issues</u>. New York: Pilgrim, 1982.

Draws upon the writings of religious ethicists in order to survey the various perspectives of the abortion controversy.

138. Baum, Gregory. "Abortion: An Ecumenical Dilemma." <u>Commonweal</u> 30 Nov. 1973: 231-35.

Catholic theologians argue that the use of violence, as a licit means of birth control, is politically and culturally irresponsible.

139. Bauman, Karl E., et al. "Legal Abortions and Trends in Age-Specific Marriage Rates." <u>American Journal of Public Health</u> Jan. 1977: 52-53.

An examination of the relationship between legal abortions and age-specific marriage rates; contends that if legal abortions lead to postponement of marriage, the relationship between legal abortions and marriage rate trends should be stronger for younger than for older women.

140. _____. "The Relationship Between Legal Abortion and Marriage." <u>Social Biology</u> 22 (1975): 117-24.

Presents an analysis of the relationship between legal abortion and trends in the crude marriage rate among states in the United States. The hypothesis is that trends in marriage rates declined more in states with large numbers of legal abortions than in states with relatively few legal abortions.

141. Bausch, William J. "The Absence of Sweat: Abortion on Demand." <u>U.S. Catholic</u> Apr. 1972: 39-40.

Abortion on demand is an outgrowth of a society which reflects its value system in the laws it enacts and the traditions it follows. Abortion is a national question involving a country's basic values.

142. Beck, Melinda. "More Debate on Abortion." <u>Newsweek</u> 24 Sept. 1984: 27.

Bishop James C. Timlin, Diocese of Scranton, Pennsylvania, criticizes Geraldine Ferraro's stand on abortion; other prominent Roman Catholic leaders (political and clerical) explain their views.

143. Beck, Melinda, and Diane Weathers. "America's Abortion Dilemma." <u>Newsweek</u> 14 Jan. 1985: 20+.

Twelve years after a landmark court decision, the agonizing moral issue still divides the nation and defies compromise.

144. Behrens, Carl. "The Future of Abortion: Alternatives." Current Sept. 1973: 28-31.

Postulates that social change and technological advance lie behind the changes in the attitude towards, and the legal status of, abortion.

145. Belcastro, Philip A. The Birth-Control Book. Boston: Jones, 1986.

Seeks to increase knowledge about birth control, not to influence behavior.

146. Bender, David L., and Bruno Leone, eds. Teenage Sexuality: Opposing Viewpoints. Opposing Viewpoints Series. St. Paul: Greenhaven, 1988.

Presents opposing viewpoints about teenage attitudes toward sex, their sexual and reproductive rights, teenage pregnancy, sex education, and school-based clinics.

147. Benderly, Beryl Lieff. Thinking About Abortion. New York: Doubleday, 1984.

Provides many thought-provoking overviews of what has been written on abortion by authors ranging from biologists to philosophers.

148. Benecke, Mary Beth. "Rhythm: Ideal and Reality." America 15 Oct. 1977: 240-41.

Artificial contraceptives are often indicted for dehumanizing love, yet in the rhythm method such dangers are often not recognized.

149. Bennett, Owen. "Some Additional Arguments Against Abortion." Homiletic and Pastoral Review Jan. 1973: 50-53.

Discusses abortion-on-demand legislation under consideration or enacted in various states.

150. Benson, M. D. Coping with Birth Control. New York: Rosen, 1988.

Discusses various aspects of sexual activity and birth control for both male and female teens.

151. Berg, Elizabeth. "One Child? Sure! Two? Why Not? Three?... Maybe." _Parents_ Dec. 1986: 130+.

A couple discusses motives, disadvantages, and advantages (to their first child and to themselves) in having a second and third child.

152. Berger, Carol Altekruse, and Patrick F. Berger. "The Edelin Decision." _Commonweal_ 25 Apr. 1975: 76-78.

The Edelin verdict forces both sides to reexamine their positions very carefully and to do some hard thinking about when human life begins and the consequent rights of the fetus.

153. Berger, Gary S., William E. Brenner, and Louise Keith, eds. _Second-Trimester Abortion: Perspectives After a Decade of Experience_. Boston: PSG, 1981.

Articles deal with the scientific objectivity toward the health problems of women in relation to the abortion question.

154. Bermel, Joyce. "In the Aftermath of _Roe_ vs. _Wade_, a List of Ethical Issues." _Hastings Center Report_ Feb. 1983: 2-3.

How have attitudes toward health care altered in the decade since the abortion decisions of 1973? The author offers a suggestive list of recent developments that have had "a profound effect on the ministry of health care in Catholic hospitals."

155. Bernard, Anne. "The Born and the Unborn Alike." _America_ 26 Mar. 1977: 270-72.

Author argues, "Can't we get off our respective high horses, those of us who weep for the unborn and those of us who weep for the born, and come together? Our voices, joined, would grow a great deal louder, and, at last, credible."

156. Bernardin, Archbp. Joseph L., and Rabbi Richard S. Sternberger. "Ban All Abortions?" _U.S. News and World Report_ 27 Sept. 1976: 27-28.

Comprises the text of a debate between Archbishop Bernardin, president of the National Conference of Catholic Bishops (NCCB), and Rabbi Sternberger, chairperson of the Religious Coalition for Abortion Rights (RCAR).

157. Bernardin, Joseph L. Cardinal. "Consistent Ethic of Life: 'Morally Correct, Tactically Necessary.'" _Origins_ 12 July 1984: 120-22.

Demonstrates that the linkage between abortion and other issues
is both morally correct and tactically necessary to shape a
position cónsciously designed to generate interest in the
abortion question in individuals who thus far have not been
touched.

158. Bessis, Sophie. "Tomorrow's World." <u>World</u> <u>Press</u> <u>Review</u> Oct.
      1984: 40-41.

      Discusses the population question and cites rich-poor
      inequities.

159. "Beyond Personal Piety." <u>Christianity</u> <u>Today</u> 16 Nov. 1979: 13.

      Holds that the 1973 U.S. Supreme Court decision legalizing
      abortion settled the argument for many. But that decision
      should not settle anything for conscientious Christians.

160. Biale, Rachel. "Abortion in Jewish Law." <u>Tikkun</u> July-Aug.
      1984: 26-28.

      Concludes that in Jewish law there are a range of possible
      rulings on abortion, and that they are contradictory.

161. Bingham, Rebecca Saady. "The Abortion Battle Heats Up." <u>USA</u>
      <u>Today</u> Nov. 1979: 39-41.

      The question is, will abortion be legal by 1981? The 1980
      elections may be the deciding factor.

162. "Birth Control at School: Pass or Fail?" <u>Ebony</u> Oct. 1986: 37+.

      Proponents say contraceptives are necessary to fight teen preg-
      nancy; opponents argue that the pill has no right at school.

163. "Birth Control Blues." <u>Time</u> 4 Feb. 1974: 54.

      A Vatican spokesman has categorically denied that any revision
      of <u>Humanae</u> <u>Vitae</u>'s teaching was being planned.

164. "Birth Control Clinics in High Schools Brew Controversy Nation-
      wide." <u>Jet</u> 14 Oct. 1985: 10-11.

      Chicago's DuSable High School has become the focal point of a
      national controversy over the dispensing of contraceptives
      to students by public schools across the United States.

165. "Birth Control Clinics in Schools?" <u>U.S.</u> <u>News</u> <u>and</u> <u>World</u>
      <u>Report</u> 29 Sept. 1986: 82.

Pro and con arguments by Laurie Zabin and the Reverend Leo Maher.

166. "Birth Control for Men: The Pill, Ultrasound, Vaccines." Science Digest Aug. 1974: 62-63.

If birth control research programs now in progress fulfill their promise, men may soon be able to take the pill, get zapped by infrared or ultrasound, or even use a birth control vaccine to keep themselves from impregnating women.

167. The Birth Control Movie. Videocassette. Prod. Planned Parenthood of South Palm Beach. Perennial Education, 1982. 24 min.

Places the responsibility for subject expansion on the instructors. It can also be used with parents seeking closer parent-teen communications.

168. Birth Control: Myths and Methods. Videocassette. Churchill Films, 1986. 26 min.

To encourage sexually active teens to consider contraception, myths are explored and birth control methods are discussed.

169. "Births and Economic Growth." Futurist Sept.-Oct. 1986: 56.

Developing nations benefit by slowing population growth, according to the National Research Council (NRC).

170. "The Bishops and the Abortion Amendment." America 21 Nov. 1981: 312.

Recognizing that enactment of an amendment that would totally ban abortion throughout the country is virtually impossible, Archbishop Roach and Cardinal Cooke have decided to support the one step that is immediately feasible: restoration of the authority of Congress and the state legislatures over the subject of abortion.

171. "The Bishops' Plan for Pro-Life Activities." America 27 Dec. 1975: 454-55.

American Catholic bishops approve a three-pronged "Pastoral Plan for Pro-Life Activities." The plan calls for three types of effort: 1) to inform and educate the general public about the abortion issues; 2) to help women who have problems with their pregnancies or who have had abortions; 3) to secure anti-abortion laws from the legislative, judicial, and administrative departments of government.

172. Biskupic, Joan. "Abortion Protagonists Gird for Crucial Court
      Test." Congressional Quarterly Weekly Report 8 Apr. 1989:
      753-58.

      No matter what the outcome, a new flurry of activity seems
      certain in Congress and state legislatures on the abortion
      issue.

173. _____. "Justices Give Few Clues in Key Abortion Case."
      Congressional Quarterly Weekly Report 29 Apr. 1989: 973-75.

      The questioning is pointed in arguments over a woman's rights
      versus "potential life."

174. _____. "New Limits on Abortion Rights Are Upheld by 5-4
      Majority." Congressional Quarterly Weekly Report 8 July 1989:
      1698-1700.

      The battle shifts to the states and Congress, with both sides
      vowing to elect lawmakers and governors who agree with them.

175. Bissell, Roger. "A Calm Look at Abortion Arguments." Reason
      Sept. 1981: 27-31.

      Legislation relating to abortion must hinge on the question,
      When does the right to life begin?

176. "Bitter Abortion Battle." Time 11 Dec. 1972: 32.

      The Pennsylvania legislature adopts a conservative abortion
      bill, only to have Governor Shapp veto it. State Senator
      Cianfrani is exposed as a hypocrite.

177. "Black Judge Increases Penalty Against Bishops." Jet 26 May
      1986: 8.

      A black federal judge in New York recently enlarged his
      contempt-of-court penalty against the nation's Catholic
      bishops, ordering them to pay legal fees of a pro-choice
      group challenging the church's tax-exempt status.

178. Blaes, Stephen M. "Litigation: Preparation and Response."
      Hospital Progress Aug. 1973: 70+.

      Questions of how the Catholic hospital responds to abortion-
      demanding litigation generates mixed emotions.

179. Blake, Judith. "Teenage Birth Control Dilemma and Public
      Opinion." Science 18 May 1973: 708-12.

Presents public views on the controversy surrounding unwanted, illegitimate pregnancies among minors as reported to the President and Congress by the Commission on Population Growth and the American Future (CPGAF), which recommended a birth control policy to lessen unwanted pregnancies among unmarried minors.

180. Blank, Robert H. "Judicial Decision Making and Biological Fact: Roe vs. Wade and the Unresolved Question of Fetal Viability." Western Political Quarterly 37 (1984): 584-602.

Examines one instance of a major U.S. Supreme Court decision which relied heavily on biological fact in making its ruling and which now, over a decade later, remains one of the most divisive political issues "irresolvable by ordinary political processes." The most serious challenge to the Court's ruling might evolve from advances in prenatal intervention and in neonatal intensive care that are altering the biological basis upon which the Court built its decision.

181. Blockwick, Jessma Oslin. Pro-Choice Is Pro-Life. Nashville: Abingdon, 1979.

A study contending that while abortion is an issue with many aspects, at heart it is a religious issue.

182. Bluford, Robert, Jr., and Robert E. Petres. Unwanted Pregnancy: The Medical and Ethical Implications. New York: Harper, 1973.

Investigates the causes, methods, and moral implications of abortion on demand.

183. Blumberg, Bruce D., and Mitchell S. Golbus. "Psychological Sequelae of Elective Abortion." Western Journal of Medicine Sept. 1975: 188-93.

Women undergoing abortion for socioeconomic or psychosocial reasons appear to be at minimal risk for long-term negative psychological sequelae. In contrast, women in whom abortion is carried out because of exposure to rubella and the risk of fetal malformation, maternal organic disease, or the prenatal diagnosis of a genetically defective fetus are at greater risk and may need supportive psychotherapy.

184. Bond, Jon R., and Charles A. Johnson. "Implementing a Permissive Policy: Hospital Abortion Services After Roe v. Wade." American Journal of Political Science 26.1 (1982): 1-24.

Three hypotheses are tested--community preferences, incentives and disincentives, and organizational norms--that past research identifies as possible explanations of variations in hospital abortion policies after <u>Roe</u> v. <u>Wade</u> (1973).

185. Bonnette, Dennis. "Is the United States to Become the Fourth Reich?" <u>Social Justice Review</u> July-Aug. 1980: 152-57.

Compares the wartime genocidal Nazi atrocities with those of pro-abortionists in the United States.

186. "Books, Babies, Birth Control, and How Some Schools Are Handling All Three." <u>Seventeen</u> Sept. 1986: 104-05.

A Minnesota high school offers in-building day-care centers for teenage student-mothers.

187. Bopp, James, Jr., ed. <u>Restoring the Right to Life: The Human Life Amendment</u>. Provo: Brigham Young UP, 1984.

Discusses the legal and ethical ramifications of abortion, the impact of abortion on demand, and the possible consequences of an amendment to the U.S. Constitution restricting abortion.

188. Borras, Vickie A. "Birth Control Knowledge, Attitudes and Practice: A Comparison of Working and Middle-Class Puerto Rican and White American Women." Diss. U of Massachusetts, 1984.

Discusses the implications for birth control programs and future research.

189. Boyle, Joseph M. "That the Fetus Should Be Considered a Legal Person." <u>American Journal of Jurisprudence</u> 24 (1979): 59-71.

Addresses the question of whether those opposed to a permissive legal policy are "imposing their morality" in a way that is inconsistent with the American traditions of tolerance and justice.

190. Bozell, L. "The Life Movement: Quo Vade? II." <u>Triumph</u> May 1974: 15.

The attempt to amend the Constitution with an anti-abortion provision never was realistic. It was, quite simply, undertaken and supported because of the civic piety of the vast majority of the pro-life constituency.

191. Bracken, Michael B. "Psychosomatic Aspects of Abortion: Implications for Counseling." <u>Journal of Reproductive Medicine</u> Nov. 1977: 265-72.

Asks whether there is a need for abortion counseling in the light of more relaxed laws and the easier accessibility of abortion; examines the question of appropriate techniques for abortion counseling; delineates the needs of special abortion clients; and, lastly, looks at some of the more interesting directions abortion counseling may take in the future.

192. Bracken, Michael B., and Mary E. Swigar. "Factors Associated with Delay in Seeking Induced Abortions." American Journal of Obstetrics and Gynecology 1 June 1972: 301-09.

Women between the 11th and 20th weeks of pregnancy were significantly more likely to be under 21 years of age, single, black, Protestant, have no children or one living child, not have completed high school, not have used a contraceptive at the time of conception, and to have been referred through clinic or university services.

193. Bracken, Michael B., et al. "Abortion Counseling: An Experimental Study of Three Techniques." American Journal of Obstetrics and Gynecology 1 Sept. 1973: 10-20.

One hundred and seventy-one abortion patients were randomly assigned to three defined counseling procedures (group orientation, group process, and individual). These data were collected: circumstances surrounding the pregnancy (before counseling); reaction to the counseling session (after counseling but before abortion); response to abortion (after the abortion).

194. Bracken, Michael B., Gerald Grossman, and Moshe Hachamovitch. "Contraceptive Practice Among New York Abortion Patients." American Journal of Obstetrics and Gynecology 1 Dec. 1972: 967-77.

Data is presented describing contraception among 1,022 women during the 12 months preceding induced abortion.

195. Bracken, Michael B., Moshe Hachamovitch, and Gerald Grossman. "Correlates of Repeat Induced Abortions." Obstetrics and Gynecology Dec. 1972: 816-25.

Repeat aborters are more likely to be victims of contraceptive failure, which, in turn, is associated with unstable personal relationships and social situations.

196. Brandmeyer, Gerard A. "Politics and Abortion." Commonweal 1 July 1976: 432-33.

One of the major surprises of this presidential campaign was the early success of the pro-life movement in maneuvering abortion policy into the foreground as the burning issue which would make or break any candidate.

197. Brandt, Carol L., Francis J. Kane, and Charles A. Moan. "Pregnant Adolescents: Some Psychosocial Factors." Psychosomatics 19 (1978): 790-93.

Describes the evaluation of 47 unwed pregnant adolescents compared with a group of nonpregnant volunteers matched for age, class, and socioeconomic group.

198. Breig, James. "Family Planning Clinic at St. Peter's, Albany." Hospital Progress Dec. 1973: 28+.

St. Peter's Hospital, Albany, New York, houses a federally funded clinic that teaches the sympto-thermic method of family planning.

199. _____. "The Sin of Birth Control: Gone But Not Forgotten." U.S. Catholic Jan. 1979: 6-12.

Breig suggests that perhaps the biggest gap between the teaching church and the learning church is in the morality of contraception.

200. Breitman, P. How to Persuade Your Lover to Use a Condom: And Why You Should. New York: St. Martin's, 1987.

Intended for all sexually active people, regardless of gender, orientation, race, age, or life-style.

201. Bremner, William J., and David M. de Kretser. "The Prospects for New, Reversible Male Contraceptives." New England Journal of Medicine 11 Nov. 1976: 1111-17.

Reports on research being done on a new method of male contraception.

202. Brennan, William. The Abortion Holocaust: Today's Final Solution. St. Louis: Landmark, 1983.

Postulates that a knowledge of the kinship between past and current atrocities represents an indispensable step toward halting the modern resurrection of one of history's most monstrous chapters.

203. _____. "The Silent Holocaust." Liguorian Sept. 1982: 14-19.

Some enlightening parallels that link the holocausts of history with the senseless killing of unborn babies today.

204. Brennan, William C. "Abortion: Missouri HB 1470." Social Justice Review July-Aug. 1972: 129-32.

Text of Brennan's testimony at House hearing on Abortion Bill 1470, Jefferson City, Missouri, March 8, 1972.

205. _____. "The Vanishing Protectors." Social Justice Review Nov. 1973: 239-44.

Written in the first person, this article imagines the musings of an unborn, unwanted child talking to its mother, doctor, clergyman, U.S. Supreme Court justices, and so on, prior to its abortion.

206. Brewer, Michael F. "The Abortion Controversy: Ancient Practice--Current Conflict." Current Sept. 1973: 26-29.

Abortion is as old as history. Acrimony surrounds it, understandably so. Modern medicine has made it relatively safe, but undergoing it raises serious religious, legal and ethical questions.

207. "Brief Attack: Meese Goes After Abortion Law." Time 29 July 1985: 24.

The Justice Department says, "The basis for Roe v. Wade is so far flawed and is such a source of instability in the law that this court should reconsider that decision and on reconsideration abandon it."

208. Briscoe, Clarence E. Abortion: The Emotional Issue. Bryn Mawr: Dorrance, 1984.

Examines why and how a woman chooses to have an abortion.

209. Brix, James A. "Looking Past Abortion Rhetoric." Christian Century 24 Oct. 1984: 986-88.

Abortion is an issue so emotional, so divisive, that Christians who would normally engage in dialogue about the most controversial of matters find it easier to change the subject when this one comes up.

210. Broderick, Albert. "A Constitutional Lawyer Looks at the Roe-Doe Decisions." Jurist 33 (1973): 123-33.

Attempts to demonstrate that the Roe-Doe decisions were reached without respectable foundation in law and constitute (as a dissenting justice bluntly wrote) "an improvident and extravagant exercise" of "raw judicial power."

211. Brody, Boruch A. Abortion and the Sanctity of Human Life: A Philosophical View. Cambridge: MIT, 1975.

Presents the major viewpoints on abortion, with each argument measured against two standards: Is it logically valid? Are its premises true?

212. Brogger, Svend. "Health, Population and Development." World Health June 1984: 18-20.

During the past 10 years, the subject of family planning--along with other population issues--has become respectable. Now the problems of fertility and morality must receive due consideration from the planners, up to and beyond the year 2000.

213. Bromberg, Sarah. Abortion, Morality and Science. Berkeley: Dianic, 1984.

Rejects the scientific community's claims to authority in the belief that today's women have the maturity and insight to know truth and propriety in their own lives and to make decisions about their own abortion or birthing.

214. Brooke, C. P. "Legalized Abortion." Catholic Mind May 1972: 24-34.

The author, both a lawyer and a physician, treats the medical and legal aspects of abortion.

215. Browder, Clifford. The Wickedest Woman in New York: Madame Restell, the Abortionist. Hamden: Archon, 1988.

A biography of Ann Lohman, alias Madame Restell, who practiced openly as an abortionist in New York for nearly 40 years in the middle of the nineteenth century.

216. Brown, Harold O. J. Death Before Birth. Nashville: Nelson, 1977.

Examines the problems of child abuse in the light of current attitudes toward abortion.

217. _____. "An Evangelical Looks at the Abortion Phenomenon." America 25 Sept. 1976: 161-64.

Protestants, no less than Catholics, can say that their
tradition firmly condemns abortion.

218. Brown, Judie, and Paul Brown. Choices in Matters of Life and
Death. Avon: Magnificat, 1987.

Authors' answers to readers' questions about the facts they
need to know before deciding on an abortion.

219. Bryce, Edward. "Abortion and the Hatch Amendment." America
6 Mar. 1982: 166-68.

After years of trying to defend the rights of the unborn by
defining personhood, the American Catholic bishops have
switched their strategy. The new proposal has sparked
criticism from both pro-life and pro-choice groups.

220. Buckley, Michael. "Current Technology Affecting Supreme Court
Abortion Jurisprudence." New York Law School Law Review
4 (1982): 1221-60.

In this article, Roe and its progeny are analyzed so that
the current state of abortion jurisprudence may be ascertained.
Secondly, the advancements in fetal technology, and fetology
generally, since 1973 are surveyed. Finally, implications of
the changing fetal sciences on the Roe decision are analyzed
and discussed.

221. Buckley, William F. "The Abortion Decision." Catholic Digest
May 1973: 41-42.

A general article chiding the U.S. Supreme Court decision.

222. _____. "Dear Bob, You Should Stand Alone." National
Review 25 Apr. 1986: 63.

Columnist William F. Buckley, Jr., offers his perspective on
Sen. Robert Packwood's pro-choice policy.

223. Bueler, William M. "The Need for an American Population
Policy." USA Today Sept. 1985: 44-46.

No decision this society could make in the next generation,
short of avoiding nuclear catastrophe, could win such gratitude
from future generations as the institution of a policy aimed
first at stopping population growth and then at reducing the
population to an optimum level.

224. Bunson, Maggie. "Abortion and American Pluralism." Social
Justice Review Nov.-Dec. 1981: 198-204.

Contends that the American pluralist system, that process by which Americans debate and discuss issues sanely in a public arena, was almost destroyed by those forces which initiated and then institutionalized abortion on demand.

225. "The Burger Course." National Review 9 Aug. 1985: 18.

The Justice Department petitions the U.S. Supreme Court to reverse its ruling in Roe v. Wade.

226. Burnell, George M., William A. Dworsky, and Robert L. Harrington. "Post-Abortion Group Therapy." American Journal of Psychiatry Aug. 1972: 220-23.

Two hundred fifty women who had undergone a therapeutic abortion attended a group therapy program designed to help patients cope with guilt feelings and to clear up areas of misinformation about sexual function and contraception.

227. Burns, Robert E. "The Morality of Birth Control: Unfinished Business?" U.S. Catholic Jan. 1981: 2-3.

A report on the contraception debate during the biennial synod of bishops in Rome.

228. _____. "The Prolife Agenda: Converts or Convicts." U.S. Catholic Apr. 1983: 2.

Contends that anti-abortionists are losing the battle because of exaggerated faith in legalistic remedies and that they would have greater success if they were consistent in respecting all life.

229. Burtchaell, James. "In a Family Way." Christianity Today 12 June 1987: 24-27.

The central question is this: Shall we have legal barriers that protect the unborn by restraining their mothers' freedom to abort?

230. _____. "Justifying Abortion." Sign Feb. 1982: 18+.

There are moral positions founded on principles, facts, reasoning; there are those rising out of raw, personal choice. It is impossible to argue with this second sort.

231. Burtchaell, James Tunstead. "Abortion: It Can't Be Left to Personal Choice." St. Anthony's Messenger Oct. 1984: 17-20.

Argues that abortion is much more than a matter of personal

choice, and that while all laws do curtail choice, organized society does benefit from them.

232. _____. The Limits of the Law: Reflections on the Abortion Debate. Chicago: Americans United for Life; Legal Defense Fund, 1987.

Draws from Judeo-Christian history, classic literature, and practical contemporary observation to argue that the abortion issue will not be ultimately resolved by civil law alone.

233. _____. Rachel Weeping and Other Essays on Abortion. Kansas City: Andrews, 1982.

A collection of moving, thought-provoking essays intended for the thinking person's argument against abortion.

234. _____. Rachel Weeping: The Case Against Abortion. New York: Harper, 1984.

A thinking person's argument against abortion.

235. "Bush's No-No on Abortion." Time 6 Nov. 1989: 30.

The President's twin vetoes slow the pro-choice momentum.

236. Butler, J. Douglas, and David F. Walbert, eds. Abortion, Medicine and the Law. 3rd ed., completely rev. New York: Facts on File, 1986.

Essays about the legal, ethical, and political aspects of the abortion issue.

237. Byrn, Robert M. "Confronting Objections to an Anti-Abortion Amendment." America 19 June 1976: 529-34.

A lawyer looks at the objections to a federal amendment voiced by certain Catholics and decides that, considering Wade's legal enormities, they are unpersuasive.

238. _____. "Goodbye to the Judeo-Christian Era in Law." America 2 June 1973: 511-14.

In declaring the unborn child a nonperson, the U.S. Supreme Court has purged the law of the Judeo-Christian ethic. It has also denied the unborn the shelter of the Fourteenth Amendment.

35

239. _____. "Judicial Imperialism." Hospital Progress Nov. 1977: 90+.

Forty years of U.S. Supreme Court decision on privacy and abortion.

240. _____. "Wade and Bolton: Fundamental Legal Errors and Dangerous Implications." Catholic Lawyer 19 (1973): 243-50.

Claims that a reading of Wade leads to the conclusion that the United States Supreme Court was influenced by its interpretation of the Anglo-American history of the law of abortion and that the Court's understanding of history is both distorted and incomplete.

241. Byrne, Harry J. "Abortion and Contraception: Apples and Oranges." America 3 Nov. 1984: 272-75.

Argues that it is disastrous to treat abortion and contraception equally in trying to form public opinion; it is also theologically inappropriate.

242. Cairns, Allen Lord. "Fighting for Life: Ideology, Social Networks and Recruitment of Activists to a Pro-Life Movement Organization." Diss. State U of New York at Buffalo, 1981.

Focuses on the 25 leaders and activists of Pro-Life Incorporated (PLI), examining the conditions and processes related to recruitment to social movement organizations.

243. Calder, Kathleen Anne. "The Viability of the Trimester Approach." U of Baltimore Law Review 2 (1984): 322-45.

An analysis which emphasizes the development of the Roe doctrine, the current division of the United States Supreme Court, and the validity and future applicability of Roe.

244. Califano, Joseph A., Jr. "Moral Leadership and Partisanship." America 29 Sept. 1984: 164-65.

A Catholic in public life has an obligation to enforce the law or resign. Resignation would remove a Catholic voice from government.

245. Callahan, Daniel. "An Alternative Proposal." Commonweal 16 Nov. 1973: 183-85.

What the Pope might have said in Humanae Vitae, but didn't.

246. _____. "Pro-Choice vs. Pro-Life Is a Moral Dilemma, Says
Daniel Callahan: We Carry Both Traditions Within Us."
People Weekly 12 Aug. 1985: 89+.

All people carry both traditions--pro-choice and pro-life--
within them and there is merit in both positions.

247. Callahan, Joan C. "The Fetus and Fundamentals Rights."
Commonweal 11 Apr. 1986: 203-09.

Argues that the reluctance of some politicians to support anti-
abortion legislation, despite their personal opposition to
abortion, is justified because the nonreligious case for the
unborn human's right to life is much less compelling than many
abortion opponents suppose.

248. Callahan, Sidney. "Abortion and the Sexual Agenda."
Commonweal 25 Apr. 1986: 232-38.

New feminist efforts to rethink the meaning of sexuality,
femininity, and reporduction are all the more vital as new
techniques for artificial reproduction, surrogate motherhood,
and the like present a whole new set of dilemmas.

249. _____. "The Court and a Conflict of Principles: An Anti-
Abortion View." Hastings Center Report Aug. 1977: 7-8.

The United States Supreme Court decision can be seen as only
the latest legal round in the continuing and deeply disturbing
ethical and moral disagreement over abortion.

250. Callahan, Sidney, and Daniel Callahan, eds. Abortion: Understanding Differences. New York: Plenum, 1984.

Presents arguments from both sides of the abortion debate.

251. Callahan, Sidney, and Daniel Callahan. "Breaking Through the
Stereotypes." Commonweal 5 Oct. 1984: 520-23.

A husband and wife weigh and order their differing values in
the abortion question.

252. Cameron, Paul. "Abortion, Capital Punishment and the Judeo-
Christian Ethic." Linacre Quarterly 48 (1981): 316-32.

Explores abortion and capital punishment in the context of
Judeo-Christian ethics.

253. "Can States Restrict a Minor's Access to Abortion?" Editorial.
Christianity Today 3 Apr. 1987: 44+.

A woman's right to an abortion: Lower courts as well as the
hight court remain uncertain about restrictions on the rights
of unmarried, underage girls.

254. Carlin, David R., Jr. "Abortion and Dialogue." <u>America</u>
      18 Aug. 1984: 64.

      The abortion controversy in the United States is not about to
      go away. If there is any domestic issue today that cries out
      for a dialogic approach, it is abortion. Each side has its
      lunatic fringe, but by and large both are composed of toler-
      ably rational persons of good will.

255. _____. "Abortion, Religion and the Law." <u>America</u> 1 Dec.
      1984: 356-58.

      Governor Mario Cuomo advanced two arguments (impracticality of
      enforcement and religious pluralism) for permitting Catholic
      policymakers to accept some forms of legalized abortion.

256. _____. "As American as Freeways: Abortion's Roots in Our
      Culture." <u>Commonweal</u> 1 July 1989: 392-93.

      Compares and contrasts <u>Roe</u> v. <u>Wade</u> to <u>Plessy</u> v. <u>Ferguson</u>.

257. _____. "The Dilemma of an Anti-Abortion Democrat."
      <u>Commonweal</u> 18 Nov. 1983: 626-28.

      Argues: "How can we continue to support a national party, how
      can we support its candidate for president, when that party and
      that candidate adopt a pro-choice position--that is, leaving
      euphemisms aside, a pro-abortion position?"

258. _____. "Patchy Garment: How Many Votes Has Bernardin?"
      <u>Commonweal</u> 10 Aug. 1984: 422-23.

      To be consistently pro-life, one should be against abortion,
      capital punishment, and nuclear arms. This article serves to
      situate the Catholic anti-abortion position within what may
      loosely be called a liberal or progressive framework of
      political thinking, and to rescue it from the conservative
      or right-wing ideology within which it is frequently found--
      for example, that of Jerry Falwell and his Moral Majority.

259. _____. "Rules for Liberals: Making Their Voices Heard."
      <u>Commonweal</u> 21 Sept. 1984: 486-87.

      Lists a Rhode Island state senator's rules for liberal anti-
      abortionists should they join the abortion debate.

260. _____. "A Tragedy Without Villains." _Commonweal_ 6 Oct
1989: 517-18.

Discusses the political battle over abortion.

261. Carlson, John. "Three Levels of Discussion about Abortion."
Dimension 8 (Spring 1976): 37-45.

Ethical theorists often distinguish three levels of discussion
in connection with moral topics. Here this approach is applied
to abortion. For each level a relevant question is posed,
together with three positions in response to it. One of the
positions is called "A Pro-Life Position"; the others,
"Contrary Positions."

262. Carlson, Margaret. "The Battle over Abortion." _Time_ 17 July
1989: 62-63.

A bitterly divided United States Supreme Court sets the stage
for the most corrosive political fight since the debate over
Viet Nam.

263. _____. "Can Pro-Choicers Prevail?" _Time_ 14 Aug. 1989:
28.

Feminists squabble over strategy for protecting abortion
rights.

264. Carlson, Ruth Anna. "Patient, Physician, Society: Whose
Rights at Stake in 'Life' Issues." _Hospital Progress_ Dec.
1982: 53-59.

Cases regarding informed consent, sterilization, and wrongful
birth/wrongful life have filled court dockets in the past 10
years.

265. Carmen, Arlene, and Howard Moody. _Abortion Counseling and
Social Change: From Illegal Act to Medical Practice_. Valley
Forge: Judson, 1973.

Not just about abortion, but about people, their laws, their
prejudices, and the forces that sometimes change them.

266. Carmody, Denise Lardner. _The Double Cross: Ordination,
Abortion, and Catholic Feminism_. New York: Crossroad, 1986.

Sketches aspects of the Christian world view that bear directly
on abortion.

267. Caron, Wilfred R. "The Human Life Federalism Amendment--An
      Assessment." Catholic Lawyer 2 (1982): 87-111.

      Presents a legal assessment of the human life federalism
      amendment and considers the principal questions posed by others
      dedicated to the protection of the unborn.

268. _____. "Legal Assessment: Human Life Federalism
      Amendment." Origins 14 Jan. 1982: 495-500.

      Wilfred R. Caron, U.S. Catholic Conference (USCC) general
      counsel, analyzes the human life federalism amendment--often
      called the Hatch amendment--to restrict abortion, concluding
      that it is a legally sound vehicle for attaining the maximum
      protection of the unborn.

269. Carr, Pamela, and Faye Wattleton. "Which Way Black America?"
      Home Journal May 1977: 102.

      Contrasts two opposing views on the abortion question.

270. Carro, Geraldine. "Another Child? Does It Make Sense?"
      Ladies' Home Journal May 1977: 102.

      Advances common misconceptions--myths--concerning the reason(s)
      for having a second child. What are the right reasons?
      There's only one: that you really want to be a parent and
      have a talent for it.

271. Carroll, W., et al. "Right to Life: Time for a New Strategy?"
      Triumph Jan. 1975: 11-16.

      Eight activists discuss whether or not pro-lifers need to
      develop a new constitutional strategy.

272. Carson, Mary. "One Mother's View of Birth Control and Sex in
      Marriage." St. Anthony's Messenger Aug. 1974: 38-42.

      Aware that she differs from the Catholic church, a wife of 20
      years and mother of eight reflects on how she and her husband
      have wrestled with the morality of contraception.

273. Casady, Margie. "Abortion: No Lasting Emotional Scars."
      Psychology Today Nov. 1974: 148-49.

      Research indicated that an abortion rarely damages a woman's
      emotional health; it often brings improvement.

274. "The Case for a Human Life Amendment." Origins 19 Nov.
      1981: 360-72.

40

The National Conference of Catholic Bishops (NCCB) says the
question before our legislators is not whether they will
"legislate morality," it is whether the morality reflected in
the law will be one which respects all human life or one which
legitimates the destruction of particularly inconvenient and
dependent human lives.

275. Castelli, Jim. "Anti-Abortion, the Bishops and the Crusaders."
      America 22 May 1976: 442-44.

      Some bishops have expressed private reservations about the
      national anti-abortion strategy. People want to know why
      these bishops do not speak up publicly. The main reason is
      that they do not want to be misunderstood, attached, or abused
      by pro-life people.

276. _____. "Catholic Church and Abortion." Progressive
      Apr. 1974: 9.

      The most visible Catholic church response to the United
      State Supreme Court decision has been support of the concept
      of a constitutional amendment prohibiting abortion.

277. _____. "Prolife, Prochoice Groups Claim Midterm Election
      Victories." Hospital Progress Dec. 1982: 18-19.

      An analysis of the voting choices and power blocks as a result
      of the 1980 election, as well as the 1982 mid-term election.

278. Castelli, Jim, et al. The Abortion Issue in the Political
      Process: A Briefing for Catholic Legislators. Washington:
      Catholics for a Free Choice, 1982.

      A monograph intended to assist the Catholic members of Congress
      who are charged with the task of developing sound public
      policy within the context of legalized abortion.

279. Castleman, Michael. "HEW and the Sexual Revolution: Why
      Teenagers Get Pregnant." Nation 26 Nov. 1977: 549-52.

      The Department of Health, Education and Welfare (HEW) is
      planning to ask Congress for $200 million for a four-year
      campaign to "combat the epidemic of premature pregnancy."

280. Castro, Janice. "Shutting the Door on Dissent: The Vatican
      Orders an End to Debate over Abortion." Time 7 Jan. 1985: 83.

      Pope John Paul II's position on abortion is firm and uncom-
      promising: It is morally wrong and equivalent to infanticide.
      It puts the Vatican in a confrontation with 24 American nuns
      that could lead to their expulsion from religious life.

281. Cates, Willard, Jr. "Adolescent Abortions in the United
      States." Journal of Adolescent Health Care 1 (1980): 18-25.

      Despite the fact that adolescent females have a more negative
      reaction to abortion than older women, they are apparently
      more likely to use legal abortion to prevent unplanned births.

282. _____. "Late Effects of Induced Abortion: Hypothesis or
      Knowledge?" Journal of Reproductive Medicine Apr. 1979: 207-
      12.

      Describes the design complexities of the different studies on
      the long-term effects of induced abortion.

283. _____. "Legal Abortion: The Public Health Record."
      Science 26 Mar. 1982: 1586-90.

      The increasing availability and utilzation of legal abortion
      in the United States had several important effects on public
      health in the 1970s.

284. Cates, Willard, Jr., and Christopher Tietze. "Standardized
      Mortality Rates Associated with Legal Abortion: United
      States, 1972-1975." Family Planning Perspectives Mar.-Apr.
      1978: 109-12.

      Abortions performed before the sixteenth week of pregnancy
      are safer than childbirth. This remains true when abortion-
      related death rates are standardized for age and race.

285. "The Catholic Burden." Triumph May 1973: 45.

      Following Roe v. Wade, the fact is that the United
      States Supreme Court has certified a sociopolitical reality
      that is intolerable to Catholics and susceptible to correction,
      if at all, only by the most determined and sustained effort
      by the Catholic people of the United States.

286. "The Catholic Interest." Triumph Jan. 1974: 15.

      Discusses the founding of the Catholic League for Relisious
      and Civil Rights (CLRCR) and the emergence of a pro-life bloc
      in the U.S. Congress.

287. "Catholic Peace Fellowship Statement on Abortion." Catholic
      Mind Feb. 1975: 7-9.

      Reports on expressions of opposition to abortion by the
      Catholic Peace Fellowship (CPF), a group of some 6,000
      members and associates.

288. "A Catholic Woman in the White House?" Editorial. <u>Commonweal</u> 10 Aug. 1984: 419-21.

Many Catholic women feel forced to choose between the Catholic church's apparent refusal to acknowledge legitimate differences on abortion and the credibility of a strong and independent woman like Geraldine Ferraro.

289. "Catholics and Abortion." Editorial. <u>Commonweal</u> 31 May 1974: 299-300.

An editorial espousing Catholic views on the question of abortion, although it notes that abortion is not just a Catholic concern.

290. Catholics for a Free Choice. <u>My</u> <u>Conscience</u> <u>Speaks</u>: <u>Catholic</u> <u>Women</u> <u>Discuss</u> <u>Their</u> <u>Abortions</u>. Abortion in Good Faith Series. Washington: Catholics for a Free Choice, 1981.

Interviews with eight women of different economic situations, ethnic backgrounds, and ages, who tell about their abortions.

291. Cavnar, Nick. "Who Plans Your Family?" <u>New</u> <u>Covenant</u> Feb. 1984: 13-16.

Discusses family planning and <u>Humanae</u> <u>Vitae</u>.

292. "CHA to Conduct Anti-Abortion Campaign." <u>Hospital</u> <u>Progress</u> Mar. 1973: 82.

The thrust of the establishment of a series of programs and services by the Board of Trustees of the Catholic Hospital Association (CHA) is to "protect and preserve the health care apostolate of the Catholic church."

293. Chamberlain, Gary L. "The abortion Debate is Revealing Our Values." <u>New</u> <u>Catholic</u> <u>World</u> Oct. 1972: 206-08.

The abortion question raises cultural values and social responsibility; it demands of anti-abortionists a commitment to promoting viable alternatives to abortion, and it asks of American society a reordering of priorities, attitudes, and institutions to enhance a real quality of human life.

294. Chandrasekhar, Sripati. <u>A</u> <u>Dirty,</u> <u>Filthy</u> <u>Book</u>. Berkeley: U of California P, 1981.

Writings of Charles Knowlton and Annie Besant on reproductive physiology and birth control and an account of the Bradlaugh-Besant trial.

295. Child, Marion. "Birth Control: Why Shouldn't Your Husband Take a Pill?" Redbook Feb. 1973: 96-97.

For every woman who has dealt gracefully with a diaphragm, willingly tried the IUD, or been grateful for the birth control pill, there is another woman who is asking one question: Why me?

296. "Children Having Children." Editorial. America 30 Mar. 1985: 245.

Discusses phenomena, with references to Alan Guttmacher Institute findings on children having children, comparing the United States to four other industrialized democracies.

297. "Choice Decision." Editorial. Time 11 July 1983: 21.

Senator Orrin Hatch's constitutional amendment to overturn the Roe v. Wade decision falls 18 votes short of the required two-thirds majority.

298. Christian, Scott Rickly. The Woodland Hills Tragedy. Westchester: Crossway, 1985.

The full story behind the over 16,000 aborted babies found buried in a California suburb.

299. Chu, Daniel. "Choice vs. Life." People Weekly 5 Aug. 1985: 70-72.

A survey article on the abortion question, with reference to society's perceptions since Roe v. Wade.

300. Chung, Chin Sik, and Patricia G. Steinhoff. The Effects of Induced Abortion on Subsequent Reproductive Function and Pregnancy Outcome. Hawaii: East-West Center, 1983.

Reports on an eight-year (1971-78) follow-up study of the effects of induced abortion on subsequent pregnancies among women in Hawaii.

301. "Church and State in Boston." Editorial. America 4 Oct. 1980: 180.

Humberto Cardinal Medeiros issues an anti-abortion pastoral letter two days before the election in Massachusetts.

302. Church, George J. "Five Political Hot Spots: In Some States the Abortion Battle Is Already Near Boiling Point." Time 17 July 1989: 64.

Abortion is expected to become a fighting issue in almost every state. But in a handful, it is coming to a head right now.

303. The Churches Speak on - Abortion: Official Statements from Religious Bodies and Ecumenical Organizations. Detroit: Gale, 1989.

A series of monographs which contain the major official pronouncements of North American religious bodies and ecumenical organizations on the abortion issue.

304. Clark, Carole P. "Perspectives of Viability." Arizona State Law Journal 1 (1980): 128-59.

In Roe v. Wade, the U.S. Supreme Court reached a compromise between recognizing a woman's privacy right to terminate her pregnancy and the state's power to protect unborn life. Viability was firmly established as a key concept to the issue of abortion. Yet the Court failed to furnish a workable definition of viability.

305. Clark, Matt. "Contraceptives: On Hold." Newsweek 5 May 1986: 68.

Liability fears are cutting off research.

306. _____. "New Doctors' Dilemma." Newsweek 3 Mar. 1975: 24-25.

Late abortions (second and third trimesters) are matters of complex concern inasmuch as medical research and practice make it possible to save premature infants. The case involves Dr. Kenneth C. Edelin.

307. _____. "Report on Abortion." Newsweek 17 Feb. 1975: 97.

Reputedly, this is the first in-depth study of the impact of the Roe v. Wade decision, showing that abortion on demand remains more of a legal theory than a medical fact in much of the United States.

308. Clayton, Richard R., and William L. Tolone. "Religiosity and Attitudes Toward Induced Abortion: An Elaboration of the Relationship." Sociological Analysis 34 (1973): 26-39

Using a sample of 821 college students at three different universities, attempts to clarify the relationship between religiosity (ideological commitment assessed by a five item Guttman-type scale) and attitudes toward induced abortion for seven situational conditions (woman's health endangered, rape, serious defect in the child, low income, unmarried, want no more children, and incest).

309. Cobliner, W. Godfrey, Harold Schulman, and Seymour L. Romney. "The Termination of Adolescent Out-of-Wedlock Pregnancies and the Prospects for Their Primary Prevention." American Journal of Obstetrics and Gynecology 1 Feb. 1973: 432-44.

Concludes that attitudes toward abortion are secondary phenomena in that they are governed by, or are derivatives of, what is tentatively being called vectors of orientation.

310. Coburn, Judith. "The Intelligent Woman's Guide to Sex." Mademoiselle Sept. 1977: 136+.

The U.S. Supreme Court has created two classes of women: moneyed women with rights to abortion and poor women without those rights.

311. Cockburn, Alexander. "Aborted Justice." New Statesman and Society 14 July 1989: 19-20.

Behind the U.S. Supreme Court's ruling on abortion lies a history of subversion of American liberalism.

312. Coffey, Patrick. "When Is Killing the Unborn a Homicidal Action?" Linacre Quarterly 43 (1976): 85-93.

Advances arguments centering on the relationship of homicidal action and the killing of the unborn.

313. Coffey, Patrick J. "Toward a Sound Moral Policy on Abortion." New Scholasticism 47 (1974): 105-12.

Innovative attempts to advance the philosophical debate on the morality of abortion have been made recently by Daniel Callahan and Germain Grisez. The intent of this article is to bring these positions to a further stage of development by showing that Grisez's moral policy, with a modification, is a more plausible line of approach than that indicated by Callahan's policy.

314. Cohen, Marshall, comp. Rights and Wrongs of Abortion. Princeton: Princeton UP, 1974.

Essays drawn from the periodical Philosophy and Public Affairs and addressing the fundamental issues of the abortion controversy.

315. Cohen, Sherrill, and Nadine Taub, eds. Reproductive Laws for
      the 1990s: A Briefing Handbook. Clifton: Humana, 1989.

      Calls for comprehensive assessment of existing birth control
      laws and services affecting reproductive choices to replace
      the current model of piecemeal legislation.

316. Cohodas, Nadine. "'Pro-Life' Interest Groups Try a New Tactic
      in Effort to Crack Down on Abortion." Congressional Quarterly
      Weekly Report 28 Feb. 1981: 383+.

      Pro-life forces have come up with a new tactic they hope will
      succeed, and Sen. Jesse Helms and Rep. Henry J. Hyde have
      introduced identical bills (S 158, HR 900) they say will
      lead to banning abortion without a constitutional amendment.

317. _____. "Array of Anti-Abortion Amendments Planned."
      Congressional Quarterly Weekly Report 2 Nov. 1985: 2201+.

      A variety of anti-abortion amendments tied to federal stop-
      gap funding bill.

318. _____. "Court's Move Heartens Anti-Abortion Forces."
      Congressional Quarterly Weekly Report 14 Jan. 1989: 87.

      The U.S. Supreme Court's January 9, 1989, decision to review a
      Missouri abortion case will prompt congressional maneuvering
      in the coming weeks.

319. Coleman, John J., III. "Roe v. Wade: A Retrospective Look
      at a Judicial Oxymoron." St. Louis University Law Journal
      29 (1984): 7-44.

      Evaluates the Roe decision and the commentary that it has
      inspired, identifies the most fundamental flaw in the decision,
      illustrates how suggested alternatives by commentators perpet-
      uate this flaw, and proposes an alternative rationale.

320. Colford, Steven W. "Media Bonanza Seen with Abortion Ruling."
      Advertising Age 10 July 1989: 1+.

      Discusses the fact that the U.S. Supreme Court's new ruling
      on abortions means unprecedented levels of local issue
      advertising next year.

321. Collins, Carol C., ed., Abortion: The Continuing Controversy.
      New York: Facts on File, 1984.

      The editor explores the meaning and possible repercussions of
      the abortion issue through the commentaries of the nation's
      newspaper editors.

322. Collins, Mary J., ed. A Church Divided: Catholics' Attitudes
     About Family Planning, Abortion and Teenage Sexuality.
     Washington: Catholics for a Free Choice, 1986.

     The public opinion data presented in this report shows that the
     attitudes of Catholics toward sexuality and reproduction are
     closer to the attitudes held by non-Catholic Americans than to
     the positions taken by the institutional church.

323. "Colorado Bishops Endorse Amendment No. 3." Origins 20 Sept.
     1984: 223-24.

     The bishops of Colorado's three dioceses endorse a state
     constitutional amendment to prohibit the use of state funds
     for elective abortions.

324. "Colorado Voters Amend the State's Constitution to Outlaw Public
     Funding of Abortions." Christianity Today 18 Jan. 1985: 46-47.

     Colorado voters defeat Amendment 3 to ban public funding of
     abortions.

325. Colson, Charles. "Abortion Clinic Obsolescence." Christianity
     Today 3 Feb. 1989: 72.

     Just as these principled pro-lifers were indicting a calloused
     American conscience, events were taking place that may soon
     render their protests impotent altogether.

326. _____. "How Prolife Protest Has Backfired." Christianity
     Today 15 Dec. 1989: 72.

     Christians screaming and waving their Bibles, faces twisted
     with hate and anger, hardly help the pro-life cause.

327. "Concerned Catholics, Concerned Hierarchy." Editorial.
     America 15 Mar. 1986: 197.

     Discusses an October 1984 ad in the New York Times and centers
     on an individual's right to dissent ad (March 2, 1986).
     Points out fallacies in thought regarding the latter ad.

328. "Conference Examines Proposed Human Life Amendment." Hospital
     Progress Oct. 1981: 22-23.

     The National Right to Life (NRL) Educational Trust Fund and
     the Center for Health Care Ethics (CHCE) examine the human
     life amendment's legal and social ramifications.

329. Conference on Counseling in Abortion Services, 1973, New York. _Counseling in Abortion Services: Physician, Nurse, Social Worker_. New York: U Book Service, 1974.

   Proceedings of a conference called to develop an integrated model for counseling in abortion services through the examination of varied approaches used at the present time and to explore the relationship of counseling to the patients' needs and characteristics.

330. Conley, Patrick T., and Robert J. McKenna. "The Supreme Court on Abortion--A Dissenting Opinion." _Catholic Lawyer_ 19 (1973): 19-28.

   A detailed rebuttal of the Court's reasoning in arriving at the _Roe_ v. _Wade_ decision.

331. "Connecticut Abortion Laws Ruled Unconstitutional." _Christian Century_ 10 May 1972: 539.

   Connecticut's 112-year-old abortion laws have been struck down by the 2-1 decision of a U.S. circuit court of appeals, which termed the statutes a violation of a woman's right "to determine whether or not to have a child once conception has occurred."

332. Connell, Noreen. "A Lesser Life and Other Lies: Feminists and Families." _Nation_ 16 Aug. 1986: 106-08.

   Comments concerning the call for the women's movement to focus more on pro-family issues.

333. Conner, John S. "Freedom Through Value." _Catholic Lawyer_ 1 (1980): 78-87.

   Discusses the idealism, practical impact, and consequences of the pro-life position.

334. Connery, John R. "Abortion: A Philosophical and Historical Analysis." _Hospital Progress_ Apr. 1977: 49-50.

   The question of when the fetus becomes a human being is posed: At the moment of conception or the moment of birth?

335. _____. _Abortion: The Development of the Roman Catholic Perspective_. Chicago: Loyola UP, 1977.

   Traces the development of the Catholic stand on abortion from the pre-Christian era to the mid-twentieth century.

336. _____. "A Seamless Garment in a Sinful World." *America* 14 July 1984: 5-8.

Pacifism, abortion, and capital punishment are three separate issues, even though they are part of a consistent pro-life ethic.

337. Connors, Joseph M. "Operation Rescue." *America* 29 Apr. 1989: 400+.

Within the pro-life effort a new project of massive civil disobedience is targeting abortion clinics directly.

338. "Consciousness Raising for Catholics." *America* 6 Oct. 1973: 231.

American Catholic bishops reschedule and expand the "Respect Life" program.

339. "Constitutional Right to Life from the Moment of Conception." *Social Justice Review* Mar. 1972: 408-18.

A substantial part of the public testimony given by various individual citizens to the Constitutional Amendment Committee, Missouri House of Representatives, February 6, 1972, on behalf of House joint resolution HR 92.

340. "Contraception Choices Now." *Changing Times* Nov. 1986: 121-28.

The range of easily available birth control methods is diminishing, and so are one's options.

341. "Contraception on Campus." *Society* May-June 1986: 3.

A new national Gallup survey of more than 600 college students at 100 campuses nationwide shows that more than 66 percent of today's college women claim to be sexually active, yet remain surprisingly uninformed about contraception.

342. Cooke, Bernard. "Contraception and the Synod." *Commonweal* 21 Nov. 1980: 648-50.

The bishops' synod on the family is finished, and two things are clear: on important issues such as contraception and divorce there is genuine and growing episcopal concern and no definitive clarity.

343. Cooke, Terence Cardinal. "The Impact of Abortion." *Origins* 16 Oct. 1980: 283-85.

The impact of abortion on marriage and family life is described
by Terence Cardinal Cooke.

344.   _____. "Natural Family Planning Is the Way to Go."
International Review of Natural Family Planning 7 (1983):
190-99.

Discusses the moral, religious, and social importance of family
planning.

345.   _____. "Will Church Institutions Be Forced to Make Medical Payments for Abortion?" Origins 2 Mar. 1978: 577+.

Terence Cardinal Cooke discusses a U.S. House of Representatives bill which would require all employers, including
churches and church-related organizations, to provide medical
payments and paid leave time for abortions, and stresses that
the National Conference of Catholic Bishops (NCCB) cannot
comply with it.

346. Coots, Max A. "On Abortion." Progressive Nov. 1974: 20-21.

A "state-of-the-art" article on social-legal thought in regard
to the abortion issue, which is alive and well and living in
three proposed amendments to the Constitution.

347. Copelon, Rhonda. "Abortion Rights." Ms. Oct. 1983: 146.

Urges women to work to reintegrate reproductive and sexual
rights into the concept of equality.

348. Copelon, Rhonda, and Kathryn Kolbert. "The Gathering Storm:
Roe v. Wade." Ms. Apr. 1989: 89-93.

In Webster v. Reproductive Health Services, the U.S. Supreme
Court has agreed to consider "whether Roe v. Wade should be
overruled."

349. Coriden, James A. "Church Law and Abortion." Jurist
33 (1973): 184-98.

Three questions related to abortion in the law of the Catholic
church serve as a framework for this article: 1) What have been
the prohibitions and penal sanctions against abortion in the
history of the church? 2) What has been the sacramental
discipline regarding the baptism of an expelled fetus? 3) What
is the relationship between these ordinances and the moral
teaching or pastoral practice of the church?

350. Cormier, Robert. "Three Against Abortion: None of Them
      Catholic." St. Anthony's Messenger June 1976: 18-22.

      A black Methodist doctor, a Jewish rabbi, and a Protestant
      mayor add their voices to the pro-life campaign, demonstrating
      that abortion is not just a Catholic issue.

351. Corsaro, Maria. A Woman's Guide to a Safe Abortion. New York:
      Holt, 1983.

      A useful guide to the best options for terminating a pregnancy
      in any geographic area of the United States.

352. Cory, Laurie. "Court-Ordered Sterilization Performed at St.
      Vincent's Hospital." Hospital Progress Dec. 1972: 22-24.

      A court-ordered sterilization operation has been performed in
      a Catholic hospital, apparently for the first time in the
      country. Bishop Eldon B. Schuster of Great Falls, Montana,
      commented, following the issuance of the judge's order, that
      "we have no choice but to abide by the law."

353. Costikyan, Barbara, et al. "Abortion: Your Right Under
      Attack." Cosmopolitan Oct. 1985: 222-27.

      Offers responses to these questions: How strong is the right-
      to-life movement? Will we be forced to surrender control over
      our own bodies? Who are the participants in this difficult,
      divisive debate?

354. Cottrell, Jack W. "Abortion and the Mosaic Law." Christianity
      Today 16 Mar. 1973: 6-9.

      The most crucial question in the abortion debate is when (or
      even whether) the fetus is to be considered a human being. To
      answer this we are directed to the Bible.

355. "Countdown: The Wars Within the States." Newsweek 17 July
      1989: 24.

      A state-by-state survey/report on pro-choice and pro-life
      leanings.

356. Cripps, Edward J. "The Church Faces World Population Year,
      1974." America 17 Nov. 1973: 370-72.

      A growing appreciation of the "population problem" as involving
      not just "birth control," but broader issues of development
      and international justice, offers the Catholic church an
      opportunity to contribute and to learn.

357.   Crocker, Laura.   "*Harris* v. *McRae*: Whatever Happened to the
       Roe v. *Wade* Abortion Right?"   *Pepperdine Law Review*
       3 (1981): 861-97.

       Examines the abortion controversy from the time of the *Roe*
       decision up to the enactment of the Hyde amendment, the various
       arguments and corresponding levels of review by which the U.S.
       Supreme Court upheld the Hyde amendment, the drastic conse-
       quences that *Harris* v. *McRae* will pose for indigent
       women, and the U.S. Supreme Court's "two-tiered" approach
       for equal protection clause analysis.

358.   Cuca, Roberto.   *Family Planning Programs: An Evaluation of
       Experience*. Washington: World Bank, 1979.

       A review of the evolution of a family-planning policy and
       program activity in those countries in which there is an
       official family-planning policy.

359.   Cuddy, D. L.   "Black Genocide."   *America* 3 Oct. 1981: 181.

       It has been reported that white legislators are supporting
       abortion rights as a means of "getting rid of those black
       welfare babies before they get here." When looked at in
       context, it adds up to blatant genocide.

360.   Culliton, B. J.   "Antiabortionists Challenge March of Dimes."
       Science 7 Nov. 1975: 538.

       Anti-abortionists are claiming that by endorsing amniocentesis
       the March of Dimes Foundation is encouraging abortion.   The
       foundation replies to the contrary.

361.   Culliton, Barbara J.   "Abortion and Manslaughter: A Boston
       Doctor Goes on Trial."   *Science* 31 Jan. 1975: 334-35.

       Recounts the trial of Dr. Kenneth C. Edelin for manslaughter
       in a Boston abortion case. The prosecutor alleges that the
       fetus was old enough to be viable, and the defense claims that
       the fetus never lived. Both sides agree that the fetus was 17
       to 24 weeks old.

362.   _____.   "Abortion: Liberal Laws Do Make Abortion Safer
       for Women." *Science* 13 June 1975: 1091.

       The health effects of abortion are related to the legality of
       the procedure.

363.   _____.   "Edelin Conviction Overturned."   *Science* 7 Jan.
       1977: 36-37.

The Massachusetts Supreme Judicial Court overturns Edelin's conviction and acquits Edelin on the grounds that there simply was not enough evidence to find him guilty.

364. _____. "Edelin Trial." Science 7 Mar. 1975: 814-16.

Concludes that the jury which found Dr. Edelin guilty of manslaughter was "not persuaded by scientists for the defense."

365. _____. "Manslaughter: The Charge Against Edelin of Boston City Hospital." Science 25 Oct. 1974: 327+.

A general overview article on the Edelin case.

366. Cumming, Joseph B., Jr. "'Right-to-Life'--Two Crusaders." Newsweek 3 Mar. 1975: 29.

Recounts the presentation made by a right-to-life husband-and-wife team at a Georgia ladies' auxiliary meeting.

367. Cunningham, Paige Comstock. "Reversing Roe vs. Wade: It May Take More Than a Single Court Decision to Counter Abortion on Demand." Christianity Today 20 Sept. 1985: 20-22.

Covers four questions: 1) How, exactly, can the current legal situation be changed? 2) What is involved in overturning a constitutional ruling? 3) How long might it take? 4) Is there a legal strategy that pro-lifers should keep in mind?

368. Cuomo, Mario M. "Abortion and the Law." Origins 25 Oct. 1984: 301-03.

Governor Mario Cuomo claims that "perhaps the greatest good to come from the current debate on abortion...will be the enunciation of better, more realistic and practical ways of dealing with it."

369. _____. "A Governor Responds." America 28 Oct. 1989: 265.

Pro-Choice Catholic public officials versus the Catholic church.

370. _____. "An Interview with Mario Cuomo." With Karen Sue Smith and Patrick Jordan. Commonweal 31 May 1985: 329-33.

Discusses realities of the abortion debate in the political and governmental spheres.

371. Curran, Charles E. "Abortion: Law and Morality in Contemporary Catholic Theology." <u>Jurist</u> 33 (1973): 162-83.

    Attempts to present the state of abortion in Catholic theology, indicating the ways in which Catholics can and should approach both the legal and moral aspects of abortion.

372. _____. "After <u>Humanae Vitae</u>: A Decade of 'Lively Debate.'" <u>Hospital Progress</u> July 1978: 84-89.

    The encyclical <u>Humanae Vitae</u> caused great agitation in the Catholic church, and this article reflects one aspect of the controversy--the recent developments in moral theology.

373. _____. "Ten Years Later: Reflections on the Anniversary of '<u>Humanae Vitae</u>.'" <u>Commonweal</u> 7 July 1978: 425-30.

    Discusses the encyclical <u>Humanae Vitae</u> and its effect on the life of the Catholic church over the ten-year period since the encyclical was promulgated.

374. Curtis, Walter W. "We Need a Right to Life Amendment." <u>U.S. Catholic</u> June 1974: 14-15.

    Argues that a right-to-life amendment would establish that the unborn child is legally a person and would extend protection afforded by the Fifth and Fourteenth Amendments to the unborn child throughout the entire course of the pregnancy.

375. Cvetkovich, George, et al. "On the Psychology of Adolescents' Use of Contraceptives." <u>The Journal of Sex Research</u> 11 (1975): 256-70.

    Discusses the cognitive-emotional development typical of the adolescent years, particularly the egocentric nature of intuitive adolescent thought.

376. Cyrus, Virginia. "Margaret Sanger's Fight for the Right to Choose." <u>Know News</u> 6 May 1975: 11.

    Briefly outlines Margaret Sanger's career in the birth control movement and views the "Right to Choose" campaign as a legacy of her work.

377. Czepiga, Paul T. "The Fetus Under Section 1983: Still Struggling for Recognition." <u>Syracuse Law Review</u> 4 (1983): 1029-65.

    Provides a legal background to the question of fetal life versus human life.

378. Daily, Edwin F., and Nick Nicholas. "Use of Conception Control Methods Before Pregnancies Terminating in Birth or a Requested Abortion in New York City Municipal Hospitals." American Journal of Public Health Nov. 1972: 1544-45.

Reveals that the younger a postpartum or abortion patient is, the less likely she is to have used contraception in the two years prior to the termination of the pregnancy.

379. Daly, K. Diane, Ann M. Prebil, and Thomas W. Hilgers. "NFP Programs Provide Consumer Choice, Benefit Hospital." Hospital Progress Oct. 1980: 56+.

Natural family planning (NFP) deals with the very beginnings of life and the family and has a two-fold purpose, achieving pregnancy as well as avoiding pregnancy; NFP services belong within the context of the family-centered health care system.

380. Daly, Mary. "Abortion and Sexual Caste." Commonweal 4 Feb. 1972: 415+.

Women did not arbitrarily choose abortion as part of their platform. It has arisen out of the realities of their situation.

381. Darst, Stephen. "He Runs for Their Lives." Catholic Digest Mar. 1974: 45-47.

Dr. John C. Willke finds that speaking against abortion is an exhausting task; this article chronicles a day in his life.

382. Dauber, Bonnie, Marianne Zalar, and Phillip J. Goldstein. "Abortion Counseling and Behavioral Change." Family Planning Perspectives Apr. 1972: 23-27.

Discusses evidence suggesting that counseling just prior to, during, and following legal abortion can help prevent future unwanted pregnancies.

383. Davis, John Jefferson. Abortion and the Christian: What Every Believer Should Know. Phillipsburg: Presbyterian and Reformed, 1984.

Covers the abortion legal situation, reports on how major views differ, gives relevant medical data, and relates the scriptural implications.

384. Davis, Kenneth S. "The Story of the Pill: How a Crash Program Developed an Efficient Oral Contraception in Less Than a Decade." American Heritage Aug.-Sept. 1978: 80-91.

56

Includes the backgrounds of Margaret Sanger, Mrs. Stanley
(Katharine Dexter) McCormick, and Dr. Gregory Goodwin Pincus.
These three had a crucial meeting in 1951 to determine whether
a physiological contraceptive could be developed for mass use.
In June 1960, the U.S. Food and Drug Administration formally
approved the birth control pill for use as an oral contraceptive.

385.   Davis, Lenwood G., comp. History of Birth Control in the United
       States: A Working Bibliography. Exchange Bibliography 861.
       Monticello: Council of Planning Librarians, 1975.

       A selective bibliography of materials on the history of birth
       control in the United States.

386.   Davis, Nanette J. From Crime to Choice: The Transformation of
       Abortion in America. Contributions in Women's Studies 60.
       New York: Greenwood, 1985.

       Changing attitudes toward abortion and the continued social
       control of abortion are themes of this study.

387.   Davis, Ron Lee, and James G. Denney. A Time for Compassion: A
       Call to Cherish and Protect Life. Old Tappan: Revell, 1986.

       Weaves together stories of women and their decision on
       abortion, the findings of medicine and the social sciences,
       penetrating social analysis, and challenging theological
       reflection.

388.   Daynes, Byron W., and Raymond Tatalovich. "Religious Influence
       and Congressional Voting on Abortion." Journal for the
       Scientific Study of Religion 23 (1984): 197-200.

       Research shows that political ideology is the most important
       reason for a congressperson's supporting or opposing abortion.
       Further research indicates that religious affiliation is the
       second most important predictor of a congressperson's vote on
       abortion legislation.

389.   DeAmicis, Lyn A., et al. "A Comparison of Unwed Pregnant
       Teenagers and Nulligravid Sexually Active Adolescents Seeking
       Contraception." Adolescence 16 (1981): 11-20.

       Compares respondents in regard to school attendance; prevalence
       of broken homes and the occurrence of crises in the period
       preceding the pregnancy; sexual history; knowledge and practice
       of contraception; motivation for pregnancy; and the reaction
       of parents and boyfriend toward the pregnancy.

390. DeCelles, Charles. "Conservatives and Liberals on Prolife Issues." _America_ 2 May 1981: 365-68.

Argues that there is simply no way that the human life amendment can become a reality unless it is supported by an ecumenical coalition, with both liberal and conservative backing. Catholics campaigning alone for pro-life legislation hardly have a prayer. Catholic conservatives alone, forget it. Coalitions work, and the wider the better.

391. _____. "The Fallacy of Legalized Abortion as a Lesser Evil." _Social Justice Review_ Jan.-Feb. 1983: 3-5.

The fact is that laws against abortion are very effective in curbing abortions. Conversely, the lifting of anti-abortion laws strongly encourages the multiplication of abortions.

392. Decker, Raymond G., and Walter R. Trinkaus. "The Abortion Decision: Two Years Later." _Commonweal_ 14 Feb. 1975: 384-92.

Two opposing views on abortion, based on the _Roe_ v. _Wade_ decision, with comparisons to the _Dred Scott_ decision.

393. DeDanois, Vivian. _Abortion and the Moral Degeneration of the American Medical Profession_. Albuquerque: American Classical College P, 1977.

An attack on the physicians who perform abortions.

394. _____. _Abortion: The Claims of the Body and the Deceit of Choice_. New and expanded ed. 2 vols. A Science of Man Library Book. Albuquerque: American Classical College P, 1978.

A series of essays dealing with the moral and ethical aspects of abortion from a research study sponsored by the New Psychology Foundation (NPF).

395. _____. _Good and Abortion_. Albuquerque: American Classical College p. 1979.

Contends that abortion is not only a crime against society, but a crime against oneself and against God.

396. Dedek, John F. _Human Life: Some Moral Issues_. New York: Sheed. 1972.

Discusses the sanctity of life and the principle of double effect as it relates to the abortion question.

397.   "Defense of a Seamless Garment." _Time_ 19 Dec. 1983: 62.

       Joseph Cardinal Bernardin defends the linking of opposition to
       both abortion and capital punishment by arguing that these
       "pro-life" policies constitute a "seamless garment."

398.   DeGeorge, Richard T.   "Legal Enforcement, Moral Pluralism and
       Abortion." _American Catholic Philosophical Association
       Proceedings_ 49 (1975): 171-80.

       Examines the U.S. Supreme Court decision in the case of _Roe_ v.
       Wade; considers some principles concerning the relation of
       law and morality; attempts to draw some conclusions concerning
       the legal enforcement of moral views on abortion in a morally
       pluralistic society.

399.   Degnan, Daniel A.   "Law, Morals and Abortion."   _Commonweal_
       31 May 1974: 305-08.

       Alternatives in light of the U.S. Supreme Court's decision.

400.   _____.   "Prudence, Politics and the Abortion Issue."
       America 16 Feb. 1985: 121-24.

       The safeguarding of human fetal life creates an urgent demand
       for action in the field of law and politics. Simply put, this
       article maintains that our political leaders must be held to
       account for their stands on abortion.

401.   _____.   "When (If) 'Roe' Falls: Can There Be Compromise?"
       Commonweal 5 May 1989: 267-69.

       Raises the question, "If... human life, including unborn human
       life, cries out for legal protection, is it morally permissible
       to accept a compromise on abortion?" and proceeds to answer it.

402.   Dellinger, Walter.   "Day in Court." _New Republic_ 8 May 1989:
       11-12.

       The anticipated outcome of _Webster_ v. _Reproductive Health
       Services_ is being billed by some as a reasonable compromise.

403.   DeMarco, Donald.   _Abortion in Perspective: The Rose Palace or
       the Fiery Dragon_. Cincinnati: Hiltz, 1974.

       Brings to light some of the deeper philosophical implications
       of the abortion issue which are seldom discussed and rarely
       recorded.

404.   _____. "Abortion: Legal and Philosophical Considerations." American Ecclesiastical Review Apr. 1974: 251-67.

Explores the presuppositions of democracy and authoritarianism
and then relates them to the abortion issue.

405.   _____. "The Contraceptive Mentality." Homiletic and
Pastoral Review July 1983: 56-63.

The "contraceptive mentality" implies that a couple have not
only the means to separate intercourse from procreation, but
the right or responsibility as well.

406.   _____. "Parallels in Treachery." Sisters Today Oct.
1973: 82-89.

The abortionists' plot to kill the unborn bears a striking
resemblance in style, development and logic to the Romans'
conspiratorial plan to kill Caesar. Six major stages in the
development of the plot to kill Caesar are compared to the
abortionists' plot to kill the unborn.

407.   _____. "The Right to Be Born." Sisters Today Apr. 1973:
490-95.

Human beings are conceived and brought to birth owing not to
the power of parents but to their love, which cooperates with
the power of the universe.

408.   DeMarco, Donald T. "The Roman Catholic Church and Abortion: An
Historical Perspective." Homiletic and Pastoral Review July
1984: 59-66; Aug.-Sept. 1984: 68+.

Traces the historical development of the Catholic teaching on
abortion. Part I emphasizes that the Catholic church's teaching that direct, induced abortion is always a grave evil has
been clear, emphatic, and unwavering. Part II contends that
never and in no case has the church taught that the life of
the child must be preferred to that of the mother.

409.   Dembo, Myron H., and Beverly Lundell. "Factors Affecting
Adolescent Contraception Practices: Implications for Sex
Education." Adolescence 14 (1979): 657-64.

Explores the major reasons for limited contraception practices
among adolescents and discusses implications for improving
sex education. Three areas are identified for discussion: lack
of information, cognitive-emotional development, and acceptance
of sexuality.

410. Demerath, Nicholas J. Birth Control and Foreign Policy: The Alternative to Family Planning. New York: Harper, 1976.

Seeks to show evidence that family planning as promulgated at present should be abandoned and that societal strategies of fertility reduction should be adopted.

411. Dendinger, Donald C., and Timothy Mathern. "Abortion: Toward Developing a Policy in a Catholic Social Service Agency." Social Thought 6.4 (1980): 33-46.

Counseling and referral services in regard to the problems of pregnancy and abortion are explored within the context of Catholic social service agencies and the profession of social work.

412. Denes, Magda. In Necessity and Sorrow: Life and Death in an Abortion Hospital. New York: Basic, 1976.

Explores the paradoxical nature of abortion.

413. _____. "Performing Abortions." Commentary Oct. 1976: 33-37.

A medical doctor, working in an abortion hospital, recalls her activities, work, and inner thoughts on one of her routine workdays.

414. Dennehy, Raymond Leo, ed. Christian Married Love. San Francisco: Ignatius, 1981.

A series of articles on the birth control controversy from the moral and religious viewpoints of the author.

415. Denney, Myron K. A Matter of Choice: An Essential Guide to Every Aspect of Abortion. New York: Simon, 1983.

Focuses on the social aspects related to abortion for the woman with an unwanted or unplanned pregnancy.

416. Dennis, Frances. "The IPPF: 21 Years of Achievement." Journal of Biosocial Science 5 (1973): 413-19.

Dennis traces the history of the International Planned Parenthood Federation (IPPF).

417. DeParle, Jason. "Beyond the Legal Right." Washington Monthly Apr. 1989: 28+.

Discusses why liberals and feminists do not like to talk about the morality of abortion.

418.   DeParrie, Paul. The Rescuers. Brentwood: Wolgemuth, 1989.

Stories of ordinary people who risked their reputations and freedom to save babies from abortion.

419.   Devereaux, George. A Study of Abortion in Primitive Societies. Rev. ed. New York: Intl. Universities P, 1976.

A typological, distributional and dynamic analysis of the prevention of birth in 400 preindustrial societies, which demonstrates a variety of possible solutions to this conflict-ridden situation.

420.   Devlin, William. "America: There's a Nigger in the Woodpile." Triumph May 1973: 27.

The American commitment to justice has once again officially lapsed. Our nation still has its disadvantaged. But, more shameful than that, she once again has them de jure.

421.   _____. "Which Amendment?" Triumph Jan. 1974: 12+.

Points out that after a year of discussion, there is still no consensus on a pro-life amendment and asks: What are the prospects of an amendment: What kind of amendment is most desirable?

422.   Diamond, E. "Right to Life vs. Upjohn." Editorial. Linacre Quarterly 41 (1974): 147-48.

Specifies the differences between the Catholic medical community and institutions and the Upjohn Company.

423.   Diamond, E. F., and E. C. Diamond. "Abortion: The Search for a Consensus." International Review of Natural Family Planning 8 (1984): 95-101.

Conflicting viewpoints as to the prevailing opinion among American citizens on the issue of abortion have largely related to a failure to refine the issue. However, there seems to be little doubt that the majority of Americans would accept abortion under certain circumstances.

424.   Diamond, James J. "Abortion, Animation, and Biological Hominization." Theological Studies 36 (1975): 305-24.

With the discovery in 1827 of the human ovum, many scholars

with an interest in pinpointing the beginning of human life considered the question closed. There has been a debate over mediate versus immediate animation, yet rational psychologists are no closer to a certain identification of the precise time of ensoulment.

425. _____. "Pro-Life Amendments and Due Process." America 19 Jan. 1974: 27-29.

No pro-life amendment can give a fetus more protection than the Constitution already grants the rest of us. But that is a great deal, and it opens the way for due process for our unborn fellow citizens.

426. Diamond, Milton, et al. "Sexuality, Birth Control and Abortion: A Decision-Making Sequence." Journal of Biosocial Science 5 (1973): 347-61.

Reports that coitus was anticipated by the majority of women, but pregnancy was unplanned. Two-thirds of the women who did not want to become pregnant were not using a contraceptive method; yet, regardless of whether pregnancy was planned or unplanned, one of three women chose to have an abortion.

427. Dienes, C. Thomas. Law, Politics, and Birth Control. Urbana: U of Illinos P, 1972.

Spans more than 100 years of birth control developments and discusses how these activities were interrelated with politics and national and state laws.

428. Diller, Lawrence, and Wylie Hembree. "Male Contraception and Family Planning: A Social and Historical Review." Fertility and Sterility Dec. 1977: 1271-79.

Calls for a greater emphasis on male contraception, citing the prevalence of the vasectomy to illustrate the male concern for birth control.

429. "Diocesan-wide NFP Program Reaches Broad Population Groups." Hospital Progress Apr. 1984: 26+.

Discusses the establishment and development of a natural family planning (NFP) program in a Pennsylvania diocese.

430. DiPerna, Paula. "Abortion: The Great Debate." Ladies' Home Journal Nov. 1985: 142+.

A special magazine-sponsored investigation examining all sides of the emotion-packed issue of the 1980s: abortion.

431. "Disagreement over Proposed Human Life Bill." Origins 2 July
      1981: 100-05.

      A memorandum questioning the constitutionality of the proposed
      human life bill has become a bone of contention between one of
      the bill's sponsors, Rep. Henry Hyde (R-Ill.), and the author
      of the memorandum, U.S. Catholic Conference (USCC) general
      counsel, Wilfred Caron.

432. "Dissent and Reaction." Editorial. America 19 Jan. 1985:
      37.

      Some Catholics say that dissent is possible in regard to a
      person's abortion decision; however, the Sacred Congregation
      for Religious and Secular Institutes (SCRSI) says no.

433. "Diversity Claimed." Christian Century 6 Mar. 1985: 240.

      Catholics for a Free Choice (CFC) claim that the results of a
      survey of Catholic theologians and scholars on abortion
      "prove once again that committed Catholics in fact have
      widely disparate viewpoints on this most sensitive issue."

434. Djerassi, Carl. "Abortion in the United States: Politics or
      Policy?" Bulletin of the Atomic Scientists Apr. 1986: 38-41.

      Deals with the legal and geopolitical implications of abortion,
      its present inevitability, the difficulties in reaching the
      day when it will be largely unnecessary, and the morality of
      the issue.

435. _____. "Fertility Control Through Abortion: An Assess-
      ment of the Period 1950-1980." Bulletin of the Atomic
      Scientists Jan. 1972: 28+.

      Contends that studies reveal that the perseverance of a highly
      motivated and frequently desperate woman seeking termination
      of an unwanted pregnancy crosses all socioeconomic and
      developmental levels, and her ingenuity far surpasses that of
      legislatures and law enforcement bodies.

436. _____. The Politics of Contraception. New York: Norton,
      1980.

      A work of information and advocacy for birth control that will
      educate the general reader.

437. _____. "Searching for Ideal Contraceptives." Society
      Nov.-Dec. 1985: 41-43.

Focuses on the "ideal" contraceptive for teenagers and poses
three questions: 1) Can this be defined? 2) Can it be created?
If yes, 3) When?

438. "Do Catholics have Constitutional Rights?" Editorial.
 Commonweal 8 Dec. 1978: 771-73.

Claims that in _McRae_ v. _Califano_ First Amendment rights of
religion, speech, press, and political activity are being
tampered with.

439. Dobell, Elizabeth Rodgers. "Abortion: The Controversy We Can't
Seem to Solve." _Redbook_ June 1979: 42+.

The results of a recent _Redbook_ poll look beyond the raging
debate on abortion. They tell us what Americans think about
this vital issue--and they may help you clarify your own stand.

440. "Dobson Tells Reagan to Focus on the Family." _Christianity
Today_ 2 Mar. 1984: 37.

Christian psychologist James Dobson suggests ways the government could better meet the needs of American families and
tells President Reagan that the government could do more to
promote adoption as an alternative to abortion.

441. "The Doctors' Dilemma." _Newsweek_ 17 July 1989: 25+.

Doctors are divided like everyone else--and fear the courts
have too much faith in science.

442. "Documentation: Missouri House Bill No. 1211." _Jurist_ 35
(1975): 110-14.

Planned Parenthood v. _Danforth_, 392 F. Supp. 1362 (E.D. Mo.
1975). This statute attempts to exercise virtually all of
the possible means of state regulation and control of abortion
which appear to be permissible after the _Roe_ decision. It
represents the most successful attempt to date by a state
to reassert meaningful regulation and control over abortion
after _Roe_.

443. Doerflinger, Richard. "Who Are Catholics for a Free Choice?"
America 16 Nov. 1985: 312-17.

A brief history of the group that sponsored the ad proclaiming
a "diversity of opinions regarding abortion exists among
committed Catholics" highlights the question of freedom
versus authority in the Catholic church.

444. Doerr, Edd. "Abortion Rights." Humanist Mar.-Apr. 1985:
      39-40.

      An examination of abortion vis-a-vis the separation of church
      and state in the United States.

445. _____. "Abortion Rights at the Crossroads." Humanist
      Nov.-Dec. 1985: 39-40.

      Thornburgh v. American College of Obstetricians and Gynecol-
      ogists and Diamond v. Charles: Madeline Kochen of the New York
      Civil Liberties Union argues that the challenged statutes
      violate the First Amendment requirement that the government
      remain neutral with regard to theological differences and
      "interfere ideologically and practically with a woman's right
      to freely exercise her religion and conscience in making the
      abortion decision, while placing no similar obstacles in the
      path of the women whose faith compels childbirth."

446. _____. "Abortion: Right or Wrong?" USA Today Jan. 1989:
      51-53.

      At the heart of the public policy controversy over abortion
      is the question of when a fetus becomes a person.

447. _____. "Answering Silent Scream." Humanist May-June
      1986: 37.

      Relates The Silent Scream video with interviews with Isaac
      Asimov, Michael Bennett, Patricia Goldman-Rakic, Clifford
      Grobstein, and Dominick Purpura, and makes the point that a
      functioning brain is critical to personhood.

448. _____. "Black Monday." Humanist Sept.-Oct. 1989: 39.

      Recounts how the U.S. Supreme Court decided in a 5-4 ruling in
      Webster v. Reproductive Health Services, that the fundamental
      liberty to terminate problem pregnancies is no longer immune
      from legislative infringement.

449. _____. "Church and State." Humanist Mar.-Apr. 1979: 62.

      Six years after Roe v. Wade, demonstrators of various persua-
      sions "parade" their viewpoints on the anniversary of the
      historic decision.

450. _____. "Good News, Bad News." Humanist Sept.-Oct. 1983:
      36+.

      The U.S. Supreme Court rules unconstitutional state and local laws which place unnecessary obstacles in the way of women choosing to terminate problem pregnancies.

451. _____. "Silence." Humanist May-June 1983: 43-44.

Maintains that the most dangerous silence is that of those who should know better but shirk their duty to stand up for freedom, including the freedom of abortion.

452. _____. "Silent Scream, Population, Parochiaid." Humanist July-Aug. 1985: 41-42.

Reflects on church and state questions, using The Silent Scream as a point of reference.

453. Doerr, Edd, and James W. Prescott. Abortion Rights and Fetal "Personhood". Long Beach: Centerline, 1989.

A series of papers presented at an Americans for Religious Liberty (ARL) Conference which will contribute significantly to public discourse on the abortion rights debate.

454. Doherty, Dennis J. "The Morality of Abortion." American Ecclesiastical Review Jan. 1975: 37-47.

Seeks to help those who are absolutely opposed to abortion to assess the force of their conviction.

455. Dolan, Edward F., Jr. Matters of Life and Death. New York: Watts, 1982.

A book for young adults which contains a brief comparison of the experiences Margaret Sanger and others underwent during the current abortion struggle.

456. Dominian, Jack. "Birth Control and Married Love." Month Mar. 1973: 98-103.

Discusses the interface of birth control and married love in the life of practicing Catholics.

457. Donceel, Joseph F. "Catholic Politicians and Abortion." America 2 Feb. 1985: 81-83.

Shows that although it is difficult to see how a Catholic can be pro-choice with respect to abortion, Catholic politicians may remain in good standing in their church even while allowing non-Catholics to be pro-choice within certain limits and for serious reasons.

458.   _____. "Why Is Abortion Wrong?" America 16 Aug. 1975:
        65-67.

        The idea that the human person is present in the fetus from
        conception has not always been the teaching of the Catholic
        church, and has no necessary part in the present debate.
        The author also advances other historical reasons for the
        church's stance.

459.   Donovan, Patricia. "Half a Loaf: A New Antiabortion Strategy."
        Family Planning Perspectives Nov.-Dec. 1981: 262-68.

        The right-to-life movement is at a critical point in its
        crusade to prohibit abortion. Senator Jesse Helms (R.-NC) and
        Rep. Henry J. Hyde (R.-IL) are trying to shortcut the amendment
        process by getting Congress to pass, by a simple majority vote,
        the so-called human life statute. Meanwhile, pragmatic anti-
        abortion activists in Congress are backing a proposed constitu-
        tional amendment which would authorize Congress and the states
        to regulate or prohibit abortion.

460.   Dooling, John Francis. Cora McRae et al., plaintiffs, Against
        Secretary of Health, Education and Welfare, Defendant, Against
        James F. Buckley, et al. 2 vols. Brooklyn: U.S. District
        Court, Eastern District of New York, 1979.

        Debates on the Hyde amendment, which stated that no funds
        appropriated under this Act should be used for abortions.

461.   Dornblaser, Carole, and Uta Landy. The Abortion Guide: A

        Handbook for Women and Men. New York: Playboy, 1982.

        Contains information on the abortion procedure, as well as
        personal stories of people who have gone through the abortion
        experience, for those women faced with an unwanted pregnancy.

462.   Doyle, John P. "Taxes--Where the Dollars Go--Abortions Yes,
        Private Schools No." Liguorian Sept. 1975: 7-11.

        Contrasts the use of tax monies for abortions, but not to
        subsidize private school education, which is "equally" a
        civil right of American citizens.

463.   Doyle, John P., et al. "Fight for Life: Missouri, March 8,
        1972 (Missouri House Bill 1470)." Social Justice Review June
        1972: 89-94.

        Statements from four physicians supporting the anti-abortion
        cause in Missouri.

464. Doyle, Marsha Vanderford. "In-House Rhetoric of Pro-Life and Pro-Choice Special Interests Groups in Minnesota: Motivation and Alienation." Diss. U. of Minnesota, 1982.

    The focus of this study is the rhetoric produced by the abortion controversy in Minnesota.

465. Drill, Victor A. "History of the First Oral Contraceptive." Journal of Toxicology and Environmental Health Sept. 1977: 133-38.

    Oral contraceptives have now been used clinically for over 15 years. The present brief review discusses the discovery and development of the first oral contraceptive.

466. Drinan, Robert F. "The Abortion Decision." Commonweal 16 Feb. 1973: 438-40.

    Drinan, a Jesuit, U.S. congressman, and former dean of Boston College Law School, cites how, in Roe v. Wade, the justices tried to balance poverty and pregnancy.

467. _____. "Abortions on Medicaid?" Commonweal 9 May 1975: 102-03.

    The defeat of the Bartlett amendment reinforces the fact that Catholics in the U.S. Congress are not united on any legal-moral approach to the use of federal funds for abortions.

468. Drogin, Elasah. Margaret Sanger, Father of Modern Society. Coarsegold: CUL, 1980.

    Recounts the life of the woman who founded the international birth control movement.

469. Dryfoos, Joy G. "What President Bush Can Do About Family Planning." American Journal of Public Health June 1989: 689-90.

    Encourages President Bush to move rapidly to promote a "kinder and gentler" nation by ensuring that the family-planning program is finally allowed to achieve its potential.

470. Dubois, Christine. "What Different Christian Churches Believe About Abortion." U.S. Catholic Aug. 1985: 33-38.

    Dubois ponders: None of the mainline Protestant churches believes that abortion is a good thing. But why do some of them consider it "a necessary option in a sinful world"?

471. Dudar, Helen. "Abortion for the Asking." Saturday Review of
      the Society. Apr. 1973: 30-35.

      A narrative of the events taking place in a New York abortion
      clinic, interspersed with medical explanations and legal
      arguments.

472. Duffey, Michael K. "Abortion and the Christian Story." Linacre
      Quarterly 51 (1984): 60-69.

      Considers the practice of abortion in terms of adhering to a
      particular way of life.

473. Duggan, George H. "Humanae Vitae and After." Linacre
      Quarterly 40 (1973): 58-62.

      Duggan agrees with Derrick, who said he thought the Humanae
      Vitae encyclical would probably not have any long-term conse-
      quences of a dramatic nature. The church has not been rent
      by open schism, and although there have been some notable
      defections, those who have rejected the papal teaching have
      contented themselves with "responsible dissent."

474. Dunigan, Vincent J. "Natural Family Planning Basis for a
      Happy Married Life." Priest Jan. 1982: 12-17.

      Claims that natural family planning (NFP) is not a technology
      but a way of life, a path of development--a life-style which
      involves a deeply human ordering of sexual energy which
      combines self-knowledge and concern for one's spouse in a
      mutually supportive, tender, loving atmosphere.

475. Durbin, Karen. "The Intelligent Woman's Guide to Sex."
      Mademoiselle Mar. 1975: 41.

      Argues that abortion is a fact in our society. Shall we
      impose upon it once again the conditions that prevailed until
      two years ago--criminality, and the resulting barbarism, greed,
      and gross injustice?

476. Dyck, Arthur J., and George H. Williams. "The Right to Life:
      The Harvard Statement." Catholic Digest Mar. 1972: 29-32.

      Progress in the laws defending the rights of the unborn is
      reversed by the trend toward abortion.

477. Dykeman, Wilma. Too Many People, Too Little Love: Edna Rankin
      McKinnon: Pioneer for Birth Control. New York: Holt, 1974.

478. Ebaugh, Helen Rose Fuchs, and C. Allen Haney. "Church Attendance and Attitudes Toward Abortion: Differentials in Liberal
and Conservative Churches." Journal for the Scientific Study
of Religion 17 (1978): 407-13.

National survey finds that frequency of church attendance is
positively related to disapproval of legalized abortion for
members of fundamentalist churches; no relationship exists
between church attendance and attitudes toward abortion for
members of liberal churches.

479. _____. "Shifts in Abortion Attitudes: 1972-1978."
Journal of Marriage and the Family 42 (1980): 491-99.

Trends in attitudes toward abortion on the part of the American
population are analyzed, with emphasis upon a comparison of
attitudes before and after the 1973 Roe and Doe U.S. Supreme
Court decisions.

480. Eclipse of Reason: Award-Winning Documentary About Women and
Life and Death in the Womb. Videocassette. Dir. R. Anderson.
Intro. Charleton Heston. Prod. Charles Warren. Bernadell,
1987. 8 min.

Through a fiberoptic camera, shows a 4-1/2-month-old fetus
apparently being dismembered with forceps during an abortion.

481. "Ecumenical War over Abortion." Time 29 Jan. 1979: 62-63.

Both sides in the McRae v. Califano lawsuit on the Medicaid
issue believe that opponents threaten their basic rights.

482. "Edelin Abortion Verdict." National Review 14 Mar. 1975: 260-
63.

Jury verdict in the Edelin case once again sets off a national
debate on abortion. The debate raises the question of whether
the case was really about abortion, or whether it was a manslaughter case.

483. "Edelin Case." Nation 8 Mar. 1975: 260-61.

The trial and conviction of Dr. Kenneth C. Edelin in Boston on
a manslaughter charge may, in the end, help to reconcile the
seemingly irreconcilable abortion and anti-abortion forces.

484. Edelin, Kenneth. "Questions No One Asked Dr. Kenneth Edelin
on the Witness Stand." Ed. Gloria Steinem. Ms. Aug. 1975:
76+.

An interview with Dr. Edelin following his conviction for manslaughter.

485. Edelstein, Robert, Edward S. Herman, and Mary W. Herman. "Moral Consistency and the Abortion Issue." Commonweal 22 Mar. 1974: 59-61; 17 May 1974: 261-64.

Protecting human life before and after birth--the Pennsylvania scene with John Cardinal Krol.

486. "Edges of Life, 2." Commonweal 1 Aug. 1980: 421.

The U.S. Supreme Court rules on the Hyde amendment. A discussion of the legally coercive prohibition of abortion by the state and the potentially economically coercive refusal of payment for abortion.

487. Edmonson, Daisy, and Olivia Schieffelin Nordberg. "Birth Control: What You Need to Know." Parents Oct. 1986: 156.

Which birth control methods are reliable? How safe are they? Here are the facts you need to find the contraceptive that works best for you.

488. Edmunds, Lavinia. "Birth Control on TV." Ms. Nov. 1985: 20.

The three major TV networks refuse to air ads designed as public service announcements by the American College of Obstetrics and Gynecology (ACOG) to prevent teenage and other unintentional pregnancies. Meanwhile, stations in Atlanta, Miami, and other cities, along with Cable News Network, were putting in requests for the ACOG announcements.

489. _____. "Voters Alert: Abortion, Gay Rights, ERA (for a change)." Ms. Sept. 1986: 30.

A short survey article dealing with anti-abortion referenda in various states.

490. Ehrlich, Elizabeth. "If Pro-Choice Is Mainstream, Now's the Time to Prove It." Business Week 17 July 1989: 64.

The U.S. Supreme Court's July 3 ruling in Webster v. Reproductive Health Services throws the abortion issue out of the lofty realm of constitutional law and into the grittier political arena of lobbying and lawmaking.

491. Eleven Million Teenagers: What Can Be Done About the Epidemic of Adolescent Pregnancies in the United States. New York: Guttmacher Inst., 1976.

Directly addresses the issue of what adolescent pregnancies
cost Americans and America in health, economic, social, and
human terms.

492. Elizari, F. J. "The Ten Years of Humanae Vitae." Theology
      Digest 28 (1980): 33-37.

      Reviews and appraises the major developments in regard to
      Humanae Vitae during this decade.

493. Ellington, Jenefer. We Are the Mainstream: Dissent in the
      Catholic Church. Washington: Catholics for a Free Choice,
      1981.

      Looks at the institutional history of the Catholic church and
      measures it against the experiences of its membership, past
      and present.

494. Elliot, Elizabeth, and Wendy Susco. "Legal Briefs: Questions
      and Answers." Working Woman 4 Mar. 1979: 16.

      An abortion update: What's changed--and what hasn't--since the
      U.S. Supreme Court stepped in.

495. Elliott, Robin A. "Bringing the Sexual Revolution Home--
      Rejoinder." America 14 Oct. 1978: 243.

      Argues that the "imposition of moral codes by fiat of govern-
      ment" is precisely what Planned Parenthood's programs for
      teenagers are. Using public funds, Planned Parenthood inter-
      poses itself between parents and children, teaches children
      that premarital sex is a "liberating" experience, (and) shuts
      parents completely out of the decision-making process under
      the guise of..."confidentiality."

496. Emerson, Thomas I. "The Power of Congress to Change Constitu-
      tional Decisions of the Supreme Court: The Human Life Bill."
      Northwestern University Law Review 2 (1982): 129-42.

      Discusses that portion of the human life bill, as reported by
      the subcommittee, which provides: 1) Congress finds that
      the life of each human being begins at conception. 2) Con-
      gress further finds that the Fourteenth Amendment to the
      Constitution of the United States protects all human beings.

497. Emmens, Carol A. The Abortion Controversy. New York: Messner,
      1987.

      Examines the issue of abortion, including its moral, legal,
      social, and medical aspects.

498. "Employee Benefit Encourages Adoption as Abortion Alternative."
     Hospital Progress Mar. 1984: 29-30.

     The employee benefits program at the Holy Cross Health System
     includes payment of up to $1,000 to any employee adopting a
     child, to be used to defray adoption expenses.

499. "The End of Roe?" National Review 24 Mar. 1989: 12-13.

     Roe remains the nakedest, least-principled exercise of what
     Justice Byron White called "raw judicial power" in the history
     of the Republic.

500. Engel, Randy. "Will Your Government Phase Out Large Families?"
     Liguorian May 1972: 39-42.

     A hypothetical bill introduced in Congress, "The Voluntary
     Family Limitation Act," is used to illustrate what the future
     might hold.

501. English, Dierdre. "The War Against Choice: Inside the Anti-
     abortion Movement." Mother Jones Feb.-Mar. 1981: 16-32.

     Reviews the variety of programs and groups concerned with the
     anti-abortion movement.

502. Enright, Vincent L. "Natural Family Planning at the Grass-
     roots." Priest Sept. 1982: 30-32.

     Discusses various family-planning programs and support in
     dioceses in Pennsylvania and the Rochester diocese in New York.

503. "ERA and Abortion: Pennsylvania Court Ruling." Origins 29 Mar.
     1984: 699-704.

     A Pennsylvania state court has ruled unconstitutional that
     state's laws limiting the public funding of abortion to cases
     where the mother's life is endangered by the pregnancy or where
     the pregnancy is a result of rape or incest.

504. Erdahl, Lowell O. Pro-Life/Pro-Peace: Life-Affirming Alterna-
     tives to Abortion, War, Mercy Killing, and the Death Penalty.
     Minneapolis: Augsburg, 1986.

     The coverage of the issues of abortion, war, mercy killing, and
     the death penalty encourages serious reflection by everyone
     concerned about the issues of life and peace.

505. Erens, Pamela. "Anti-Abortion, Pro-Feminism?" Mother Jones
     May 1989: 31+.

Argues that feminists advocate choice versus right-to-lifers who oppose abortion, women's rights, and sexual freedom.

506. Estreicher, Samuel. "Congressional Power and Constitutional Rights: Reflections on Proposed "Human Life" Legislation." Virginia Law Review Feb. 1982: 333-458.

The constitutionality of the "human life" proposal does not depend on one's view of the wisdom or legitimacy of Roe and its progeny. The issue is simply whether Congress can undo Roe v. Wade by ordinary legislation.

507. Etzioni, Amitai. "The Fetus: Whose Property?" Commonweal 21 Sept. 1973: 493.

A three-judge federal court ruled on August 15, 1973, in Miami, Florida, that a woman does not need the consent of her husband to obtain a legal abortion. The ruling goes far beyond removing the government as an agent in deciding what a woman and her physician may choose to do; it also removes the husband.

508. Evangelicals for Social Action Staff. Completely Pro-Life: Building a Consistent Stance. Downers Grove: Inter-Varsity, 1987.

Attempts to articulate a consistent pro-life stance on public-policy issues that flow from a biblical definition of life.

509. Evans, J. Claude. "The Abortion Debate: A Call for Civility." Editorial. Christian Century 21 Mar. 1979: 300-01.

Argues that both sides in the abortion controversy share a fallacy in their arguments; that is, each side wants legislatures to make laws supporting its position.

510. _____. "The Abortion Decision: A Balancing of Rights." Editorial. Christian Century 14 Feb. 1973: 195-97.

Summarizes the U.S. Supreme Court's decision by examining the focus and conclusions it arrived at in its historic ruling.

511. _____. "Defusing the Abortion Debate." Editorial. Christian Century 31 Jan. 1973: 117-18.

Suggests that the best way to defuse the abortion issue is to keep it in national debate and not emotionalize it into a life-and-death issue.

512. Evans, Joyce. "Prolife Compassion or Crusade?" America 11 Dec. 1982: 373-74.

No matter how noble the goal, the dynamics of any group can lead to a narrow focus on winning that leaves little room for recognizing the victims.

513. Ezzard, Nancy V., et al. "Race-Specific Patterns of Abortion Use by American Teenagers." American Journal of Public Health Aug. 1982: 809-14.

As legal abortion became more widely available nationally, abortion rates and ratios increased for all American teenagers; the rates and ratios for teenagers of black and other races increased faster than those for white teenagers.

514. Facione, Peter A. "Callahan on Abortion." American Ecclesiastical Review May 1973: 291-301.

Daniel Callahan, in his book Abortion: Law, Choice, and Morality (New York: Macmillan, 1970), has successfully tackled the complex and polemic-scarred issue of abortion. He presents and interprets the relevant medical, psychological, biological, legal, sociological, political, moral, philosophical, and religious material.

515. Falik, Marilyn. Ideology and Abortion Policy Politics. New York: Praeger, 1983.

Challenges the assumption that "abortion politics" is a single-issue campaign and demonstrates that the abortion policy debate underscores conflicting orientations toward fundamental aspects of social and political life.

516. "False Advertising." Time 20 Oct. 1986: 43.

Right-to-life organizations in Texas are prohibited from listing themselves in the telephone yellow pages under the "abortion information" heading.

517. Faludi, Susan. "Where Did Randy Go Wrong?" Mother Jones Nov. 1989: 22+.

Background article on Randall Terry of Operation Rescue, outlining his life experiences and their influences on his present position of being a militant anti-abortionist.

518. Falwell, Jerry. If I Should Die Before I Wake. Nashville: Nelson, 1986.

Traces the ordeal of one Georgia girl from her first sexual encounter to the birth of her son.

519.   _____. "A Pragmatic Proposal." Editorial. <u>Fundamental-ist Journal</u> Mar. 1983: 8.

Jerry Falwell says, "Reality has forced me to understand that strategy changes had to be made if any chance of a significant pro-life victory is to be realized."

520.   "Family Planning: United Nations World Survey." <u>UNESCO Courier</u> July 1974: 46-48.

A survey by wide geographic areas, not by country.

521.   "Family Planning Funds Are Cut." <u>World Health</u> Mar. 1986: 31.

The Agency for International Development (AID) withholds $10 million from a $46-million allocation for the budget of the United Nations Fund for Population Activities.

522.   "The Fanatical Abortion Fight." <u>Time</u> 9 July 1979: 26-27.

The momentum has swung to the pro-life groups, and the struggle has shifted to the political arena.

523.   Farber, Daniel A. "Abortion Economics: A Fresh Analysis." <u>New Republic</u> 14 and 21 July 1986: 15-16.

The intellectual movement called "law and economics" is used in novel ways to address legal and moral issues, including abortion.

524.   Farr, Louise. "I Was a Spy at a Right-to-Life Convention." <u>Ms</u>. Feb. 1976: 77+.

Anyone who disagrees with the right-to-lifers' logic is "pro-death."

525.   Farrell, Mary H. J. "Birth Control: Surprising News!" <u>Good Housekeeping</u> May 1985: 315.

Sterilization has now overtaken the birth control pill as the birth control choice of married women.

526.   Fathalla, M. F. "The Ethics of Family Planning." <u>World Health</u> June 1984: 27-29.

With the development of government-based family-planning programs, the ethical debate has moved away from the question of why and now concerns how: How is the human right of access to family-planning services being met?

527. Faux, Marian. Roe v. Wade: The Untold Story of the Landmark
      Supreme Court Decision That Made Abortion Legal. New York:
      Macmillan, 1988.

      An account of the events leading up to the U.S. Supreme Court's
      1973 decision to overturn state laws banning abortion during
      the first six months of pregnancy.

528. Fawcett, James T., ed. Psychological Perspectives on Popula-
      tion. New York: Basic, 1973.

      Eighteen original essays sponsored by the Population Council.

529. "Federal Abortion." Editorial. America 24 Oct. 1981: 232-33.

      Congress is encouraged to eliminate payments for abortions for
      federal employees.

530. Feen, Richard H. "The Historical Dimensions of Infanticide
      and Abortion: The Experience of Classical Greece." Linacre
      Quarterly 51 (1984): 248-54.

      As the practice of abortion and infanticide are becoming
      commonplace in the American family, we are returning to a
      pre-Christian moral universe. This article reviews the Greek
      experience on this matter.

531. Feen, Richard Harrow. "The Classical Roots of the Personhood
      Debate." Faith and Reason 9 (1983): 120-27.

      Marshalls important evidence for pro-life by showing that the
      debate over abortion was very much in earnest in the classical
      world, with much to be said in favor of the unborn.

532. Feinberg, Joel, ed. Problem of Abortion. Belmont: Wadsworth,
      1973.

      A collection of essays on the abortion question.

533. Feldman, David M. Marital Relations, Birth Control, and
      Abortion in Jewish Law. New York: Schocken, 1974.

      Offers insights into and value judgments on areas of human
      concern--marital relations, birth control and abortion--
      insights which can be enlightening to a generation beset by
      confusion and self-questioning.

534. "Fertility and Contraception." Scientific American Oct. 1972:
      46.

The modernization of contraceptive practices in the United States dramatized by a 36-percent decline in the rate of unwanted childbearing between the five-year periods ending in 1965 and 1970, has been a major factor in the remarkable decrease in the American birthrate during the past decade.

535. Ficarra, Bernard Joseph. *Abortion Analyzed*. Old Town: Health Educator, 1989.

A study in the approach to a problem, abortion, that has divided modern medical practice in America.

536. Field, Mary Jane. *The Comparative Politics of Birth Control: Determinants of Policy Variation and Change in the Developed Nations*. New York: Praeger, 1983.

Details some of Margaret Sanger's earlier visits to Europe, her adoption of medical supervision for birth control, and her neo-Malthusian ideas.

537. "Fight over Abortions--Heating Up Again." *U.S. News and World Report* 19 Dec. 1977: 68.

The fight over abortions seems certain to be renewed next year--and possibly for many years ahead--when the annual budget request for the Department of Health, Education and Welfare (HEW) comes up for consideration again.

538. Fightlin, Marshall. "Spirituality and Family Planning." *Homiletic and Pastoral Review* June 1983: 24-29.

The term "family planning" designates a process, usually on-going, by which married couples make decisions about conceiving children. In this article, the term refers to a process by which a married couple decides here and now whether pregnancy should be consciously sought or avoided.

539. Figley, Charles R., and Linda M. Scroggins. "Putting the 'Family' in Family Planning Services." *Advances in Planned Parenthood* 13 (1978): 75-77.

Suggests that the American family is evolving rather than dying and that human services programs, like family-planning centers, must reevaluate their relationship to the family unit. This paper promotes the adoption of a family-planning delivery system centered upon relationships.

540. Fimian, Charles. "The Effects of Religion on Abortion Policy-Making: A Study of Voting Behavior in the U.S. Congress, 1976-1980." Diss. Arizona State U, 1983.

A study of the effects of religion on the votes cast by members of the U.S. Congress on abortion-funding legislation during the period 1976-80.

541. Finkel, Madelon Lubin, and David J. Finkel. "Male Adolescent Contraceptive Utilization." Adolescence 13 (1978): 443-51.

The contraceptive utilization of a sample of sexually active, urban high school males (black, Hispanic, and white) is examined.

542. Finkel, Madelon Lubin, and Steven Finkel. "Sex Education in High School." Society Nov.-Dec. 1985: 48-52.

Contends that the rationale behind formal instruction in sex education is that increased knowledge about human reproduction, sexual behavior, and contraception could dispel misconceptions, myths, and half-truths while encouraging more informed, responsible decision making about individual sexual activity and behavior.

543. Finlay, Barbara Agresti. "Sex Differences in Correlates of Abortion Attitudes Among College Students." Journal of Marriage and the Family 43 (1981): 571-82.

Data from a sample of students at a large southern university are analyzed for differences between males and females in correlates of abortion attitudes. Males' abortion attitudes are related primarily to their degree of conventionality in sexual and nonsexual matters. Females' abortion attitudes are related to a broader set of attitudinal variables.

544. Finn, Joseph L. "A Physician Looks at the Abortion Problem." Dimension 5 (Spring 1973): 14-24.

Provides a medical consideration of abortion.

545. Finnis, John M. "Conscience, Infallibility and Contraception." Month Dec. 1978: 410-17.

An opposite point of view: a study by Dr. Finnis, who believes that Humanae Vitae reproduced "an irreformable teaching infallibly taught by the Church."

546. Fischman, Susan H. "Delivery or Abortion in Inner-City Adolescents." American Journal of Orthopsychiatry 47 (1977): 127-33.

This study of an urban group of unwed black adolescent girls who chose to deliver or abort a pregnancy focuses on factors in that decision associated with personal, social, and familial characteristics.

547. Fisher, William A., ed. Adolescents, Sex and Contraception. Hillsdale: Erlbaum, 1983.

Addresses the question of why so many adolescents who do not want to conceive still fail to use contraception despite their increased education about it and its availability.

548. Flaherty, Francis J. "Abortion, the Constitution and the Human Life Statute." Commonweal 23 Oct. 1981: 586-93.

Reviews the strategy for developing and offering the Helms-Hyde bill, otherwise known as the human life statute, which would declare a fetus to be a human person from the moment of conception.

549. Fleming, Alice Mulcahey. Contraception, Abortion, Pregnancy. Nashville: Nelson, 1974.

Introduces the facts about sexual intercourse, contraception, abortion and its alternatives, pregnancy, and childbirth.

550. Fletcher, Joseph. "Abortion and the True Believer." Christian Century 1 Jan. 1975: 1126-27.

Essentially a debate over the question of whether or not a fetus is a person and, consequently, what, if any, rights ought to be assigned to uterine life.

551. Flexner, Eleanor. Century of Struggle: The Woman's Rights Movement in the United States. Rev. ed. Cambridge: Harvard UP, 1975.

Deals with Margaret Sanger's efforts in the field of population control and her early efforts for birth control.

552. "Florida Baptists Group Says All Abortions Immoral." Jet 9 Dec. 1985: 29.

Abortions are immoral, even if the pregnancy threatens the life of the mother or is the result of incest or rape.

553. "Foes of Abortion Start a Prolife Insurance Company." Christianity Today 3 Feb. 1984: 43.

A northern Illinois insurance agent and three doctors have

formed an insurance company that will not offer abortion
coverage to any policyholder.

554. Foltz, Kim. "TV, Sex and Prevention." Newsweek 9 Sept. 1985:
72.

Some television stations cautiously start to air advertisements for contraceptives to determine whether the public finds
them offensive.

555. Forbes, Malcolm S., Jr. "'Natural' Birth Control." Editorial.
Forbes 28 Apr. 1986: 45.

A population growth strategy by itself is not going to make
a poor country rich. When a country becomes more prosperous,
birth rates fall. As people become better off, the population
"problem" takes care of itself.

556. Ford, James H., and Michael Schwartz. "Birth Control for
Teenagers: Diagram for Disaster." Linacre Quarterly 46 (1979):
71-81.

The accuracy of studies on teenage pregnancy by Zelnick and
Kantner for Planned Parenthood is attacked and refuted on the
basis that results do not support their conclusions.

557. Ford, John C., and Germain Grisez. "Contraception and the
Infallibility of the Ordinary Magisterium." Theological
Studies 39 (1978): 258-312.

Argues that the received Catholic teaching on contraception has
been proposed infallibly by the ordinary magisterium.

558. Ford, Maurice deG. "Rocking the Roe Boat: Hearing the
Missouri Case." Commonweal 2 June 1989: 326-28.

Describes the emotion surrounding the U.S. Supreme Court's
chambers, and the arguments in them, as the Webster v. Reproductive Health Services case is heard.

559. Ford, Nancy. "The Evolution of a Constitutional Right to an
Abortion, Fashioned in the 1970s and Secured in the 1980s."
Journal of Legal Medicine 4 (1983): 271-322.

Traces the historical evolution of the right to an abortion,
paying particular attention to the various standards of
judicial review that have been utilized by the U.S. Supreme
Court and lower courts in abortion cases. Reviews the
constitutionality of specific types of abortion regulation.
Analyzes, in the final section, the U.S. Supreme Court's most
recent abortion decisions: City of Akron v. Akron Center

for <u>Reproductive</u> <u>Health,</u> <u>Inc.,</u> <u>Planned</u> <u>Parenthood</u> <u>Association</u>
v. <u>Ashcroft,</u> and <u>Simopoulos</u> v. <u>Virginia</u>.

560. Fornos, Werner. "The Moral Implications of Our Population
Policy." <u>Humanist</u> Jan.-Feb. 1987: 30-32.

It is time for the United States to regain the moral high
ground in the battle for effective family planning in the
Third World.

561. Foss-Goodman, Deborah Anne. "Males and Contraception: The
Relationship Between Contraceptive Knowledge, Attitudes and
Behavior." Diss. Albany: SUNY, 1984.

Reflects the results of a questionnaire surveying the contraceptive knowledge, attitude, history, and behavior of 500
undergraduate males at the College of William and Mary in
Virginia.

562. Fowler, Paul B. <u>Abortion:</u> <u>Toward</u> <u>an</u> <u>Evangelical</u> <u>Consensus</u>.
Portland: Multnomah, 1987.

Contends that the beliefs and values underlying every pro-
choice or pro-abortion position are antithetical to central
themes of Scripture.

563. Fowler, Richard A., and H. Wayne House. <u>The</u> <u>Christian</u>
<u>Confronts</u> <u>His</u> <u>Culture</u>. Chicago: Moody, 1983.

Strategies, counseling tips, and case studies are presented in
the areas of feminist rights, right-to-life issues, and homo-
sexuality to aid the Christian in applying the material to the
Catholic church's position on those issues.

564. Fox, Greer Litton. "Sex-Role Attitudes as Predictors of Contraceptive Use Among Unmarried University Students." <u>Sex</u> <u>Roles</u>
June 1977: 265-83.

Findings suggest that nontraditional sex-role-related
attitudes, in conjunction with an internal locus of control
orientation, are predictive of effective contraception for
women respondents. Neither variable, alone or jointly,
explain the contraceptive behavior of men respondents.

565. _____, ed. <u>The</u> <u>Childbearing</u> <u>Decision:</u> <u>Fertility</u> <u>Atti-</u>
<u>tudes</u> <u>and</u> <u>Behavior</u>. Beverly Hills: Sage, 1982.

Will be beneficial to those who desire an appreciation and
general characterization of the many facets of fertility-
related decisions.

566. Fraker, Susan, Lucy Howard, and Elaine Sciolino. "Abortion: Who Pays?" Newsweek 4 July 1977: 12-13.

A report on the immediate and long-term effects of the U.S. Supreme Court's denial of the use of federal funds for Medicaid abortions.

567. Frame, Randy. "Presbyterians Consider Four Views on Abortion." Christianity Today 15 Dec. 1989: 52-55.

Reviews alternative options on the abortion question.

568. _____. "Prolife Activists Escalate the War Against Abortion." Christianity Today 9 Nov. 1984: 40-42.

During an election year, pro-lifers intensify their picketing efforts and venture into civil disobedience.

569. _____. "Prolife Leaders Say 1986 Has Been a Very Good Year." Christianity Today 21 Nov. 1986: 30+.

More people are coming to regard abortion as a violation of the civil rights of the unborn.

570. _____. "School-Based Health Clinics: An Idea Whose Time Has Come?" Christianity Today 7 Mar. 1986: 42-44.

Opponents maintain that providing contraceptives to teens might cause more pregnancies than it prevents.

571. _____. "Strategists Work to Sound Death Knell for Abortion." Christianity Today 18 May 1984: 74.

Pro-life leaders want to make sure that if and when ground is prepared, the legal seeds for reversal are planted with prudence. The key element in this strategy is the principle of gradualism.

572. Francke, Linda Bird. "Abortion and Men." Esquire Jan. 1978: 58-60.

Excerpt from Linda Bird Francke's forthcoming book, The Ambivalence of Abortion (New York: Random, 1978). Men, like women, often have fears and emotional needs which require special--yet different--counseling.

573. _____. The Ambivalence of Abortion. New York: Random, 1978.

84

Explores the emotional and psychological aspects of abortion, alluding briefly to the historical and sociological aspects of the issue.

574.   Francome, Colin. <u>Abortion</u> <u>Freedom:</u> <u>A</u> <u>Worldwide</u> <u>Movement</u>. Boston: Allen, 1984.

Examines legal changes concerning contraception and abortion rights that have occurred worldwide.

575.   _____. <u>Abortion</u> <u>Practice</u> <u>in</u> <u>Britain</u> <u>and</u> <u>the</u> <u>United</u> <u>States</u>. Boston: Allen, 1986.

Concentrates heavily on young, single teenagers and attempts to explode the myths about teeenage sexuality--myths to which abortion has so often contributed.

576.   Frank, Elizabeth Pope. "The Tragedy That Did Not Have to Happen." <u>Good</u> <u>Housekeeping</u> June 1979: 78+.

The story of a young woman who conceived out of wedlock, did not marry, and aborted herself. She was then indicted for conducting an illicit abortion and subsequently acquitted.

577.   Frech, Frances. "How I Handle Abortion Hecklers." <u>Liguorian</u> Apr. 1974: 23-27.

Relates how the author disarms or otherwise confronts pro-abortion persons in audiences she addresses.

578.   Freedman, Sheldon. "Jewish Religious Tradition and the Issue of Abortion." <u>Dimension</u> 5 (Summer 1973): 90-93.

The text of testimony before the Abortion Law Commission on February 24, 1972, which represents the National Rabbinical Council (NRC) of America's pronouncements that it is against Jewish law to destroy, or harm in any way, an embryo <u>in</u> <u>utero</u>.

579.   "Freeing the Prisoners." <u>Time</u> 20 Mar. 1972: 89-90.

New medical and legal attitudes are rapidly giving women virtually complete freedom from involuntary conception or motherhood.

580.   Freeman, Ellen W. "Abortion: Subjective Attitudes and Feelings." <u>Family</u> <u>Planning</u> <u>Perspectives</u> May-June 1978: 150-55.

The decision to terminate a pregnancy is neither casual nor easy: most women see abortion as a difficult but necessary alternative to an unintended birth. Their ambivalence is no reason to counsel against the abortion; most resolve their problems soon after the procedure. Lack of support by partners can be a major source of distress.

581. Friedman, Cornelia Morrison, Rhoda Greenspan, and Fay Mittleman. "The Decision-Making Process and the Outcome of Therapeutic Abortion." American Journal of Psychiatry Dec. 1974: 1332-37.

American literature on abortion suggests that an immediate negative response to abortion is not uncommon among women undergoing this procedure and that short-term unhappiness and guilt may be part of the normal response.

582. Friesen, Duane K. Moral Issues in the Control of Birth. Newton: Faith and Life, 1974.

A study designed to help readers think about abortion, learn some facts about it, consider their attitudes toward it, and, perhaps, reach some decision on it.

583. Frohock, Fred M. Abortion: A Case Study in Law and Morals. Westport: Greenwood, 1983.

Examines abortion in terms of political philosophy, justice, and moral positions.

584. "From the Courts to Congress." America 25 June 1983: 2.

In striking down restrictions on abortions imposed by local ordinances in Akron, Ohio, the U.S. Supreme Court's decision clearly leaves Congress and a constitutional amendment the only remaining avenue for limiting abortions.

585. Fuqua, David. "Justice Harry A. Blackmun: The Abortion Decisions." Arkansas Law Review 2 (1980): 276-96.

Does not support any argument, pro or con: Instead, it analyzes the jurisprudential philosophy of the major abortion decisions written by Justice Blackmun, with an emphasis on explaining the decisional expediency of Roe v. Wade.

586. "Furor over Abortion--Hotter Than Ever." U.S. News and World Report 4 Mar. 1974: 43-44.

Asks: What are the rights of an unborn child? The question is stirring debate and a nationwide drive by anti-abortion forces to overturn a historic U.S. Supreme Court ruling.

587. Fylling, Petter, and Torunn Svendsby. "Contraceptive Practice Before and After Therapeutic Abortion." *Fertility and Sterility* July 1979: 24-27.

   Of 180 women who underwent therapeutic abortion in a certain period in 1977, 71.7 percent were unmarried and 63.9 percent were unmarried primigravidas (women pregnant for the first time).

588. Gaetano, David. "Why Abortion Sit-ins?" *Columbia* May 1979: 18-23.

   Discusses what is behind the confrontation between pro-lifers and abortion clinics.

589. Gaffney, Edward M. "Law and Theology: A Dialogue on the Abortion Decisions." *Jurist* 33 (1973): 134-52.

   The subject matter of the U.S. Supreme Court's abortion decisions calls for careful scrutiny from disciplines other than the law, which deal with human life and human values. And so, a theologian comments on the Court's abortion decisions from the perspective of his science.

590. Gaffney, James. "Human Embryos: Their Moral Status." *America* 19 Oct. 1985: 236-38.

   Insights gleaned from an understanding of moral development can help clarify our thinking about the abortion issue.

591. Gager, Virginia D. "In Defense of the Unborn." *Marriage* June 1973: 38-45.

   Reviews the recent *Roe* v. *Wade* decision and exposes the flaws and inconsistencies in the U.S. Supreme Court's logic.

592. Gallagher, Janet. "The Fetus and the Law--Whose Life Is It Anyway?" *Ms.* Sept. 1984: 62+.

   A feminist attorney examines the complex and sometimes heart-rending conflicts that arise when the law starts questioning a pregnant woman's rights.

593. Gallagher, John P. "Why the NFP Movement Has Grown." *International Review of Natural Family Planning* 7 (1983): 200-04.

   Gives social reasons why the natural family planning (NFP) movement has grown.

594. Gallagher, Maggie. "One Step Forward..." National Review
     13 Mar. 1987: 29-30.

     Discusses enforcement of a 1970 law prohibiting organizations
     that promote abortions from receiving federal funds.

595. Gallahue, Louise. "Societal Trends, Church Beliefs Support
     NFP Methods." Hospital Progress Dec. 1983: 54+.

     Contends that couples' use of information about themselves to
     achieve or to avoid a pregnancy without resorting to chemicals
     or devices is in keeping with societal trends emphasizing
     living naturally to decrease environmental and social problems.
     Also contends that these trends are a major reason why people
     are turning to natural family planning (NFP).

596. Ganz, Richard L., ed. Thou Shalt Not Kill: The Christian Case
     Against Abortion. New Rochelle: Arlington, 1978.

     Seven essays examining and criticizing abortion from diverse
     perspectives.

597. Gardner, Joy. A Difficult Decision: A Compassionate Book About
     Abortion. Trumansburg: Crossing, 1986.

     Aims to provide support to the woman (or to the couple) when
     the woman finds herself unexpectedly pregnant.

598. Gardner, R. F. R. Abortion: The Personal Dilemma. New York:
     Erdmans, 1974.

     A Christian gynecologist examines the medical, social, and
     spiritual issues of abortion.

599. Garfield, Jay L., and Patricia Hennessey, eds. Abortion: Moral
     and Legal Perspectives. Amherst: U of Massachusetts P, 1984.

     Valuable because it deals with familiar, central problems, yet
     manages to exercise the mind with many new twists and turns.

600. Garn, Jake. "Debating Abortion." National Review 11 Nov. 1977:
     1299+.

     Recounts the day's activities in the U.S. Senate when abortion
     debate on the Labor-HEW Appropriations bill was held.

601. Garner-Sweet, Gail, ed. Pro-Life Feminism: Different Voices.
     Lewiston: Life Cycle, 1985.

A series of articles showing the relationship between pro-life and feminist tenets on abortion.

602. Garton, Jean S. _Who Broke the Baby?_ Minneapolis: Bethany, 1979.

Cites the pros and cons of abortion.

603. Garvey, John. "Imposing Mercy: Abortion, the Church, and the Unwanted." _Commonweal_ 11 Sept. 1981: 485-86.

Concludes that Linda Bird Francke misquoted and misunderstood the church's position concerning the conception versus ensoulment (quickening) question.

604. _____. "Pro-Life Means More Than Anti-Abortion." _U.S. Catholic_ Mar. 1980: 35-37.

Argues that to be pro-life is to take a broad stance which, of necessity and for consistency, involves capital punishment, nuclear war, problems of the hungry and the homeless.

605. Gastonguay, Paul. "Abortion: Assault on Human Life." _Liguorian_ Dec. 1972: 27-30.

According to the author, abortion is becoming a socially accepted means of taking the lives of unwanted babies, and euthanasia will evolve from relaxed abortion legislation.

606. _____. "Early Discovery of Birth Defects." _America_ 29 Sept. 1973: 218.

Explores the relationship between amniocentesis and abortion legislation.

607. _____. "The Fourteenth Amendment and Human Life." _America_ 15 Apr. 1972: 400-01.

What facts legally determine whether the human embryo is a human being and thus protected by the Fifth and Fourteenth Amendments?

608. Gaulard, Joan Marie. "Woman Rebel: The Rhetorical Control Movement, 1912-1938." Diss. Indiana U, 1978.

Provides an excellent review of Margaret Sanger's plan of action which resulted in 1938 in a series of U.S. Supreme Court decisions regarding the availability and distribution of birth control information and materials.

609.	Gaum, Gregory. "Abortion: An Ecumenical Dilemma." Commonweal
	30 Nov. 1973: 231-35.

	An ecumenical theologian asks whether one should regard the
	moral teaching of Christian churches on abortion as a Christian
	witness, even though they differ from the traditional position.

610.	Gaylor, Anne Nicol. Abortion Is a Blessing. New York:
	Psychological Dimensions, 1975.

	Seeks to persuade readers to join in the effort to keep
	abortion legal until such time as education, medical research,
	and human behavior combine to make abortion obsolete.

611.	Geary, Patrick F. "Analysis of Recent Decisions Involving
	Abortions." Catholic Lawyer 23 (1978): 237-42.

	Aims to determine what the legal effect of the abortion
	decisions has been, with a view to understanding the direction
	the legal issues are likely to take.

612.	_____. "Court Upholds Utah Law Requiring Preabortion
	Notice of Minors' Parents." Hospital Progress May 1981: 22-23.

	In a 6-3 decision, the U.S. Supreme Court held that the Utah
	statute requiring preabortion notice to a minor's parents was
	constitutionally acceptable.

613.	_____. "U.S. Supreme Court Affirms Society's Interest
	in 'Potential Life.'" Hospital Progress Aug. 1980: 22-24.

	Two U.S. Supreme Court decisions signal a new phase of the
	abortion controversy. By a vote of 5 to 4 in Harris v. McRae
	and Williams v. Zbaraz, the Court held that the Hyde amend-
	ment's limitations on the federal funding of "medically
	necessary" abortions are constitutionally valid.

614.	Gelman, David. "A New Attack on Abortion." Newsweek 2 Feb.
	1987: 32.

	The pro-lifers' grisly sequel to The Silent Scream.

615.	"A Generation of One-Child Families?" Futurist June 1985: 49-
	50.

	Maintains that in an age of slower economic growth, improve-
	ments in living standards may depend more on the skills of
	family planners than on those of economic planners.

616. Genovesi, Vincent J.   "Challenging the Legal Status of
     Abortion: A Matter of Moral Obligation?" _America_ 14 Dec.
     1985: 417-22.

     Can the sacred obligation to protect life be best fulfilled by
     passing restrictive laws directly prohibiting all or most
     abortions or by trying to bring about a change in public
     attitudes and values?

617. Gergen, David R. "More Choice, More Life." Editorial. _U.S._
     News _and_ _World_ _Report_ 17 July 1989: 68.

     An abortion issue compromise.

618. Gest, Ted. "Abortion Fight Gets Set for a New Round." _U.S._
     News _and_ _World_ _Report_ 28 Jan. 1985: 69.

     Neither side is willing to give an inch in a social war that
     has employed everything from bombs to court cases.

619. _____. "The Abortion Furor." _U.S._ _News_ _and_ _World_ _Report_
     17 July 1989: 18-22.

     The U.S Supreme Court threw the issue back to the states and
     probably changed the face of American politics for the next
     decade.

620. _____. "Abortion in America: ABC's of a Raging Battle."
     _U.S._ _News_ _and_ _World_ _Report_ 24 Jan. 1983: 47-49.

     An overview highlighting the various strategies of pro-life
     and pro-choice groups; a balanced status report of these
     movements.

621. _____. "Abortion Rights Ride Out an Attack--for Now."
     _U.S._ _News_ _and_ _World_ _Report_ 23 June 1986: 8.

     The 5-4 U.S. Supreme Court ruling on June 11, 1986, strikes
     down a Pennsylvania law requiring that women be warned of
     the risks of abortion. The new one-vote margin means that
     one death or retirement--on a Court with five members over age
     77--might endanger the _Roe_ v. _Wade_ ruling.

622. _____. "Anti-Abortion Groups Have a Bad Day in Court."
     _U.S._ _News_ _and_ _World_ _Report_ 27 June 1983: 31.

     Pregnancy terminations will increase and get cheaper--because
     of the latest decisions by the U.S. Supreme Court justices.

623.   _____. "New Abortion Fights: Why the Supreme Court
Probably Won't Overturn Roe v. Wade." U.S. News and World
Report 24 Apr. 1989: 22+.

Analyzes the reasons for the possible abortion vote of each of
the U.S. Supreme Court justices in a rehearing of Roe v. Wade.

624.   Gest, Ted, and Jeannye Thornton. "Battle over Abortion Gets
Hot Again." U.S. News and World Report 29 July 1985: 59.

One of the nation's most divisive social issues is moving from
protest marches to the courtroom.

625.   Gibb, Gerald D., and Richard J. Millard. "Divergent Perspectives in Abortion Counseling." Psychological Reports 50
(1982): 819-22.

Investigates the accuracy of observers' predictions in abortion
counseling clinics.

626.   Gilbert, Edward J. "Abortion: Legal but Still Wrong."
Liguorian Oct. 1973: 2-4.

A summary of the legal reasoning of the U.S. Supreme Court
decision and of the teaching of the Catholic church.

627.   _____. "Why We Need a Human Life Amendment." Liguorian
Nov. 1974: 17-20.

Offers a summary of the common teachings of the Catholic
church on abortion from a moral and legal viewpoint and
concludes with some specific recommendations for a visible
response to the unacceptable decision of the U.S. Supreme
Court.

628.   Gilhooley, James S. "An Abortion Alternative." America
13 Nov. 1982: 289-90.

Recounts the establishment and development of a home which
offers on-site support to unmarried pregnant women.

629.   Ginsburg, Faye D. Contested Lives: The Abortion Debate in
an American Community. Berkeley: U of California P, 1989.

Based on the author's field research with grassroots abortion
activists in Fargo, North Dakota, where protests have continued
since 1981 when the first abortion clinic opened in the state.

92

. Ginsburg, Ruth Bader. "Some Thoughts on Autonomy and Equality in Relation to Roe v. Wade." North Carolina Law Review Jan. 1985: 375-86.

The breadth and detail of the Roe opinion may, ironically, have stimulated rather than discouraged anti-abortion measures, particularly with respect to the public funding of abortion.

631. Glasow, Richard D. School-Based Clinics: The Abortion Connection. Washington: Natl. Right to Life Educ. Trust Fund, 1988.

Exposes the motives behind school-based clinics and explains how schools are being used to encourage children to kill their unborn children.

632. Glendon, Mary Ann. Abortion and Divorce in Western Law. Cambridge: Harvard UP, 1987.

Shows that in Europe and America laws on divorce and abortion have been greatly liberalized since the 1960s.

633. _____. "A World Without Roe: How Different Would It Be?" New Republic 20 Feb. 1989: 19-20.

Argues that even with a new emphasis on the U.S. Supreme Court, neither the worst fears of pro-choice partisans nor the highest hopes of pro-lifers are likely to be realized.

634. Glenn, Gary D. "Abortion and Inalienable Rights in Classical Liberalism." American Journal of Jurisprudence 20 (1975): 62-80.

Addresses the question, What should be the public policy regarding abortion of a regime dedicated to inalienable rights? More precisely, what should one think about abortion on the basis of inalienable rights?

635. Golden, Edward. "Suffer the Little Children to Come." U.S. Catholic June 1974: 25-31.

An interview with Edward Golden, the first president of the National Right-to-Life Committee (NRLC).

636. Goldenberg, David. "The Right to Abortion: Expansion of the Right to Privacy Through the Fourteenth Amendment." Catholic Lawyer 19 (1973): 36-57.

A review of the historical background of abortion and actual legal cases and court decisions which are the basis for current abortion law in the United States.

637. Goldman, Alan H. "Abortion and the Right to Life." Personal-
     ist 60 (1979): 402-06.

     The central question in the abortion issue concerns the origin
     of the right to live. Man's altered criteria for establishing
     that right enable him to see why it must be granted soon after
     birth.

638. Goldsmith, Sadja, et al. "Teenagers, Sex and Contraception."
     Family Planning Perspectives Jan. 1972: 32-38.

     Reports statistically on 377 sexually active unwed girls aged
     13 to 17 from California's Bay Area, most of them white,
     middle-class, and raised in Protestant or Catholic homes, who
     were questioned about their knowledge, attitudes, and practices
     relating to sex and birth control.

639. Goldstein, Michael S. "Abortion as a Medical Career Choice:
     Entrepeneurs, Community Physicians, and Others." Journal of
     Health and Social Behavior 25 (1984): 211-29.

     A study of physicians in Los Angeles who made the performance
     of abortions a major or sole component of their practice in the
     five years (1967-72) subsequent to the legalization of abortion
     in California. Four distinct career patterns (entrepreneurs,
     academics, workers, and community physicians) were found. The
     major finding is the existence of a subgroup of physicians
     whose primary identity is business person or entrepreneur.

640. Goldstein, Robert D. Mother-Love and Abortion: A Legal
     Interpretation. Berkeley: U of California, 1988.

     Supplements the abortion debate's rhetoric of rights with an
     ethic of love.

641. Goldzieher, Joseph W., and Harry W. Rudel. "How the Oral
     Contraceptives Came to Be Developed." Journal of the American
     Medical Association 21 Oct. 1974: 421-25.

     The birth control pill became a reality only because of
     developments in steroid chemistry, and because of vigorous
     advocates who overcame the hesitancy of the pharmaceutical
     industry to venture into such an emotionally charged arena.

642. "Good News on Abortion." New Republic 31 July 1989: 5-6.

     In Webster v. Reproductive Health Services the U.S. Supreme
     Court all but overruled Roe and once more gave the states
     substantial leeway to restrict abortion.

94

643. Goodart, Margaret Metcalf. "Contraception: The Secular Controversy." Diss. U of California at Davis, 1975.

Discusses birth control as a tool of social reform.

644. Goodman, Michael F., ed. What Is a Person? Clifton: Humana, 1988.

A series of essays dealing with contemporary issues in bio-medicine, ethics, and society.

645. Gordon, Linda. "The Politics of Population: Birth Control and the Eugenics Movement." Radical America July-Aug. 1974: 61-97.

Gordon views Sanger's "personal-political transformation" as a "microcosm of the general transformation of the birth control campaign." Although it began with radical objectives, the birth control movement linked itself with eugenics and racism. It deteriorated completely when feminism was abandoned, when "birth control" became "family planning" and was controlled by men. By the 1950s, feminist motives had disappeared, and the movement had become a government-motivated "population control" campaign.

646. _____. Woman's Body, Woman's Right: A Social History of Birth Control in America. New York: Grossman, 1976.

A social history of women, sex, and feminism.

647. Gordon, Mary Beth. "Chronicle of Life and Death--I: Nobody Wants an Abortion." Commonweal 21 Oct. 1983: 557-58.

A story of the thoughts in the mind of a young woman on the day of her friend's abortion.

648. Gorman, Michael J. Abortion and the Early Church: Christian, Jewish and Pagan Attitudes in the Greco-Roman World. Downers Grove: Inter-Varsity, 1982.

A powerful response to the early Christians' attitudes on the abortion issue.

649. "The Governor and the Bishop." Editorial. New Republic 8 Oct. 1984: 7-9.

Governor Mario Cuomo of New York takes the unusual step of challenging Archbishop John J. O'Connor publicly and forcing him to "clarify" his position that "he didn't see how a Catholic could in good conscience vote for a candidate who supports abortion."

650. Gow, Haven Bradford. "Did the Supreme Court Impose Its Morality on Us?" Liguorian Jan. 1979: 35-38.

The U.S. Supreme Court's ruling in effect imposed the moral views of pro-abortionists on those in our society who think abortion is murder, or at least the taking of potential life.

651. Grady, Thomas J. "A Life, a Life Style, and the Way of Life." Catholic Digest June 1980: 34-36.

The decision to have an abortion is only the last in a long line of selfish decisions.

652. Granberg, Donald. "The Abortion Activists." Family Planning Perspectives July-Aug. 1981: 157-63.

Abortion and anti-abortion activists compare member character-istics of the National Abortion Rights Action League (NARAL) and the National Right to Life Committee (NRLC).

653. _____. "Abortion Activists in Missouri." Social Biology 28 (1981): 239-52.

Reports on a compositional study comparing members of two opposing groups concerned about abortion. The study drew upon existing theory and analysis for help in determining what factors might be characteristic of individuals involved in a pro- or anti-abortion organization.

654. _____. "The Abortion Controversy: An Overview." Humanist July-Aug. 1981: 28-38.

In the midst of the hysteria over abortion, here is a rational look at the recent political and social aspects of the debate.

655. _____. "Comparison of Members of Pro- and Anti-Abortion Organizations in Missouri." Social Biology 28 (1981): 239-52.

Compares members of Missouri Citizens for Life (MCL) and the Abortion Rights Alliance (ARA) of Missouri in regard to education, religion, sexual equality, politics, free speech, social deviancy, suicide, and militarism.

656. _____. "Comparison of Pro-Choice and Pro-Life Activists: Their Values, Attitudes, and Beliefs." Population and Environment 5 (1982): 75-94.

Reports a survey of two statewide abortion-related organiza-tions: Missouri Citizens for Life (MCL) and the Abortion Rights Alliance (ARL).

657. _____. "Family Size Preferences and Sexual Permissiveness as Factors Differentiating Abortion Activists." Social Psychology Quarterly 45 (1982): 15-23.

Reports on a 1980 survey of members of two statewide abortion-related organizations: Missouri Citizens for Life (MCL) and the Abortion Rights Alliance (ARA). The groups differed markedly on religious affiliation and religiosity, and on attitude items pertaining to birth control, sex education, divorce, and sexual permissiveness.

658. _____. "Pro-Life or Reflection of Conservative Ideology? An Analysis of Opposition to Legalized Abortion." Sociology and Social Research 62 (1978): 414-29.

Reports an analysis of national survey data on opinions about abortion.

659. _____. "What Does It Mean to Be Pro-Life?" Christian Century 12 May 1982: 562-66.

Analyzes the positions pro-lifers should consistently take--for example, promote gun control, oppose suicide, promote physical exercise, etc.

660. Granberg, Donald, and Beth Wellman Granberg. "Abortion Attitudes, 1965-1980: Trends and Determinants." Family Planning Perspectives Sept.-Oct. 1980: 250-61.

After a slight drop in 1978, support for legal abortion rose to an average of 67 percent in 1980. Support for civil liberties and women's rights is tied to abortion approval; moral conservatism and strength of Catholic and fundamentalist Protestant commitment are linked to disapproval.

661. _____. "Pro-Life Versus Pro-Choice: Another Look at the Abortion Controversy in the U.S." Sociology and Social Research 65 (1981): 424-34.

The trend in abortion attitudes in the United States is examined using data from the National Opinion Research Center (NORC) General Social Surveys. The pro-life versus pro-choice controversy is interpreted as involving a struggle over the custody of the concept of abortion and over the way in which abortion is connotatively defined.

662. Granberg, Donald, and Donald Denney. "The Coathanger and the Rose." Transaction/Society May-June 1982: 39-46.

A comparison of pro-choice and pro-life activists in the contemporary United States.

663.   Granfield, David.   "The Legal Impact of the Roe and Doe
        Decisions." Jurist 33 (1973): 113-22.

        An assessment of the legal impact of the Roe and Doe cases is
        substantiated by reviewing each of these decisions.

664.   Gratz, Roberta Brandes. "Never Again! Never Again?" Ms. July
        1977: 54-55.

        Contends that women's hard-won right to have a legal abortion
        is in trouble. At best, it is being seriously challenged; at
        worst, it may be effectively crippled or even withdrawn
        altogether.

665.   Green, Constance M. "Faye Wattleton." Black Enterprise Apr.
        1987: 42+.

        A biographical article on the head of the Planned Parenthood
        Federation of America (PPFA).

666.   Green, Dorothy, and Mary Elizabeth Murduck, eds. The Margaret
        Sanger Centennial Conference: November 13 and 14, 1979.
        Northampton: The Sophia Smith Collection, Smith College, 1982.

        The staff of the Sophia Smith Collection used the collection's
        resources to celebrate the centenary of Margaret Sanger's
        birth.

667.   Green, Philip.   "Abortion: The Abusable Past." Nation 7 Aug.
        1989: 177-79.

        One thing remains clear: For many years still, in most if not
        all states, women are going to be obtaining legal abortions
        despite the mean-spirited harassments they and their doctors
        may have to undergo at the behest of state legislatures.

668.   Green, Shirley. The Curious History of Contraception. New
        York: St. Martin's, 1972.

        Discusses the various methods of contraception used from the
        time of the ancient Hebrews to the present day.

669.   Greep, Roy O. Reproduction and Human Welfare: A Challenge to
        Research. Cambridge: MIT P, 1976.

        A review of the reproductive sciences and contraceptive
        development; sponsored by the Ford Foundation.

670.   Greer, Germaine. Sex and Destiny: The Politics of Human
        Fertility. New York: Harper, 1984.

Includes statements that deal with the history of contraceptives and the eugenic movement.

671. Gregory, Hamilton, ed. The Religious Case for Abortion:
Protestant, Catholic, and Jewish Perspectives. Asheville:
Madison, 1983.

A series of essays and quotations which attempt to show that
the Bible does not consider abortion to be murder.

672. Grib, Philip J. Divorce Laws and Morality: A New Catholic
Jurisprudence. Lanham: UP of America, 1985.

An edited version of a doctoral dissertation (Catholic
University, 1983), which was a historical and systematic
theological critique and evaluation of the Catholic church's
moral teaching concerning civil divorce laws in the United
States.

673. Griffith, Elisabeth. In Her Own Right: The Life of Elizabeth
Cady Stanton. New York: Oxford UP, 1984.

A full-bodied portrait of a mother of 11 children, who went
from a comfortable, complacent, upper-class existence to become
perhaps the most important woman suffragist and feminist
reformer in nineteenth-century America.

674. Grisez, Germain. "A Critique of Two Theological Papers."
Homiletic and Pastoral Review July 1984: 10-15.

Grisez observes that we ought not to allow current prejudice
against the unborn to blind us to the moral truth about public
programs of abortion.

675. Grobstein, Clifford. Science and the Unborn: Choosing Human
Features. New York: Basic, 1988.

Covers the ethical evaluation of the human species from
fertilization to birth.

676. Grutka, Andrew R. "Humanae Vitae--Ten Years Later." Linacre
Quarterly 45 (1978): 10-14.

A review article on the development and acceptance/rejection
of Humanae Vitae in the years after its promulgation.

677. Gustafson, Karen. "The New Politics of Abortion." Utne Reader
Mar.-Apr. 1989: 19+.

Abortion is not just an issue of feminists and fundamentalists, but is, rather, a political tool that has been consistently used for obtaining and maintaining power.

678. Guttmacher, Alan F. "Why I Favor Liberalized Abortion." Reader's Digest Nov. 1973: 143-47.

A doctor explains how years of "exposure to the raw edges of human existence" have convinced him that legalized abortion is an essential and humane medical service.

679. Guttmacher, Alan Frank. Pregnancy, Birth and Family Planning: A Guide for Expectant Parents in the 1970's. New York: Viking, 1973.

A guide for the lay reader on the facts of conception, pregnancy, birth, and family planning.

680. Hacker, Andrew. "Of Two Minds About Abortion." Harper's Sept. 1979: 16-18.

Abortion is a controversy with a life of its own, demanding a place on the public agenda. There have been similar issues before, but none--not even Prohibition--has stirred so much soul-searching or ambiguity of feeling.

681. Hackett, George, and Ann McDaniel. "All Eyes on Justice O'Connor." Newsweek 1 May 1989: 34-35.

The first woman on the U.S. Supreme Court is the focal point for activists on both sides.

682. "Half Our Pregnancies Are Unintentional." Newsweek 10 Oct. 1983: 37.

The Alan Guttmacher Institute finds that of the 3.3 million unintended pregnancies, nearly half were terminated by abortion; the bulk of the report is devoted to various forms of contraception.

683. Hall, Elaine J., and Myra Marx Ferree. "Race Differences in Abortion Attitudes." Public Opinion Quarterly 50 (1986): 193-207.

A consistent finding in public opinion surveys of abortion attitudes has been that black respondents are less in favor of legal abortion than white respondents.

684. Hall, Ruth. Passionate Crusader: The Life of Marie Stopes. New York: Harcourt, 1977.

Presents the reader with a good deal of material about England's birth control movement, in which Marie Stopes played a leading role.

685. Hammond, Margo. "Abortion in Italy." _Commonweal_ 7 July 1978: 420-21.

Abortion is no longer a crime in Italy. The Italian Parliament--where there is, for the first time since 1947, a majority not subject to the religious outlook of the Christian Democrats--recently approved an abortion bill that allows women within the first three months of pregnancy to obtain a state-paid abortion.

686. Hanink, James Gee. "Persons, Rights and the Problem of Abortion." Diss. Loyola Marymount, 1975.

Considers the normative question of when, if ever, voluntary induced abortion is morally justifiable.

687. Hansen, Susan B. "State Implementation of Supreme Court Decisions: Abortion Rates Since _Roe_ v. _Wade_." _Journal of Politics_ May 1980: 372-95.

Discusses national trends in abortion, illegitimacy, maternal mortality rates, and birth rates since _Roe_, and then focuses on state implementation of abortion policy.

688. Hardin, Garrett. "Abortion vs. the Right to Life: The Evil of Mandatory Motherhood." _Psychology Today_ Nov. 1974: 42+.

Excerpted from _Mandatory Motherhood: The True Meaning of Right to Life_ (Beacon: 1974). Argues that requiring a woman to carry an unwanted fetus to term is evil and a violation of the mother's rights.

689. Hardin, Garrett James. _Mandatory Motherhood: The True Meaning of the Right-to-Life_. Boston: Beacon, 1974.

Counters the right-to-life concept with devastating logic and solid biological and legal evidence meant to stimulate the reader to defend or refute the arguments advanced.

690. _____. _Stalking the Wild Taboo_. 2nd ed. Los Altos: Kaufman, 1978.

An update of the 1973 edition. Challenges the popular assumptions that hinder rational consideration of abortion and other vital issues of the day.

691. Haring, Bernard. "Does God Condemn Contraception? A Question for the Whole Church." Commonweal 10 Feb. 1989: 69-71.

A protest against the inflexible position taken by the Vatican on the question of artificial contraception and against anonymous denunciations of theologians.

692. Harrington, Paul V. "The Catholic Doctor, the Catholic Hospital, and Contraception." Linacre Quarterly 40 (1973): 8-31.

Claims that when we are confronted by matters of substantial doctrine--whether of faith or of moral conduct--we must judge within that necessary framework, which is at the very foundation of our religion and church.

693. Harris, Harry. Prenatal Diagnosis and Selective Abortion. Cambridge: Harvard UP, 1975.

Discusses the promise and perils of medical advances for abortion.

694. Harris, Michael P. "New Life for Family Planning." Time 19 Sept. 1988: 96.

The Vatican is promoting birth control--naturally.

695. Harrison, Barbara Grizzuti. "Now That Abortion Is Legal..." McCall's Nov. 1973: 64+.

Is it still the wrenching, searing experience it once was, or have guilt and shame and sorrow vanished? The testimony of women who have recently exercised their new freedom of choice reveals the unforeseen emotions that follow.

696. Harrison, Beverly Wildung. Our Right to Choose: Toward a New Ethic of Abortion. Boston: Beacon, 1983.

Attempts to create an ethic of abortion rooted in women's experience and using women's well-being as a central norm.

697. Hartmann, Betsy. Reproductive Rights and Wrongs: The Global Politics of Population Control and Contraceptive Choice. New York: Harper, 1987.

Studies how best to balance the collective perils of overpopulation with the desire of individuals to determine for themselves the number of children they will have.

698.   Hatch, Orrin G.   "Senate Hearings on Abortion Amendments."
       Origins 22 Oct. 1981: 293+.

       Hearings before a subcommittee of the Senate Judiciary
       Committee on proposed amendments to the U.S. Constitution to
       restrict abortions.   These hearings represent the first effort
       by the Senate in more than six years to address this question.

699.   _____.   The Value of Life.   Washington: Natl. Committee
       for a Human Life Amendment, 1984.

       Discusses the myths and facts related to the abortion contro-
       versy and advocates that respect for all human life be restored
       to the status of a right protected under the Constitution.

700.   Hatcher, Robert A., Leslie M. Butterfield, and Monica Oakley.
       "Contraceptive Practices of 1,486 Women at the Time of First
       Act of Intercourse."   Advances in Planned Parenthood 16 (1981):
       110-16.

       Of 1,486 women interviewed at an urban municipal hospital
       family-planning clinic, 64 percent did not use a contraceptive
       at the first act of intercourse; close to half, 49.3 percent,
       had initiated sexual intercourse between the ages of 14 and 16.

701.   Hauerwas, Stanley.   "Abortion: The Agent's Perspective."
       American Ecclesiastical Review Feb. 1973: 102-20.

       Contends that abortion is fundamentally a moral problem.
       Holds that although sociological, psychological, medical, and
       legal information is necessary for any full discussion of
       abortion as an issue, no amount of facts can determine whether
       abortion is right or wrong.

702.   _____.   "Abortion: Why the Arguments Fail."   Hospital
       Progress Jan. 1980: 38-49.

       Christian opposition to abortion on demand has failed
       because, by attempting to meet the moral challenge within
       the limits of public polity, people have failed to exhibit
       their deepest convictions, which make rejection of abortion
       intelligible.

703.   Heim, David.   "Beyond Rights in Abortion Politics."   Editorial.
       Christian Century 19 July 1989: 675-76.

       One of the problematic aspects of the U.S. Supreme Court's
       1973 ruling in Roe v. Wade was that it short-circuited
       legislative efforts that might have begun addressing abortion
       in such a large context.

704. Hekman, Randall. _Justice for the Unborn: Why We Have Legal Abortion and How We Can Stop It_. Ann Arbor: Servant, 1984.

Deals primarily with the moral and ethical aspects of the abortion controversy.

705. Helgesen, Martin W. "Abortion as a Local Option." _America_ 29 Dec. 1979: 426-27.

Politicians wish the abortion issue would disappear as they search for a solution to please everyone, but some answers only add other problems.

706. Hellegers, André. "Amazing Historical and Biological Errors in Abortion Decision--Dr. Hellegers." _Hospital Progress_ May 1973: 16-17.

Excerpts from an interview with Dr. André Hellegers, director of the Kennedy Institute for the Society of Human Reproduction and Bio-Ethics.

707. Hennessee, Judith Adler. "Inside a Right-to-Life Mind." _Mademoiselle_ Apr. 1986: 173+.

Seeks to clarify certain aspects of the right-to-life position through an interview with an exemplar of the movement, who not only has thought her position through to its logical conclusion, but articulates it clearly.

708. Henshaw, Stanley K. "Abortion Services in the United States, 1979 and 1980." _Family Planning Perspectives_ Jan.-Feb. 1982: 5-15.

About one-fourth of all pregnancies--just under one-half of all unintended pregnancies--were terminated by abortion in 1980. Increases in the abortion rate, which was 30.0 per 1,000 live births in 1980, are slowing. If the trend continues, the abortion rate should stabilize this year.

709. Henshaw, Stanley K., and Jennifer Van Vort, eds. _Abortion Services in the United States, Each State and Metropolitan Area, 1984-85_. New York: Guttmacher Inst., 1988.

Compiles in a single source the results of the abortion research program of the Alan Guttmacher Institute from 1985 to 1987.

710. Henshaw, Stanley K., and Kevin O'Reilly. "Characteristics of Abortion Patients in the United States, 1979 and 1980." _Family Planning Perspectives_ Jan.-Feb. 1983: 6-16.

Discusses the number of Medicaid-financed abortions in a two-year period by age group, marital status, educational attainment, race and state of residence.

711. Henshaw, Stanley, et al. "Abortion in the United States, 1978-1979." Family Planning Perspectives Jan.-Feb. 1981: 6-18.

Although 1.5 million women obtained abortions in 1979, an estimated 641,000 in need were unable to do so, largely because of geographical and financial inaccessibility. About 3 percent of women aged 15 to 44, and 30 percent of those who were pregnant, had abortions.

712. Henshaw, Stanley K., et al. Abortion 1977-1979: Need and Services in the United States, Each State and Metropolitan Area. New York: Guttmacher Inst., 1981.

A report containing statistics on the number of reported abortions in the United States from 1977 to 1979.

713. Hensley, Jeffrey Lane, ed. The Zero People: Essays on Life. Ann Arbor: Servants, 1983.

An up-to-date handbook for those who desire to educate themselves on the abortion issue.

714. Hentoff, Nat. The Indivisible Fight for Life. Chicago: Americans United for Life, 1987.

Discusses the moral and ethical rights of the unborn child.

715. Hern, Warren M. "Abortion as Insurrection." Humanist Mar.-Apr. 1989: 18+.

Discusses the role abortion plays in the changing power relationships in American society.

716. Hern, Warren M., and Phillip G. Stubblefield. Abortion Practice. Philadelphia: Lippincott, 1984.

Deals authoritatively with all aspects of providing an abortion.

717. Hernandez, Donald J. Success or Failure? Family Planning Programs in the Third World. Westport: Greenwood, 1984.

An explanation of family-planning programs.

718. Hertel, Bradley, Gerry E. Hendershot, and James W. Grimm. "Religion and Attitudes Toward Abortion: A Study of Nurses and Social Workers." _Journal for the Scientific Study of Religion_ 13 (n.d.): 23-34.

Rates of approval of abortion by liberal and conservative Christian nurses and social workers in Tennessee are analyzed using survey data to investigate hypotheses suggested by Johnson's findings that support for the Republican party rises with church attendance among conservative Protestants, but declines with church attendance among liberals.

719. Hertel, James R. "_Humanae Vitae_: Four Years Later." _Priest_ 28 June 1972: 18-26.

Points out that in 1968, and still in 1972, no other papal utterance in living memory was so instantly greeted by such a vociferous chorus of outraged voices, with emotions running the entire gamut from modest incredulity to outright rejection of the pontiff's position in _Humanae Vitae_.

720. Hertzberg, Hendrik. "People's Choice." _New Republic_ 1 May 1989: 4+.

Chronicles the pro-choice demonstration in Washington, DC, in the spring of 1989.

721. Higgins, George G. "The Prolife Movement and the New Right." _America_ 13 Sept. 1980: 107-10.

Opposition to abortion has become a rallying point for right-wing political organizations. Catholic pro-life groups should be alert to the risk of identifying their cause with the wider right-wing agenda.

722. Higgins, James J. "Is Abortion Only a Catholic Issue?" _Liguorian_ May 1976: 24-28.

The Catholic opposition to abortion flows from the church's opposition to unjustified killing of human beings. What it is trying to do is win over the citizenry and the courts to an appreciation of some truths learned by human reason from modern biology and from human history.

723. "High Court Strikes Down Abortion Restrictions, Rules on Handicapped Infants." _Christianity Today_ 11 July 1986: 38-39.

Two U.S. Supreme Court decisions deal setbacks to the right-to-life movement, but many pro-life leaders are encouraged by signs of growing sentiment on the Court to reconsider abortion on demand.

724. Hilgers, Thomas W. "The American Academy of Natural Family Planning." International Review of Natural Family Planning 7 (1983): 306-17.

     Provides an insight into the present goals and objectives of the American Academy of Natural Family Planning (AANFP) and outlines the organization's history, purposes, code of ethics, bylaws, membership, and role as an accrediting and certifying body.

725. Hilgers, Thomas W., and Dennis J. Horan. Abortion and Social Justice. New York: Sheed, 1972.

     Presents, to the still open-minded and concerned, the full range of argumentation against abortion: biological, medical, psychological, sociological, legal, demographic, and ethical.

726. Hilgers, Thomas W., et al., eds. New Perspectives on Human Abortion. Frederick: U Publ. of America, 1981.

     A collection of essays dealing with the medical, legal, and social aspects of abortion.

727. Hill, Carlene B. "A Question of Honor: Penalizing Birth." Commonweal 23 Mar. 1984: 174-75.

     Contends that abortion is a moral wrong widely viewed as politically essential to establishing parity between men and women in the world.

728. Himes, Kenneth R. "Single-Issue Politics and the Church." America 9 May 1987: 377-81.

     Single-issue activists sometimes have focused not on a political principle but on a strategy for bringing about their objective. This tactic may increase polarization in the body politic. Tension is occasioned by what appears to be the exclusive focus of some Catholic bishops on abortion.

729. Hinds, Judith, ed. Towards Smaller Families: The Crucial Role of the Private Sector. Draper Fund Report 15. Washington: Population Crisis Committee, 1986.

     A series of essays outlining critical activities which show the greatest promise for slowing population growth.

730. Hitchcock, James. "The American Press and Birth Control: Preparing the Ground for Dissent." Homiletic and Pastoral Review July 1980: 10-26.

Examines media coverage of Vatican II and _Humanae Vitae_ in light of the birth control debate in the American Catholic church.

731. Hodgson, Jane E., ed. _Abortion and Sterilization: Medical and Social Aspects_. New York: Greene, 1981.

Presents arguments to legitimize abortion and sterilization for the sake of those who need and seek the service and discusses their social and political history and public health aspects.

732. Hoffman, Paul. "Nixon vs. Rockefeller: The Politics of Abortion." _Nation_ 5 June 1972: 712-13.

Provides background on concerns and thinking in the New York State Legislature in regard to the liberalized abortion law.

733. Hoffmeier, James K., ed. _Abortion: A Christian Understanding and Response_. Grand Rapids: Baker, 1988.

A collection of essays designed to increase the reader's understanding of the facts, issues, principles, and values that should be part of any discussion of abortion.

734. Hogan, Griff. "Abortion and the Handicapped: Present Practice in the Light of History." _Social Thought_ 6 (1980): 37-46.

The subject of the handicapped complicated the abortion debate by introducing the issue of "selective abortion." If the fetus were normal, no abortion would be performed.

735. Holden, Constance. "AID Tightens Antiabortion Measures." _Science_ 15 Mar. 1985: 1318-19.

The Agency for International Development (AID), in implementing the Reagan administration's antiabortion policy abroad, could cut $50 to $80 million from family-planning programs.

736. _____. "AID Turns Down IPPF." _Science_ 4 Jan. 1985: 37.

The Agency for International Development (AID) rejects a request for $17 million from the International Planned Parenthood Federation (IPPF), alleging that the group "promotes" abortion, contrary to administration policy.

737. _____. "Congress to Reexamine Antiabortion Amendment." _Science_ 24 July 1981: 421.

The human life amendment passes the U.S. Senate subcommittee by a vote of 3 to 2; next it goes to the full Judiciary Committee.

738. _____. "Contraception Research Lacking." _Science_ 13 Sept. 1985: 1066.

Argues that while research on natural family planning (NFP) is finally getting some long-awaited attention, contraception research worldwide has been stagnant for the past 15 years.

739. _____. "Koop Finds Abortion Evidence 'Inconclusive.'" _Science_ 10 Feb. 1989: 730-31.

Right-to-lifers fail to get the hoped-for evidence to reverse _Roe_ v. _Wade_ when the U.S. Supreme Court reconsiders the issue this spring.

740. _____. "A 'Prolife' Population Delegation?" _Science_ 22 June 1984: 1321-22.

The White House is promoting a right-wing, anti-abortion agenda at the United Nations world population conference in Mexico City.

741. _____. "'Right-to-Life' Scores New Victory at AID." _Science_ 13 Sept. 1985: 1065-67.

Agency for International Development (AID) rules are bent to accommodate natural family planning (NFP) groups that oppose "artificial" birth control.

742. Hollerback, Paula E. _Factors That Determine the Appropriateness of New Technology to Consumer Needs_. New York: Population Council, 1982.

Examines proposed research on the acceptability of future planned birth technologies and policy implications of the existing research.

743. Holmes, Helen B., Betty B. Hoskins, and Michael Gross, eds. _Birth Control and Controlling Birth: Women-Centered Perspective_. Clifton: Humana, 1980.

A collection of edited papers dealing with the social, technological, economic, and personal aspects of the reproductive and birth control alternatives available to women.

744. Horan, Dennis J. "Critical Abortion Litigation." _Catholic Lawyer_ 26 (1981): 198-208.

Discusses various pieces of legislation and important common elements in human life concerns.

745. _____. "Dignity of Life Developments." Catholic Lawyer 3 (1982): 239-42.

Deals with various proposed human life amendments and other abortion-related legislation, and contains an outline of cases presented at the diocesan attorneys' meeting.

746. _____. "Human Life 'Federalism' Amendment: Its Language, Effects." Hospital Progress Dec. 1981: 12-14.

A legal analysis that seeks to answer two questions: 1) What is the legal effect of the language proposed in the Hatch human life amendment? 2) What effect will that language have on the performace of abortions in the United States?

747. _____. "Human Life Federalism Amendment: I. Legal Aspects." Catholic Lawyer 2 (1983): 115-17.

Discusses the two pro-life initiatives pending in Congress, the Hatch amendment and the human life bill, and points out that the pro-life supporters of each clash rather than support a unified result. Argues that the two initiatives depend on each other because, standing alone, each bill is inadequate.

748. _____. Two Ships Passing in the Night: An Interpreta-vist Review of the White-Stevens Colloquy on Roe v. Wade. Chicago: Americans United for Life, 1987.

Contends that the Roe v. Wade decision will stand as long as the courts refuse to examine the overwhelming evidence that abortion was never a liberty in American law or tradition.

749. _____. "Viability, Values, and the Vast Cosmos." Catholic Lawyer 22 (1976): 1-37.

Not a critique of Wade, the primary intent of this article is to shed light on the growing importance of the concept of viability through a discussion of cases which have arisen since that decision.

750. Horan, Dennis J., and Thomas J. Marzen. "Abortion Laws Will Bend Under New Medical, Social Pressures." Hospital Progress Dec. 1982: 48-52.

Three cases now before the U.S. Supreme Court suggest that the shape of the "right to abort" is not cast in stone. Medical technology--such as the creation of an artificial womb capable

of sustaining a human fetus throughout pregnancy--may also
alter judicial and statutory responses to abortion.

751.   Horan, Dennis J., Paige C. Cunningham, and Edward R. Grant, eds.
     Abortion and the Constitution: Reversing Roe v. Wade Through
     the Courts. Washington: Georgetown UP, 1987.

     Sets out not only to criticize the historical and jurispruden-
     tial flaws of the Roe v. Wade decision, but to suggest a
     course of litigation to bring about its reversal.

752.   Horn, Jack. "Tying Abortion to the Death Penalty." Psychology
     Today Nov. 1977: 43+.

     A study by Paul Cameron raises the question, Do women who have
     had an abortion have less regard for human life than those who
     have not had one? Cameron claims the answer may be yes.

753.   Hosken, Fran P. "A Crucial New Direction for International
     Family Planning." Humanist Jan.-Feb. 1984: 5+.

     Only when women worldwide have access to information about
     themselves can superstition and ignorance--whether ancient or
     modern--be overcome and population growth rates reduced.

754.   "How Nations Govern Growth." Scholastic Update 2 Mar. 1984:
     18+.

     As Third World populations climb, governments offer payments
     and threaten penalties in an attempt to convince couples to
     have smaller families.

755.   "How Women Really Feel About Birth Control." Ladies' Home
     Journal Aug. 1986: 54+.

     A survey article relating women's feelings about birth control.

756.   Howe, Barbara H., Roy Kaplan, and Constance English. "Repeat
     Abortions: Blaming the Victims." American Journal of Public
     Health Dec. 1979: 1242-46.

     A study of 1,505 women who obtained abortions in a freestand-
     ing abortion clinic in western New York State revealed that
     women having repeat abortions were more likely to be using
     contraception at the time of conception than women having
     their first abortion.

757.   Howe, Louise K. Moments on Maple Avenue: The Reality of
     Abortion. New York: Macmillan, 1984.

A candid and objective view of abortion, a complex issue of society.

758. Hubbard, Charles W. Family Planning Education: Parenthood and Social Disease Control. St. Louis: Mosby, 1973.

Offers information concerning the sexual aspects of living: contraception, abortion, sterilization, and the venereal diseases.

759. Hubbard, Bishop Howard. "A Response to Governor Cuomo." Origins 25 Oct. 1984: 304.

Bishop Hubbard says that Catholic opposition to abortion is based on human rights and not just religious belief and that a public official who is convinced that abortion destroys a human being must be committed to doing something to remedy that horror legally.

760. Hudson-Nicholas, Sally A., and Paige Cunningham. "Is Abortion a Women's Issue?" Update on Law-Related Education 3 (1981): 6+.

Gives both pro-choice and pro-life responses to the question of abortion as a women's issue.

761. Humber, James M. "The Case Against Abortion." Thomist Jan. 1975: 65-84.

An essay with but one purpose: to attempt to defend the view that abortion is morally wrong.

762. Hunt, Maria Vida. "The Impossible Choice." McCall's July 1985: 44+.

The story of a woman who was told she was carrying a defective baby, and who came close to having an abortion. Subsequently, she gave birth to a perfectly normal son.

763. Hunter, Allen. "Virtue with a Vengeance: The Pro-Family Politics of the New Right." Diss. Brandeis U, 1985.

Examines the development of and the reasons for the pro-family politics of the late 1970s.

764. Hunter, Nan. "What Akron Does/Does Not Say." Nation 20-27 Aug. 1983: 137-39.

An examination and analysis for the layperson of the key points in the Akron decision.

765. Hurley, Karen. "Birth Control: Let's End the Silence." St. Anthony's Messenger Oct. 1973: 10-15.

For many, especially the young, the moral dimensions of contraception have been pushed out of consciousness. The author calls for a reexamination of consciences and of the values upheld by Humanae Vitae.

766. Hurst, Jane. History of Abortion in the Catholic Church: The Untold Story. Abortion in Good Faith. Washington: Catholics for a Free Choice, 1983.

A discussion of the history of Catholic thinking on abortion.

767. Hursthouse, Rosalind. Beginning Lives. New York: Blackwell in assoc. with Open U, 1987.

Argues that it is not possible to settle the abortion issue merely by settling the moral status of the fetus.

768. "The Hyde Amendment." Editorial. America 8 Mar. 1980: 181.

Predicts that the Hyde amendment will be found unconstitutional by the U.S. Supreme Court.

769. Hyde, Henry J. "The Human Life Bill: Some Issues and Answers." Symposium on Life and Death: Issues and Implications. New York Law School Law Review 4 (1982): 1077-1100.

Representative Hyde reviews his human life bill and defends his position.

770. Hynes, Kathleen. An Ethical Inquiry: Where to Draw the Line. Washington: Catholics for a Free Choice, n.d.

A pamphlet written for people who are concerned about the value conflicts of the abortion question, but who do not have formal training in philosophy or theology.

771. Ide, Arthur Frederick. Abortion Handbook: History, Clinical Practice and Psychology of Abortion. Las Colinas: Liberal, 1986.

Addresses the pro-life issues of the abortion controversy.

772. "If Not Abortion, What Then?" Christianity Today 20 May
      1983: 14-23.

      A composite sketch drawn from interviews centering around a
      young girl's abortion/pro-life decision.

773. Imber, Jonathan B. Abortion and the Private Practice of
      Medicine. New Haven: Yale UP, 1986.

      The moral confusion generated by the legalization of abortion
      is the concern in this sociological study of the attitudes of
      physicians toward performing abortions.

774. Imber, Jonathan Bruce. "Strategies of Despair: Abortion in
      America and in American Medicine." Diss. U of Pennsylvania,
      1979.

      Contends that the birth control movement condemned abortion
      practice and promoted the use of contraception.

775. "In Center of Latest Dispute on Abortion: Nixon, Rockefellers."
      U.S. News and World Report 22 May 1972: 50.

      President Nixon publicly rejects two of the principal
      recommendations made by the U.S. Commission on Population
      Growth and the American Future headed by John D. Rockefeller
      III.

776. "In God's Image: A Statement on the Sanctity of Human Life."
      Origins 9 Aug. 1984: 151-53.

      Against the background of an election year, the bishops of New
      Jersey issue a statement urging a pro-life public policy.

777. Institute of Medicine (U.S.). Legalized Abortion and the
      Public Health: Report of a Study by a Committee of the
      Institute of Medicine. Washington: Natl. Acad. of Sciences,
      1975.

      Study emphasis is on the health effects of abortion, not on the
      alternatives to it.

778. International Fertility Research Program. Traditional Abortion
      Practices: Three Studies of Illegal Abortion in the Developing
      World. Research Triangle Park: Intl. Fertility Research
      Program, 1981.

      Offers three fresh perspectives on abortion seekers and
      traditional service providers and the acceptability of
      induced abortion as a family planning method.

779. "Is Abortion a Catholic Issue?" Editorial. Christianity
     Today 16 Jan. 1976: 29.

     Argues that the anti-abortion laws struck down by the U.S.
     Supreme Court had been enacted with a broad base of popular
     support quite irrespective of sectarian divisions.

780. "Is Abortion the Issue?" Harper's July 1986: 35-43.

     The considered opinions of a panel of women invited by Harper's
     magazine to discuss the question of legalized abortion and to
     speculate on the possibility of finding common ground.

781. Isaacson, Walter. "Holding Firm on Abortion." Time 27 June
     1983: 14.

     Defines the limits of a state's authority to regulate the
     performance of abortions.

782. _____. Pro and Con. New York: Putnam, 1983.

     A summary of the pros and cons of the major unsettled questions
     relating to the abortion controversy, with statistics and
     quotations from authorities on the subject to reinforce the
     points made.

783. "It's Up to Congress Now." National Review 8 July 1983:
     793.

     Reviews the U.S. Supreme Court's thinking in striking down
     the Akron case, thus reaffirming Roe v. Wade.

784. Jacobs, Douglas, et al. "A Prospective Study on the Psycho-
     logical Effects of Therapeutic Abortion." Comprehensive
     Psychiatry Sept.-Oct. 1974: 423-34.

     Discusses the general psychological aftereffects of "abortion
     on demand" rather than specific areas of emotional decline in
     poor-risk, psychologically impaired patients.

785. Jacoby, Tamar. "A New Majority Ticks Off the Reagan Agenda."
     Newsweek 17 July 1989: 26-27.

     Some hold that precedent is being undermined by sharply
     narrowing it.

786. Jaffe, Frederick S. Abortion Politics: Private Morality and
     Public Policy. New York: McGraw, 1981.

An analysis of the development of public policy on abortion since the Roe v. Wade decision.

787. _____. "Knowledge, Perception, and Change: Notes on a Fragment of Social History." Mount Sinai Journal of Medicine July-Aug. 1975: 286-99.

Time: the 1950s to the 1970s. Technologically, there was a switch to the birth control pill; politically, there was an end to "doctrinal arguments" with the Catholic church; sociologically, there was a greater emphasis on clinics for the poor.

788. "Jane Roe and Mary Doe." Nation 5 Feb. 1973: 165.

Jane Roe and Mary Doe, residents of Texas and Georgia, respectively, who wanted abortions, disallowed by the laws of their states, have prevailed in a matter of enormous religious, ethical, and social importance.

789. Jeffery, Mac. "Birth Control News: Once-a-Month Pill." Harper's Bazaar Aug. 1978: 24+.

The F2 alpha analog does not prevent conception, but rather terminates it, albeit in its very early stages.

790. Jelen, Ted G. "Respect for Life, Sexual Morality, and Opposition to Abortion." Review of Religious Research 25 (1984): 220-31.

Catholics, people with at least a high school education, and frequent church attenders are most likely to oppose abortion on "right-to-life" grounds. Fundamentalists, people who did not finish high school, and infrequent church attenders are most likely to oppose abortion because easily available abortions seem to render sexual promiscuity less costly or risky.

791. Jensen, Joan M. "Archives: The Evolution of Margaret Sanger's Family Limitation Pamphlet, 1914-1921." Signs: Journal of Women in Culture and Society 6 (1981): 548-67.

Traces "the metamorphosis of Margaret Sanger's pamphlet from strategy paper for working-class women to prescriptive manual for women in the middle class." Includes a reprint of the first edition of Family Limitation with notes indicating changes made through the tenth editorial.

792. Joffe, Carole. "Abortion Work: Strains, Coping Strategies, Policy Implications." Social Work Nov. 1979: 485-90.

As a result of the moral and social conflicts surrounding

abortion, workers involved in counseling potential abortion recipients are subject to certain strains which must be considered, along with the methods of coping developed by staff and administration, in formulating any policy on abortion.

793. _____. "The Moral Vision of the Pro-choice Movement: A Response to Ruth Anna Putnam." Tikkun Sept.-Oct. 1989: 82-83.

The pro-choice movement should shift from a focus on "rights" to a broader discussion that includes an explicit moral dimension.

794. _____. "What Abortion Counselors Want from Their Clients." Social Problems 26 (1978): 112-21.

Discusses some of the responses of abortion counselors to their work, and describes the role clients play in shaping the meaning of this work.

795. Johnson, Charles A., and Jon R. Bond. "Policy Implementation and Responsiveness in Nongovernmental Institutions: Hospital Abortion Services After Roe v. Wade." Western Political Quarterly 35 (1982): 385-405.

Seeks to contribute to a better understanding of the linkage between policy implementation and community preferences by analyzing hospital abortion policies after Roe v. Wade. Two questions guide the study: 1) To what extent are hospital abortion policies responsive to community preferences? 2) What community and organizational variables influence hospital responsiveness to community preferences on this health issue?

796. Johnson, Douglas, and Paige Comstock Cunningham. "E.R.A. and Abortion: Really Separate Issues?" America 9 June 1984: 432-37.

Many voters who would otherwise support an equal rights amendment fear that it could be used to undermine laws restricting public funding for abortion. Several cases prove that these fears are well founded.

797. Johnson, John G. "The Dynamics of the Abortion Debate." America 13 Feb. 1981: 106-09.

The controversies about abortion policy are already complex and passionate, but the failure to distinguish different methods of discourse makes them muddled as well.

798. Jones, Elise F., and Charles F. Westoff. "How Attitudes
      Toward Abortion Are Changing." Journal of Population 1 (1978):
      5-21.

      The 1975 National Fertility Study is the third in a series of
      probability-sample surveys of married women in their childbear-
      ing years, taken at five-year intervals, to include a virtually
      identical panel of questions on attitudes toward abortion. The
      first section of this report describes aggregate change in
      attitudes toward abortion over time. Patterns of change in
      response for individuals from 1970 to 1975 are examined in
      the next section.

799. Jones, Maggie. "Getting the Message Across." World Health
      Feb.-Mar. 1983: 22-24.

      Convincing people about the advantages of family planning can
      be difficult; it might take years to register the beneficial
      effects. A Japanese specialist has found a way of getting
      communities interested, and much more ready to respond to and
      rely on a family planning message.

800. Jorgensen, Stephen R., Susan L. King, and Barbara A. Torrey.
      "Dyadic and Social Network Influences on Adolescent Exposure
      to Pregnancy Risk." Journal of Marriage and the Family 42
      (1980): 141-55.

      It is hypothesized that qualities of 1) the interpersonal
      relationship of the adolescent dyad (two individuals), 2) peer
      relationships, and 3) family relationships will influence the
      degree to which adolescents are exposed to pregnancy risk in
      terms of frequency of sexual intercourse and regularity of
      effective contraceptive use.

801. Jung, Patricia Beattie, and Thomas A. Shannon, eds. Abortion
      and Catholicism: The American Debate. New York: Crossroad,
      1988.

      An anthology of essays selected to represent the range of
      Catholic thought on abortion itself and on abortion and public
      policy.

802. Kader, David. "The Law of Tortious Prenatal Death Since Roe
      v. Wade." Symposium Issue--The Law of Torts. Spec. issue
      of Missouri Law Review 4 (1980): 639-66.

      Analyzes the post-Roe v. Wade wrongful death cases involving
      the unborn and offers a corrective commentary on the confusions
      and inconsistencies which exist. Aims to contribute to the
      needed effort to develop the meaning of "person" in the law,
      and to derive a legal personality for the unborn.

803. Kagan, Julia. "The New Doubts About Abortion." McCall's June 1975: 121-23.

The recent conviction of a Boston doctor has stirred fears among physicians and hospital administrators who are reassessing their own practices--and among the women who may need their help.

804. Kahn-Edrington, Maria. "Abortion Counseling." Counseling Psychologist 8.1 (1979): 37-38.

Identifies and explains the knowledge, skills, and attitudes needed by those persons engaged in effective abortion counseling.

805. Kaler, Patrick. "The Open Letter to Katharine Hepburn." Liguorian Apr. 1982: 34-39.

A letter written in response to Katherine Hepburn's appeal for support for Planned Parenthood.

806. Kambic, Robert, and Mary Kambic. "A Catholic Hospital and Natural Family Planning." Hospital Progress Apr. 1978: 70-73.

Attempts to deal with some of the questions concerning the philosophy of natural family planning (NFP) and to offer details for providing NFP service to clients.

807. Kaminsky, Barbara A., and Lorraine A. Sheckter. "Abortion Counseling in a General Hospital." Health and Social Work 4.2 (1979): 93-103.

Describes a counseling program for hospital abortion patients and emphasizes the importance of close working relationships between the counselors and their supervising staff.

808. Kane, Francis J., and Peter A. Lachenbruch. "Adolescent Pregnancy: A Study of Aborters and Non-Aborters." American Journal of Orthopsychiatry 43 (1973): 796-803.

A study of 99 single girls seeking abortion and 33 single girls completing pregnancy. Knowledge and availability of contraception were not seen as problems, but emotional factors, such as guilt over sexual activity, reactions to loss, and severe acting-out character disorders, contributed to pregnancy in both groups.

809. Kantner, John F. "From Here to 2000: A Look at the Population Problem." Johns Hopkins Medical Journal Jan. 1979: 18-24.

An overview of the efforts of the Planned Parenthood Federation (PPF) and other organizations to reduce fertility.

810. Kantner, John F., and Melvin Zelnik. "Contraception and Pregnancy: Experience of Young Unmarried Women in the United States." Family Planning Perspectives 5 (1973): 21-35.

Examines the profile of the sexual life of young, never-married women by questioning those who are sexually experienced to see to what extent they attempt to avoid pregnancy through the use of contraception; the methods they employ in doing so; and the sources from which they have obtained contraception.

811. Kantrowitz, Barbara, and Nikki Finke Greenberg. "Only but Not Lonely: Changing Views of the One-Child Household." Newsweek 16 June 1986: 66-67.

With the average number of children per family dipping below two for the first time in decades, only children are far more common, and psychologists and educators are beginning to revise their theories about the drawbacks of growing up alone.

812. Kantrowitz, Barbara, et al. "Kids and Contraceptives." Newsweek 16 Feb. 1987: 54+.

A series of articles discussing birth control, sexually trans- mitted diseases, various contraception choices, and the strong element of peer pressure.

813. _____. "Three's a Crowd." Newsweek 1 Sept. 1986: 68+.

As demanding his-and-her careers become a way of life, more and more couples are opting out of parenthood. The rate of child- lessness in this country reaches the highest it has been since the Depression.

814. Kantzer, Kenneth S. "Planned Parenthood Attacks a Parent's Need to Know." Editorial. Christianity Today 20 May 1983: 11-13.

Asks the question: For what reasons should parents be informed if clinics give minors prescription contraceptives?

815. _____. "A Winning Prolife Strategy." Christianity Today 15 Dec. 1989: 19.

Following the Webster decision, many pro-lifers looked forward to an easy slide towards strong pro-life legislation throughout the United States. It has not happened.

816. _____. "Within Our Reach." Editorial. Christianity
     Today 19 Apr. 1985: 20-23.

     An American consensus is shaping up on what to do about
     abortions; the consensus is against abortion on demand.

817. Kash, Sara. "Birth-Control Survey: Sterilization Tops List in
     U.S." Ms. Jan. 1984: 17.

     The method of contraception women choose, and why, is the
     subject of a new study of 6,790 women, ages 18 to 44, by the
     Alan Guttmacher Institute in New York City.

818. Katafiasz, Karen. "It's Time to Speak Out for All Life." St.
     Anthony's Messenger Oct. 1973: 26-27.

     Challenges readers to live as Christians and recognize our own
     failures to respect and defend human life wherever it exists.

819. Katenkamp, Jane Blank. Respecting Life: An Activity Guide.
     Washington: U.S. Catholic Conference, 1985.

     Covers topics such as leadership training for parish pro-life
     coordinators, Catholic teaching on human life issues, program
     planning, suggestions for prayers, liturgies, homilies and
     educational activities.

820. Kaufman, Sherwin A. "What You Should Know About Abortion."
     Parents Apr. 1973: 62-64.

     A doctor discusses some of the implications of the legalization
     of early abortions.

821. Kay, Bonnie Jean. "An Evaluation of Long-Range Aspects of
     Abortion Services in Chicago, Illinois: An Interdisciplinary
     Approach." Diss. Northwestern U, 1975.

     A report concerned with a contemporary health problem: repeated
     elective abortion.

822. Kaye, Tony. "The Birth Dearth." New Republic 19 Jan. 1987:
     20.

     Conservatives conceive a "crisis". The next conservative
     crusade: low fertility rates.

823. Keerdoja, Eileen, and Ying Ying Wu. "Dr. Waddill: Triple
     Jeopardy?" Newsweek 7 Jan. 1980: 10.

The jury at the trial of a California obstetrician deadlocks twice on a first-degree murder charge, but a third trial for wrongful death looms.

824.   Kelbley, Charles. "Abortion: Agreeing to Disagree." _Newsweek_ 16 Dec. 1985: 9.

Whether one is for or against morality, the author contends that there are grave doubts about the morality of a given position. When philosophers, theologians, and scientists cannot agree, then the problem should be resolved in favor of freedom, not prohibition.

825.   Keller, Allan. _Scandalous Lady: The Life and Times of Madame Restell, New York's Most Notorious Abortionist_. New York: Atheneum, 1981.

Academic historians may find this book unscholarly, but popular history buffs will enjoy this fascinating chapter of social history in New York.

826.   Kellogg, Mary Alice. "I Had an Abortion." _Seventeen_ Oct. 1984: 144+.

A popular account by a woman who chose to have an abortion.

827.   Kelly, James R. "Beyond the Stereotypes." _Commonweal_ 20 Nov. 1981: 654-59.

Right-to-life activists are commonly characterized as sectarian, morally naive, politically conservative, and best understood in the reductive social-psychological terms of "status politics." This article is an interview with right-to-life pioneers.

828.   _____. "Catholic Abortion Rates and the Abortion Controversy." _America_ 4 Feb. 1989: 82-85.

Suggests that Catholics, despite their strong anti-abortion ethic, make use of abortion in about the same proportions as everyone else.

829.   _____. "Winning _Webster_ vs. _Reproductive Health Services_: The Crisis of the Pro-Life Movement." _America_ 19 Aug. 1989: 79-83.

After the _Webster_ decision the pro-life activists must persuade their critics that their cause is more than an anti-abortion movement.

830. Kelly, Kent. Abortion: The American Holocaust. Southern Pines: Calvary, 1981.

Facts on abortion presented in the form of hard-hitting ideas which demand a reaction from the reader.

831. Kelly, Kevin. "The Consequences of Treating a Fetus as a Human Being." Whole Earth Review (1986): 64-70.

A readers' survey on abortion.

832. Kennedy, J., A. McNally, and M. Brennan. "Judicial Power and Public Conscience." Symposium. Sign Mar. 1973: 26-27.

The Roe v. Wade decision of the U.S. Supreme Court on abortion is evaluated in the light of the relationship between public and private morality.

833. Kennedy, Jeremiah. "Abortion and the Court." Sign Sept. 1977: 22.

The right-to-life movement has become one of the most powerful political lobbies in the country.

834. Kennedy, John E., and Michael Nicolazzo. "Abortion: Toward a Standard Based upon Clinical Medical Signs of Life and Death." Journal of Family Law 23 (1985): 545-63.

Viability is reached when there is a reasonable likelihood of the fetus's sustained survival outside the womb, with or without artificial support.

835. Kenyon, Edwin. The Dilemma of Abortion. Boston: Faber, 1986.

Presents a critical study of how the British Abortion Act is working, pointing up its similarities to abortion laws in other countries.

836. Kerenyi, Thomas D., Ellen L. Glascock, and Marjorie L. Horowitz. "Reasons for Delayed Abortion: Results of Four Hundred Interviews." American Journal of Obstetrics and Gynecology 1 Oct. 1973: 299-311.

Covers the abortion patients' demographic backgrounds, facts related to pregnancies, contraceptive practices, and sexual attitudes and behavior and summarizes the findings of the inquiry related to the first two areas.

837. Kessler, Alexander, and Tabitha Standley. "Contraception: Fad and Fashion." World Health June 1984: 24.

Argues that little attention is given to a factor that has had a considerable influence on family planning, that is, fads and fashions.

838. Kilby-Kelberg, Sally, and Edward Wakin. "A Nurse's Biography of an Abortion." U.S. Catholic Feb. 1973: 19-21.

A registered Catholic nurse tells about assisting a young girl at the time of her abortion, and about the conflicts she experienced.

839. Killey, John F. "Catholic Sexual Ethics: The Continuing Debate on Birth Control." Linacre Quarterly 41 (1974): 8-25.

Asks for a reconsideration of the dissent from Humanae Vitae and also questions the lines of reasoning for the acceptance of contraception.

840. Kinsley, Michael. "Danse Macabre." New Republic 19 Nov. 1977: 13+.

The Hyde amendment, if it is enacted in any of its present forms, may deny abortions not only to people on Medicaid, but also to Labor Department and Health, Education and Welfare (HEW) Department employees and their families who, otherwise, are entitled to abortion care under their government health plans.

841. _____. "The New Politics of Abortion." Time 17 July 1989: 96.

Politicians have the U.S. Supreme Court to thank for the fact that the abortion issue is now a nightmarish gauntlet that has to be run between two ravening mobs.

842. Kippley, John F. "Couple to Couple League, Hospitals Cooperate in Teaching NFP." Hospital Progress Mar. 1983: 57+.

Catholic and other hospitals have added natural family planning (NFP) services to the community programs they offer.

843. _____. "Preaching on Humanae Vitae." Homiletic and Pastoral Review Mar. 1978: 15-19.

Points out that Humanae Vitae is rarely mentioned from the pulpit because priests hesitate to push it unless they are able to provide some practical help.

844.   Kirchner, Corinne, and John Colombotos. The Abortion Issue:
       Religious and Political Correlates of Physicians' Attitudes.
       New York: American Sociological Assoc., 1973.

       Papers presented at the annual meeting of the American
       Sociological Association (ASA), New York, August 1973, on the
       abortion issue.

845.   Kirk, Russell. "Abortion at MSU." National Review 11 May
       1973: 527.

       Discusses Michigan State University (MSU) policy on student
       abortions and the law.

846.   Klaus, Hanna. "A Medical Cop-out?" America 16 Aug. 1975: 68-
       70.

       Doctors who accept only the role and responsibilities of
       technicians contribute to oversimplifications welcomed by many
       in our society.

847.   _____. "A Second Look at Humanae Vitae." Homiletic
       and Pastoral Review Oct. 1973: 59-67.

       The encyclical "Of Human Life" speaks of the integral vision
       of humanity. What it proposes is not optional for human
       nature but completes it.

848.   _____. "Why Natural Family Planning Is Different."
       Marriage and Family Living Apr.-May 1980: 14-15.

       Advances reasons why natural family planning (NFP) is so unlike
       other methods of contraception.

849.   Klein, Joe. "Abortion and the Archbishop." New York 1 Oct.
       1984: 36-43.

       A background article on some of the influential factors in the
       life and work of Archbishop John J. O'Connor, with strong
       references to his anti-abortion stand.

850.   _____. "Born Again: How an Abortion Crusader Became a
       Right-to-Lifer." New York 7 Jan. 1985: 40.

       Dr. Bernard Nathanson recounts how he came to the conclusion,
       after performing or directing 75,000 abortions, that abortion
       is wrong.

851.   Klotz, John W. Christian View of Abortion. St. Louis:
       Concordia, 1973.

Advocates that when the question of an abortion arises, the
Christian must probe reasons and resources.

852. Knight, James W. *Preventing Birth: Contemporary Methods and
Related Moral Controversies*. Salt Lake City: U of Utah,
1989.

Aims to contribute to the general understanding of the
scientific and social aspects of contemporary birth control
methods and to the public discussion of a number of the moral
issues that are related to those methods.

853. Knowles, John H. "Public Policy on Abortion." *Society* 11 July
1974: 15-18.

The U.S. Supreme Court's ruling constitutes a mandate to
government and to the health system to respond affirmatively
with an active program to ensure that individuals are able to
gain access to abortions performed under the safest, most
dignified and humane conditions.

854. Koerbel, Pam. *Abortion's Second Victim*. Wheaton: Victor, 1986.

Designed to help women who have had an abortion deal with the
emotional aftermath they face.

855. Kolbenschlag, Madonna. "Abortion and Moral Consensus: Beyond
Solomon's Choice." *Christian Century* 20 Feb. 1985: 179-83.

An insightful article examines the collective conscience of
the church and American society. It concludes with Solomon's
wise advice: Let those who are most intimately affected by
the consequences of a decision make that decision.

856. Komisar, Lucy. "Sellout on Abortion." *Newsweek* 9 June 1975:
11.

After the 1973 U.S. Supreme Court decision on abortion, the
Senate voted, and the House went along in conference, to assure
federally aided public and private hospitals that they could
refuse to perform or permit abortions or sterilizations on the
grounds of the religion or conscience of the hospital's
directors. The real issue is how some of the country's leading
politicians have responded to the anti-abortion lobby by
selling out the poor.

857. Koop, C. Everett. "Abortion Is Always Wrong." *Sign* Sept.
1978: 20-23.

Excerpt from *The Right to Live; The Right to Die* (Tyndale,
1980). A surgeon whose life has been dedicated to preserving

the lives of babies born with severe defects tells why he reversed his position on acceptance of abortion in "hard" cases.

858. _____. "The Perils of a Convenient Society." *New Covenant* Mar. 1981: 8-11.

Koop contends that one of the main factors causing the decline of society was the *Roe* v. *Wade* decision of the U.S. Supreme Court.

859. Koop, C. Everett, and Francis A. Schaeffer. *Whatever Happened to the Human Race?* Old Tappan: Revell, 1979.

Analyzes the widespread implications and loss of human rights brought on by today's practices of abortion, infanticide, and euthanasia.

860. Kopecky, Gini. "The Battle over Abortion." *Glamour* June 1983: 218+.

Discusses why, ten years after *Roe* v. *Wade*, the battle is more brutal than ever.

861. Koslow, Sally. "Contraceptives." *Ladies' Home Journal* Sept. 1979: 82+.

Women share their experiences with contraceptives, and experts give sound and reassuring advice on today's and tomorrow's contraceptives.

862. Kramer, Michael. "Reagan's War on Abortion: Future Shock?" *New York* 24 Sept. 1984: 27+.

Contends that religion in government is something quite different from religion in politics. The former is the willingness of elected leaders to use their governmental authority to impose their theological views on society at large.

863. Krason, Stephen M. "Abortion and National Policymaking: Reflections on the Congress Reversing the Rule of *Roe* v. *Wade* and *Doe* v. *Bolton*." *Social Justice Review* Mar.-Apr. 1983: 35-44.

The Human Life Bill versus the human life amendment: Krason believes that it is time for the pro-life movement to reconsider its amendment strategy and to place its primary emphasis on the passage of a federal anti-abortion statute.

864. _____. "Abortion: Politics, Morality and the Constitu-
tion: A Critical Study of <u>Roe</u> vs. <u>Wade</u> and <u>Doe</u> vs. <u>Bolton</u>
and a Basis for Change." Diss. Catholic U, 1983. Lanham: UP
of America, 1984.

A published dissertation on the anti-abortion movement.

865. _____. "The Supreme Court's Abortion Decision: A Critical
Study of the Shaping of a Major American Public Policy and a
Basis for Change." Diss. State U of New York, 1983.

A comprehensive, critical study of the U.S. Supreme Court's
1973 abortion decisions, <u>Roe</u> v. <u>Wade</u> and <u>Doe</u> v. <u>Bolton</u>.

866. Krastel, John. "Return to Realism: A Prolife Agenda." <u>America</u>
7 Feb. 1981: 101-02.

The 1980 elections have done much for the pro-life movement:
they brought new legislators, new visibility, and new success
to the drive to eliminate the killing of the unborn. Much
remains to be done, however, in this civil rights struggle.

867. Krauss, Elissa. "Clinics: Run for Women, Not Profit." <u>Ms</u>.
Sept. 1975: 106.

The Feminist Women's Health Centers (FWHC), begun in 1973 with
two abortion clinics, developed into a network of centers with
additional clinics. Each center shares a common philosophy
and commitment to self-help and women-controlled women's
health care. The clinics provide early-term abortion by
vacuum aspiration.

868. Krauthammer, Charles. "The Church-State Debate." <u>New Republic</u>
17 Sept. 1984: 15-18.

The governor and the bishops appeal to heaven in an abortion
debate initiated by John Cardinal O'Connor's statement: "I
don't see how a Catholic in good conscience can vote for a
candidate who explicitly supports abortion."

869. Kreeft, Peter. <u>The Unaborted Socrates: A Dramatic Debate on
the Issues Surrounding Abortion</u>. Downers Grove: Inter-Varsity,
1983.

Uses the Socratic technique to strip away the emotional issues
and get to the heart of the rational objections to abortion.

870. Kress, Robert. "The Antifeminism of Abortion." <u>Marriage and
Family Living</u> Feb. 1976: 2-5.

The question raised here is precisely this: Does abortion-on-demand really make for the liberation of women?

871. Kuykendall, George. "Thinking About Abortion." Cross Currents 27 (1978): 403-16.

A social development of the last 30 years has been the revolution in attitudes towards and laws about abortion. Reasons Christians today give for adopting new beliefs about abortion are discussed.

872. Lacayo, Richard. "A Day of Reckoning on Roe." Time 8 May 1989: 24.

The high court faces the abortion question--and asks a few questions of its own.

873. _____. "The Shifting Politics of Abortion." Time 23 Oct. 1989: 35-36.

With two major victories, the pro-choice majority shows that it is not so silent.

874. _____. "Whose Life Is It?" Time 1 May 1989: 20-24.

The long, emotional battle over abortion approaches a climax as the U.S. Supreme Court prepares for a historic challenge to Roe v. Wade.

875. Lader, Lawrence. Abortion II: Making the Revolution. Boston: Beacon, 1973.

Traces the development of the abortion movement from 1965 to the U.S. Supreme Court decision of January 22, 1973 (Roe v. Wade), and credits the author's part in it to the inspiration of Margaret Sanger.

876. _____. "Abortions Denied." Nation 17 July 1976: 38-39.

Contends that the refusal of public hospitals to obey the law on abortion has created a highly discriminatory system of health care, and that the most effective way to ensure that public hospitals obey the law would be to institute an omnibus court suit in key states seeking to apply the penalty that hurts most: a monetary penalty.

877. Lake, Alice. "Contraception: The Hope That Failed." Ladies' Home Journal Aug. 1984: 83+.

Twenty-five years ago, women were promised that safe, effective, easy-to-use birth control was at hand. For many women, contraception is a decision that they must evaluate again and again.

878. _____. "For Teenagers Only: Confidential Birth Control Clinics." Good Housekeeping June 1976: 132+.

Pregnancy among high school girls is now at epidemic stage. Here is how one city--Grand Rapids, Michigan--is dealing with the problem.

879. Lake, Randall A. "Order and Disorder in Anti-Abortion Rhetoric: A Logological View." Quarterly Journal of Speech 70 (1984): 425-43.

Seeks to help redress the abortion debate through an examination of the "moral landscape" painted by anti-abortion rhetoric.

880. Lake, Randall Alan. "The Ethics of Rhetoric and the Rhetoric of Ethics in the Abortion Controversy." Diss. U of Kansas, 1982.

Examines the relationships between the fields of ethics and argumentation as these relationships are manifested in the abortion dispute.

881. Lamar, Jacob V., Jr. "Silent No More: Speaking Out for Abortion." Time 27 May 1985: 32.

Reports on a year-long campaign entitled "Abortion Rights: Silent No More." The campaign, which kicked off last month with a series of nationwide "speak-outs," is designed to counter the growing tendency of anti-abortion advocates to dominate the public debate.

882. Landau, Richard. "Equal Protection." National Review 19 Jan. 1973: 87+.

The Massachusetts Supreme Judicial Court faces the basic question: Does a viable fetus have rights under law that are independent of its mother's?

883. Lane, Thomas A. "Population and the Crisis of Culture." Homiletic and Pastoral Review Apr. 1975: 61-65.

Answers the question: What can be said of a society which teaches its youth that the inconvenience of bearing a child can be avoided by abortion?

884. "Last Days of Roe?" National Review 2 June 1989: 14+.

A commentary on U.S. Supreme Court's hearing of the Webster v. Reproductive Health Services case.

885. Lauer, Margaret. "Getting Rid of Old Habits." Mother Jones Feb.-Mar. 1985: 10.

The National Coalition of American Nuns (NCAN) rejects the claim that to be pro-choice is to be pro-abortion.

886. Lawrence, Marsha A. "A Study of Movement and Countermovement Organizations in the Abortion Movement." Thesis (MA). North Texas State U, 1983.

Begins to fill the gap in sociological literature on movements and countermovements by exploring the dynamic environment of two movement organizations.

887. Lawrence, Michael. "The Impossible Dream." Triumph Mar. 1975: 9-11.

Argues that the U.S. Supreme Court's decision in the United States v. Vuitch settles the abortion controversy as a legal matter. The law of the land is now, de jure or de facto, abortion on demand.

888. _____. "The Pro-Life Movement at the Crossroads." Triumph June 1973: 11-15.

These questions must be answered if the pro-life movement is to continue: What direction must it take to transform itself into an effective national movement? How can it remain true to its own rock-bottom spiritual conviction in a sociopolitical climate actively and officially faithful to an opposite spirit?

889. Lawton, Kim A. "Arguments over Abortion Delay Civil Rights Bill." Christianity Today 16 May 1986: 46-47.

Pro-life groups want an "abortion-neutral" amendment to the Civil Rights Restoration Act, while the National Organization for Women (NOW) opposes the amendment, saying it weakens the act.

890. _____. "Could This Be the Year?" Christianity Today 7 Apr. 1989: 36-38.

According to U.S. Supreme Court observers, the 1973 Roe v. Wade decision could be restricted--and perhaps overturned-- this term.

891.   _____. "High Court Accepts Cases on Abortion, Obscenity, and Church Hiring Practices." Christianity Today 12 Dec. 1986: 53-55.

Church-and-state issues emerge as a dominant theme in the U.S. Supreme Court's current term, its first under Chief Justice William Rehnquist.

892.   _____. "High Court Strikes Down Abortion Restrictions, Rules on Handicapped Infants." Christianity Today 11 July 1986: 38-39.

Two U.S. Supreme Court decisions deal setbacks to the right-to-life movement, but many pro-life leaders are encouraged by signs of growing sentiment on the Court to reconsider abortion on demand.

893.   _____. "Promises to Keep." Christianity Today 3 Feb. 1989: 44-45.

President Bush's appointment of Louis Sullivan as secretary of Health and Human Services (HHS) disappoints pro-life supporters.

894.   _____. "Scanning the Prolife Battlefields." Christianity Today 16 June 1989: 52-53.

Reports that much public attention in the abortion debate has been focused on the U.S. Supreme Court. However, the battle over abortion continues on a variety of other fronts.

895.   _____. "Taking It to the States." Christianity Today 3 Nov. 1989: 36-38.

In light of the U.S. Supreme Court's Webster decision, pro-life activists focus on states as the new abortion battlefields.

896.   Leach, Judith. "The Repeat Abortion Patient." Family Planning Perspectives Jan.-Feb. 1977: 37-39.

Repeat abortion patients are more often dissatisfied with themselves, more often perceive themselves as victims of bad luck, and more frequently express negative feelings toward the current abortion than women who are obtaining abortions for the first time.

897.   Leahy, Peter James. "The Anti-Abortion Movement: Testing a Theory of the Rise and Fall of Social Movements." Diss. Syracuse U, 1975.

Tests a theory of the rise and fall of social movements with data from the anti-abortion movement.

898. Leber, Gary. "We Must Rescue Them." Hastings Center Report Nov.-Dec. 1989: 26-27.

Describes the strategy of Operation Rescue.

899. Ledbetter, Donald L. Abortion Is Murder. La Puente: Abbott, 1980.

Outlines the spiritual facts a person should consider before consenting to an abortion.

900. Ledbetter, Rosanna. A History of the Malthusian League, 1877-1927. Columbus: Ohio State UP, 1976.

A study of the organization which advocated the voluntary limitation of families by birth control methods as the only solution to the problems of the poor.

901. _____. "The Organization That Delayed Birth Control: A History of the Malthusian League, 1877-1927." Diss. Northern Illinois U, 1972.

Gives extensive evidence that the efforts of Charles Robert Drysdale and his son, Charles Vickery Drysdale, were important in the shaping of the birth control movements.

902. Lee, Francis G. "What About an Abortion Amendment?" America 8 Mar. 1975: 166-68.

Maintains that the U.S. Supreme Court, despite popular myth, is not infallible. The proposed amendments to reverse its abortion decisions have merit, but they need rethinking if they are going to work.

903. "Legal Abortion: How Safe? How Available? How Costly?" Consumer Reports July 1972: 466-70.

A discussion confined to what Consumers Union (CU) learned from doctors, public health officials, and abortion referral specialists across the country about the safety, availability, and costs of abortion.

904. Legge, Jerome S. Abortion Policy: An Evaluation of the Consequences for Maternal and Infant Health. Albany: State U of New York P, 1985.

Discusses basic definitions and concepts of abortion as a public policy issue.

905. Legge, Kate. "Abortion Debate." World Press Review Feb. 1989: 46.

Contends that the reversal of Roe v. Wade would return legal responsibility for abortion to the state legislatures, resulting in a potentially messy patchwork of regulations.

906. Lehrman, Lewis E. "The Right to Life and the Restoration of the American Republic." National Review 29 Aug. 1986: 25-28.

Supports the concept that the right to life is a basic outgrowth of the Constitution and, in the abortion question, does not violate the separation of church and state doctrine.

907. Leiter, Naomi. "Elective Abortion." New York State Journal of Medicine Dec. 1972: 2808-2910.

Shares ideas distilled from the author's recent experience with more than 300 clinic and private patients whom she saw for psychiatric evaluation prior to a therapeutic abortion and from the follow-ups she was able to obtain.

908. Leo, John. "The Moral Complexity of Choice." U.S. News and World Report 11 Dec. 1989: 64.

Two premises are discussed: 1) that there are too many abortions in America; 2) that abortion is a serious moral issue that is too often treated in a frivolous way.

909. _____. "Sharing the Pain of Abortion." Time 26 Sept. 1983: 78.

Contends that men whose partners have an abortion feel isolated and angry at themselves and their partners. He reports on a university professor who was involved in an abortion and concludes that abortion is a great, unrecognized trauma for males, perhaps the only major one that most men go through without help.

910. Lerner, Gerda. The Female Experience: An American Documentary. Indianapolis: Bobbs, 1977.

Contends that Sadie Sacks died from a self-induced abortion, the incident which sparked Margaret Sanger's involvement with birth control.

134

911. Leslie, Connie, with Diana Camper. "A New 'Squeal' Rule."
     Newsweek 7 Feb. 1983: 24.

     Federally funded family-planning clinics will be required to
     notify the parents of "unemancipated" teenagers under 18
     within 10 days when they are given prescriptions for
     contraceptives.

912. Letich, Larry. "Bad Choices." Tikkun July-Aug. 1989: 22-25.

     Asks: How did legal abortion, something that over 15 million
     American women have undergone, remain controversial enough to
     approach repeal?

913. Levicoff, Steve. Building Bridges: The Pro-Life Movement and
     the Peace Movement. Eagleville: Toviah, 1982.

     A statement on the growing alliance between pro-life and peace
     activists.

914. Lewin, Nathan. "Abortion and Dr. Edelin: Miscarriage of
     Justice." New Republic 1 Mar. 1975: 16-19.

     The Massachusetts prosecutor's office agreed from the outset
     of the case that Dr. Edelin's conduct was entirely legal. But
     the prosecutor insisted that the doctor violated the state's
     laws against homicide.

915. "A License to Live." Editorial. Christianity Today 26 July
     1974: 22-23.

     Euthanasia (first voluntary and then compulsory), forcible
     family limitation, and genetic controls--the pro-abortion
     forces decry these warnings as unrealistic and hysterical.

916. Lieberman, E. James. Sex and Birth Control: A Guide for the
     Young. New York: Crowell, 1973.

     A study of sexuality and birth control intended for the young
     adult population.

917. Lieberman, Janet J. "A Short History of Contraception."
     American Biology Teacher Sept. 1973: 315+.

     Gives a concise world view of contraception. Includes a brief
     history of Margaret Sanger's efforts (under "Pioneers of Birth
     Control").

918. "Life and the Fourteenth Amendment." Editorial. America
     16 May 1981: 397.

The Fourteenth Amendment's second sentence declares, in part, that no state shall "deprive any person of life, liberty, or property, without due process of law." But who is a person? And when does life begin?

919. "Life in New York." Editorial. Triumph June 1972: 45.

Attacks the pro-abortion decision of Gov. Nelson Rockefeller and the New York State Legislature.

920. "Life in the Dark Age: Governor Rockefeller's Veto." Christian Century 31 May 1972: 624.

Offers a critical analysis of Gov. Nelson Rockefeller's veto of a bill to repeal New York's abortion law, and comes to the conclusion that he made a mistake.

921. "Life Issues After the Election." Editorial. America 10 Nov. 1984: 285.

The issues of religion and politics, theology and policy, public morality and personal choice will be with us long after the current election is over.

922. "Life, Not Dissent, Is Absolute." Editorial. America 19 Oct. 1985: 229.

Holds that there is a right to dissent in the Catholic church, but that it is not absolute. Based on a well-formed personal conscience, an individual Catholic can dissent from church teaching; but there can be no well-formed conscience that ignores objective morality.

923. Lincoln, C. Eric. "Why I Reversed My Stand on Laissez-Faire Abortion." Christian Century 25 Apr. 1973: 477-79.

Argues that unrestricted abortion is but one more example of the retreat from responsibility which seems characteristic of the times.

924. Lindemann, Constance. Birth Control and Unmarried Young Women. New York: Springer, 1974.

Presents in a readable, useful form, the author's research findings on the problem of preventing unwanted pregnancy in young unmarried women.

925. Lippis, John. The Challenge to Be Pro-Life. Washington: Natl. Right to Life Educ. Trust Fund, 1982.

Provides constructive information that should be considered before making an abortion decision.

926. Liston, Mary F. "Abortion Decisions--Impact on Nursing Practice, Maternal and Child Care." Jurist 33 (1973): 230-36.

    Explores the impact of the U.S. Supreme Court's decisions on abortion in relation to the nursing practice.

927. Littlewood, Thomas B. The Politics of Population Control. Notre Dame: U of Notre Dame P, 1977.

    Discusses political motivations for birth control that arose in the United States in the 1960s.

928. Llewellyn-Jones, Derek. Human Reproduction and Society. New York: Putnam, 1974.

    Deals with demographic and social problems of human reproduction and the challenge posed by exponential population growth.

929. "Lobbying for the Unborn." Christianity Today 20 July 1973: 44.

    Discusses various legislative steps being taken by U.S. congressmen to amend the Constitution.

930. Lobman, Helaine F. "Spousal Notification: An Unconstitutional Limitation on a Woman's Right to Privacy in the Abortion Decision." Hofstra Law Review 2 (1984): 531-60.

    Analyzes the constitutionality of statutes requiring spousal notification prior to obtaining an abortion; explores alternative constitutional challenges to the validity of these statutes; proposes possible solutions to the inherent problems in spousal notification laws.

931. Lockwood, Sally. "Can You Change People's Minds on Abortion?" Liguorian Feb. 1975: 13-16.

    Argues that the swing to the right-to-life position seems to dramatize that when an American looks closely at both sides of the issue, thinks about it, becomes involved in it, he or she not only comes to believe in right-to-life goals, but does something about it.

932. Loebl, Suzanne. Conception, Contraception: A New Look. New York: McGraw, 1974.

Of interest not only to the mature junior reader, but to social and medical scientists, physicians, administrators, and anyone interested in population and fertility control.

933. Loesch, Juli. "Abortion and an Attempt at Dialogue." America 24 Mar. 1979: 234-36.

Contends that pro-lifers and pro-choicers have a common goal--reducing the number of abortions--and that their energies and insights should be so directed and coordinated.

934. _____. "Pro-Life, Pro-E.R.A." America 9 Dec. 1978: 435-36.

Being for the equal rights amendment (ERA) and against abortion is not easy. By linking the two positions, pro-abortion feminists have adopted a suicidal strategy which threatens passage of the ERA.

935. _____. "Pro-Life; Pro-Peace." Sign Sept. 1981: 11-14.

Argues that the antinuclear, pro-peace movement should be a natural ally of the pro-life movement.

936. _____. "Shake Hands with a Prolife Peacemaker." U.S. Catholic May 1984: 22-28.

An interview with Juli Loesch, who founded Pro-lifers for Survival (PLS), the organization which fights both abortion and nuclear weapons.

937. "The Longer March." Commonweal 5 May 1989: 259-60.

A statistically based article holding that a woman's freedom to choose abortion has become the symbol, and for many the substance, of women's freedom in general.

938. Lopez, Laura. "A Debate over Sovereign Rights: U.S. Views on Capitalism and Abortion Stir Controversy." Time 20 Aug. 1984: 34.

For the United States to redirect its financial assistance to organizations that do not promote abortion is a method of family planning, says U.S. Chief Delegate James Buckley at a United Nations-sponsored International Conference on Population in Mexico City.

939. Lotstra, Hans. Abortion: The Catholic Debate in America. New York: Irvington, 1985.

Contends that abortion is a multidimensional dilemma in which diverse values, social relations, and world views are put at risk.

940. Louisell, David W. "A Constitutional Amendment to Restrict Abortion." Catholic Mind Dec. 1976: 25-31.

Text of testimony presented by David W. Louisell, a professor of law at the University of California in Berkeley, before the subcommittee on Civil and Constitutional Rights of the House Committee on the Judiciary in the U.S. Congress. The sub-committee was, at the time, conducting hearings on the proposal for a constitutional amendment to restrict abortions.

941. Lovenduski, Joni, and Joyce Outshorn. The New Politics of Abortion. Beverly Hills: Sage, 1986.

A collection of papers on abortion policy and its impact on a variety of liberal democratic political systems.

942. Luciano, Lani. "Natural Family Planning: Dispelling Modern Myths." Sign June 1976: 6-8.

Many couples involved in natural family planning (NFP) praise its advantages. They have found that it has strengthened their marriages.

943. Luker, Kristin. Abortion and the Politics of Motherhood. California Series on Social Choice and Political Economy. Berkeley: U of California P, 1984.

A sociological study of the Roe v. Wade U.S. Supreme Court decision.

944. _____. Taking Chances: Abortion and the Decision Not to Contracept. Berkeley: U of California P, 1975.

A study of a group of 50 women who underwent abortions in a California clinic.

945. _____. "The War Between the Women." Family Planning Perspectives May-June 1984: 105-10.

For pro-choice women to achieve their goals, they must argue that motherhood is not a primary, inevitable, or natural role for women. For pro-life women to achieve their goals, they must argue that it is.

946. Lynch, Patricia, and Therese Coen. "Abortion, Politics and Family Life: An Interpretation." Diss. U of Massachusetts, 1981.

Examines the many dimensions of the American abortion controversy.

947. Lynch, Robert N. "Abortion and 1976 Politics." America 6 Mar. 1976: 177-78.

Asserts that the pro-life forces are badly in need of a victory, but that, unless and until they unite, there can be little hope for substantial progress because each group has a different constituency.

948. MacDonald, Sebastian. "The Meaning of Abortion." American Ecclesiastical Review Apr. 1975: 219-36.

Uses the relationship between contraception and abortion inversely by arguing that, in our culture, abortion is understood contraceptively, and by suggesting that the Catholic church fashion her pastoral response to abortion in these terms.

949. Mace, David Robert. Abortion, the Agonizing Decision. Nashville: Abingdon, 1972.

For counselors and clergy, to assist them in counseling the woman with an unwanted pregnancy.

950. MacGraw, Ali. "When Abortion Was Illegal." People Weekly 5 Aug. 1985: 74+.

Ali MacGraw's story of having an illegal abortion in New York State.

951. Maestri, William F. Choose Life and Not Death: A Primer on Abortion, Euthanasia, and Suicide. New York: Alba, 1985.

Examines three major moral life issues: abortion, euthanasia, and suicide.

952. Magnuson, Ed. "Pressing the Abortion Issue: Ferraro's Stand Is Attacked by Bishops." Time 24 Sept. 1984: 18-20.

Discusses the continuing debate over the proper role of religious leaders in trying to influence public policy and the conflicting pressures on elected officials who hold strong religious beliefs.

953. Maguire, Daniel C. "Abortion: A Question of Catholic Honesty."
     Christian Century 14 Sept. 1983: 803-07.

     Argues that it is a theological fact of life that there is no
     one nominative Catholic position on abortion.

954. _____. "A Catholic Theologian at an Abortion Clinic."
     Ms. Dec. 1984: 129-32.

     Weighing reality against doctrine, the author wishes to main-
     tain the legality of abortion for women who judge they need it.

955. _____. Reflections of a Catholic Theologian on Visit-
     ing an Abortion Clinic. Washington: Catholics for a Free
     Choice, 1984.

     Catholic moral theology is in grave default on the abortion
     issue.

956. Maguire, Marjorie R. "Can Technology Solve the Abortion
     Dilemma?" Christian Century 27 Oct. 1976: 918-19.

     The abortion controversy is impaled on a fallacy that a
     woman's right to terminate a pregnancy and a fetus's right to
     life are of necessity and forever mutually exclusive.

957. Maguire, Marjorie Reiley, and Daniel C. Maguire. Abortion: A
     Guide to Making Ethical Choices. Washington: Catholics for a
     Free Choice, 1983.

     Attempts to be sensitive to the needs of all women who seek to
     exercise their obligation to make a moral choice about
     abortion.

958. Mahowald, Mary B. "Abortion: Towards Continuing the Dialogue."
     Cross Currents 29 (1979): 330-35.

     Eleanor Smeal, president of the National Organization for
     Women (NOW), invites pro-choice and pro-life organizations to
     a meeting to discuss common areas of concern.

959. _____. "Is There Life After Roe v. Wade?" Hastings
     Center Report July-Aug. 1989: 22-29.

     Those whose views on the legality or morality of abortion are
     somewhere between absolute permissiveness and absolute condem-
     nation may look for ways of saving what seems worth saving of
     Roe v. Wade.

960. Maine, Deborah. "Does Abortion Affect Later Pregnancies?"
     Family Planning Perspectives Mar.-Apr. 1979: 98-101.

     Recent studies have found that having two or more abortions
     may increase a woman's risk of having a subsequent miscarriage,
     premature delivery, or low-birth-weight infant.

961. "Mainline Churches Reassess Prochoice Stand on Abortion."
     Christianity Today 14 Dec. 1984: 72.

     Reports on reasons why mainline Protestant churches may be
     changing their views on abortion.

962. Mall, David. In Good Conscience: Abortion and Moral Necessity.
     Libertyville: Kairos, 1982.

     Does not deal directly with the abortion issue, but with
     articles intended to stimulate thinking and talking about
     abortion.

963. Mall, David, and Walter F. Watts, eds. The Psychological
     Aspects of Abortion. Washington: U Publ. of America, 1979.

     Papers presented by 10 American and Canadian psychiatrists at
     a two-day symposium, at the Stritch School of Medicine of
     Loyola University, on the psychological aspects of abortion.

964. Mallory, George B., Jr., et al. "Factors Responsible for Delay
     in Obtaining Interruption of Pregnancy." Obstetrics and
     Gynecology Oct. 1972: 556-62.

     Abortions late in pregnancy are associated with higher morbid-
     ity and greater patient stress than are those performed
     earlier. Women having a late abortion were more likely to be
     younger, single, and nulliparous (to never have borne off-
     spring), and less likely to have ever used contraception than
     were women having early abortions.

965. Manier, E., W. Liu, and D. Soloman. Abortion: New Direc-
     tions for Policy Studies. Notre Dame: U of Notre Dame P, 1977.

     Five papers presented at a conference in 1973 at the Uni-
     versity of Notre Dame presenting the philosophical, political,
     and sociological aspects of the abortion question.

966. Mannion, Michael T. "Abortion and Healing." Ministries
     Apr. 1982: 22+.

     Outlines the Catholic church's role in ministering to those
     who have had abortions or who choose to bear a child out of
     wedlock.

967. _____. <u>Abortion and Healing: A Cry to Be Whole</u>. Kansas City: Sheed, 1986.

For the woman who has had an abortion, that she might better understand some of her emotions and feelings about the experience.

968. _____. <u>Spiritual Reflections of a Pro-Life Pilgrim</u>. Kansas City: Sheed, 1987.

Offers a scripturally based view of why we are called to speak out for life.

969. Mansour, Karem J., and Barbara Stewart. "Abortion and Sexual Behavior in College Women." <u>American Journal of Orthopsychiatry</u> 43 (1973): 804-14.

Twenty single young college women were studied in regard to their abortion experiences and post-abortion reactions. Nineteen had no appreciable psychological aftereffects during an average follow-up of seven months. Untoward physical effects were negligible. Over 70 percent were not using any birth control method.

970. Marcin, Mary Julia Regan, and Raymond B. Marcin. "The Physician's Decision-Making Role in Abortion Cases." <u>Jurist</u> 35 (1975): 66-76.

Explores the physician's legal role, as seen through the words of Justice Blackmun, and the physician's medical role, as seen both empirically and in current medical literature; assesses the current state of affairs in physician abortion counseling; and suggests a synthesis which blends the physician's legal and medical roles with a proper regard for the enormity of the abortion decision.

971. <u>Margaret Sanger: Registers of Papers in the Manuscript Division of the Library of Congress</u>. Washington: LC, 1977.

A basic search tool for using the Margaret Sanger manuscript collection at the Library of Congress.

972. Markson, Stephen Lawrence. "Citizens United for Life: Status Politics, Symbolic Reform and the Anti-Abortion Movement." Diss. U of Massachusetts, 1979.

Analyzes the anti-abortion movement as one way through which a cultural group acts to defend the dominance of its own moral commitments within the larger society.

973. Marshall, John, and Richard Snelling. "Abortion and Catholic Public Officials." Origins 11 Aug. 1977: 136-38.

    Discusses the role the moral convictions of a public official play in public policy, particularly when the official is a Catholic and the policy is the public funding of abortion.

974. Martin, Carol. "A Baby Girl: One Good Argument Against Abortion." Dimension 4 (Winter 1972): 144-48.

    An extract from Carol Martin's testimony before the Pennsylvania Abortion Law Commission.

975. Martinez, Elsie B. "The Ovulation Method of Family Planning." America 4 Apr. 1981: 277-79.

    Newer, more reliable natural family planning (NFP) methods are gaining acceptance, and not just by Catholics.

976. Martyn, Ken. "Technological Advances and Roe v. Wade: The Need to Rethink Abortion Law." UCLA Law Review June-Aug. 1982: 1194-1215.

    Technological advances in artificial life support systems for premature infants will result in the fetus's becoming viable at an earlier stage of the pregnancy. Thus, as medical technology progresses, a woman's right to an abortion will diminish.

977. Martz, Larry, et al. "The New Political Rules." Newsweek 17 July 1989: 21.

    Abortion is now an issue at the state level and it is a sure bet that it can no longer be dodged.

978. Marwick, Charles. "Court Backs States on Abortion." Journal of the American Medical Association 29 July 1989: 451-52.

    Interprets the Webster v. Reproductive Health Services case.

979. Marx, Jean L. "Birth Control: Current Technology, Future Prospects." Science 23 Mar. 1973: 1222-24.

    Discusses various methods of birth control.

980. Marx, Paul. "From Contraception to Abortion." Homiletic and Pastoral Review Feb. 1983: 8-13.

    Marx asks: Why do so many bishops and Catholic intellectuals

144

not see that abortion reflects an extension of the contraceptive mentality to a further stage?

981. _____. "Promoting NFP: Who Is Responsible?" <u>Homiletic</u>
<u>and Pastoral Review</u> Apr. 1982: 25-31.

Marx contends that contraception and abortifacients end up
destroying the family and concludes that the Catholic church
has a great healing medicine in natural family planning (NFP).

982. _____. "What Sisters Should Know About Abortion." <u>Sisters</u>
<u>Today</u> May 1972: 519-31.

A wide-ranging article on the history of abortion and its
social acceptance and consequences, and commentaries on the
practice of abortion in the United States.

983. Mason, Susan Elizabeth. "The Pro-Family Ideology of the
1970's." Diss. Columbia U: 1981.

Focuses on the anti-equal rights amendment and the anti-
abortion movements as two influential, conservative social
countermovements.

984. Matulis, Sherry. "I Had No Choice." <u>Redbook</u> Mar. 1987: 38+.

A rape victim's decision to have an illegal abortion in 1954.

985. Mauss, Armand L. <u>Social Problems as Social Movements</u>. New
York: Lippincott, 1975.

Historical treatment of abortion, with references to various
people throughout the world.

986. Maxtone-Graham, Katrina. <u>Pregnant by Mistake: The Stories of</u>
<u>Seventeen Women</u>. Rev. ed. New York: Remi, 1987.

A revision of the 1974 edition, with a new preface and index.
Interviews with 17 women who, having faced an unwanted pregnancy, tell what they did and how they felt.

987. May, John L. "Straight Talk on Abortion." <u>Catholic Mind</u> Mar.
1981: 42-49.

Cites various religions, and even atheism, as being opposed to
abortion; compares <u>Roe</u> v. <u>Wade</u> to the <u>Dred Scott</u> decision;
discusses the U.S. Supreme Court decision.

988. May, William E. "Abortion as Indicative of Personal and Social Identity." Jurist 33 (1973): 199-217.

Points out that in regard to abortion the ethicist is interested in what human acts or deeds do--that is, in their results. But he is even more interested in what they say. For it is through our deeds that we both disclose who we are and thus discover our identity and become, or fail to become, who we are meant to be.

989. _____. "Church Teaching and the Immorality of Contraception." Homiletic and Pastoral Review Jan. 1982: 9-18.

Contends that the analyses of Porter, Noonan, and Wright are seriously wrong and trivialize the teaching of Humanae Vitae.

990. _____. "The Morality of Abortion." Linacre Quarterly 41 (1974): 66-78.

Explains why the author, both as philosopher and as man, believes that the directly intended destruction of human fetuses is an act that human beings ought not to do if they are to act intelligently and responsibly.

991. Maynard, Joyce. "Diary of My Decision." Redbook Sept. 1979: 62+.

A woman tells why she had an abortion.

992. McBee, Susanna. "A Call to Tame the Genie of Teen Sex." U.S. News and World Report 22 Dec. 1986: 8.

The National Research Council (NRC) of the National Academy of Sciences (NAS) says that "contraceptive services to all teenagers should be available at low or no cost, and that pregnant girls should be encouraged, but not required, to have parental consent for abortion."

993. McCalister, Donald V., et al., comps. Readings in Family Planning: A Challenge to the Health Professions. St. Louis: Mosby, 1973.

Provides a context within which the reader may gain an appreciation of the nature of family planning and the challenge it poses for him or her both as a health professional and as an individual likely to engage in reproductive behavior.

994. McCartney, James J. Unborn Persons: Pope John Paul II and the Abortion Debate. Vol. 21 of American University Studies VII: Theology and Religion. n.d. New York: Lang, 1987.

Emphasizes the theological, philosophical, and personal influences of Pope John Paul's life which helped to formulate his firm defense of human life.

995. McCormack, Ellen. "The Game-Plan of Pro-Life and Anti-Life." Social Justice Review May 1975: 54-55.

Lists and discusses the basic strengths, weaknesses, and strategies of both the pro-life and pro-abortion forces.

996. McCormick, Richard A. "Abortion: A Changing Morality and Policy?" Hospital Progress Feb. 1979: 36-44.

Discusses public policy on abortion, and in doing so discusses morality, for these concepts are intimately related. Pro and con arguments concerning fetal life are offered.

997. _____. "Abortion: Rules for Debate." America 15-22 July 1978: 26-30.

Despite the desirability of a consensus on public policy, the level of argument about abortion remains deplorably low.

998. _____. "1973-1983: Value Impacts of a Decade." Hospital Progress Dec. 1982: 38-41.

A theologian reads the signs of the times: the abortion debate itself, the eugenic mentality, legislation and court cases, physicians and the debate on nuclear armament, cost containment, governmental advisory boards, the hospice movement, the nurses' revolt, expression of human sexuality.

999. _____. "Notes on Moral Theology: The Abortion Dossier." Theological Studies 35 (1974): 312-59.

A review of Roe v. Wade and Doe v. Bolton from four perspectives: 1) critiques of the U.S. Supreme Court's decision; 2) its legality and morality; 3) moral writings on abortion; 4) personal reflections.

1000. _____. "Silence Since Humanae Vitae." America 21 July 1973: 30-33.

The Humanae Vitae encyclical has provoked dissent and silence. For the sake of the Catholic church's teaching authority, it is now time to reflect on the meaning and import of these phenomena.

1001. _____. "The Silence Since "Humanae Vitae." Linacre Quarterly 41 (1974): 26-32.

Contends that from the response to <u>Humanae Vitae</u> over the past five years one thing is clear: the Catholic community is polarized, both on the issue of contraception and, even more importantly, on the nature and function of the church's magisterium and the appropriate Catholic response to authoritative teaching.

1002.   McCoy, Kathy.   "Birth Control."   <u>Seventeen</u> Sept. 1985: 75+.

A listing of possible methods of birth control.

1003.   McCuen, Gary E.   <u>Children Having Children: Global Perspectives on Teenage Pregnancy</u>.   Hudson: McCuen, 1988.

An anthology that presents an overview of the historical background on, and a description of, the teenage pregnancy issue.

1004.   McDaniel, Ann.   "Countdown on Abortion: Old Issue, 'New' Court."   <u>Newsweek</u> 23 Jan. 1989: 50.

The latest appeals to the U.S. Supreme Court set the stage for another comprehensive review of abortion law.

1005.   _____.   "The Future of Abortion."   <u>Newsweek</u> 17 July 1989: 14+.

The U.S. Supreme Court drills a crack in the foundation of <u>Roe</u>.

1006.   McDaniel, Ann, et al.   "Abortion Storm."   <u>Newsweek</u> 23 June 1986: 26-27.

The U.S. Supreme Court vote of 5-4 in Pennsylvania case heats up a highly divisive political issue.

1007.   McDonnell, Kathleen.   <u>Not an Easy Choice: A Feminist Reexamines Abortion</u>.   Boston: South End, 1984.

A very personal reexamination of the author's thinking on abortion which encourages readers to stimulate discussion on the issue.

1008.   McGovern, George, ed.   <u>Food and Population: The World in Crisis</u>.   The Great Contemporary Issues Series.   New York: Arno, 1979.

A compilation of articles from the <u>New York Times</u> to be read in the context of the birth control issue.

1009.   McGowan, Jo.   "The Planned Family Is a Misconception."   U.S. Catholic Nov. 1982: 31-32.

French scientists indicate that fertility decreases sharply beginning at the age of 30, rather than at 35 as previously thought.

1010.   McGurn, William.   "What the People Really Say."   National Review 22 Dec. 1989: 26-29.

Discusses the question of politics vis-a-vis abortions.

1011.   McHugh, James T.   "Abortion: The Inhumanity of It All."   St. Anthony's Messenger Feb. 1973: 12-22.

A family life expert gives an overview of the current status of the abortion controversy and the enduring arguments for safeguarding human life.

1012.   _____.   "Priests and the Abortion Question."   Dimension 5 (Winter 1973): 164-69.

It seems that the priest approaches abortion from the threefold perspective of theological teaching, public policy position, and pastoral concern.   The purpose of this essay is to provide a contemporary framework for analysis that will be practical for the priest engaged in pastoral work.

1013.   McIntosh, William A., Letitia T. Alston, and Jon P. Alston. "Differential Impact of Religious Preference and Church Attendance on Attitudes Toward Abortion."   Review of Religious Research 20 (1979): 195-213.

The relationships among religious preference, church attendance, and the consequences of religion are explored in terms of the acceptance or rejection of the legalization of abortion.

1014.   McKenna, Constance.   "I Support You, but I Can't Sign My Name": Pro-choice Catholics Testify.   Washington: Catholics for a Free Choice, 1982.

Explores the experiences of Catholics confronted by the reproductive crises of others in their professional or private lives.

1015.   McKernan, Martin F., Jr.   "Compelling Hospitals to Provide Abortion Services."   Catholic Lawyer 20 (1973): 317-27.

Discusses four areas: 1) the New Jersey case, Doe v. Bridgeton Hospital Association; 2) the twin opinions of the U.S. Supreme

Court in <u>Roe</u> v. <u>Wade</u> and <u>Doe</u> v. <u>Bolton</u>, vis-a-vis the compulsion of health care facilities to provide abortion services; 3) the concept of state action in this particular area; 4) suggested preventive matter for health care facilities which desire not to permit the performance of elective abortions.

1016. _____. "The Due Process Clause and the Unborn Child." <u>Dimension</u> 5 (Spring 1973): 25-34.

There are certain legal and philosophical constants which the American people have chosen to accept as guiding principles in the evolution of the national conscience. One of these constants is the principle that "no person shall be deprived of life . . . without due process of law," which is embodied in the Fifth Amendment to the Constitution of the United States and is commonly referred to as the "due process clause."

1017. _____. "Indiana Supreme Court Upholds State Abortion Law." <u>Social Justice Review</u> Oct. 1972: 197-99.

Reports on the court case of <u>Cheaney</u> v. <u>State of Indiana</u>.

1018. McLaren, Angus. <u>Sexuality and Social Order: The Debate over the Fertility of Women and Workers in France, 1770-1920</u>. New York: Holmes, 1983.

Contends that society is opposed not so much to birth control itself, but rather to the lack of social discipline which it symbolizes.

1019. McLaughlin, John. "Social-Agenda Headaches." <u>National Review</u> 23 Aug. 1985: 20.

Analyzes the social issues' agenda of the Republican party, chief among them being an anti-abortion platform and the dilemma it confronts in the political world.

1020. McLeod, Mary Alice, and Cliff Dudley. <u>I Almost Murdered This Child (by Abortion)</u>. Harrison: New Leaf, 1982.

Meant to help readers who are considering an abortion.

1021. McManus, Robert J. "Bishops, Politicians and Abortion." <u>America</u> 4 Nov. 1989: 294-97.

Details how, after <u>Webster</u> v. <u>Reproductive Health Services</u>, the American Catholic bishops and Catholic politicians approach the public policy debate about morally appropriate legislation concerning abortion.

1022. McNamara, Patrick H. "American Catholicism in the Mid-Eighties: Pluralism and Conflict in a Changing Church." Annals of the American Academy of Political and Social Science 480 (1985): 63-74.

Predicts continuing individualism in religious beliefs and practice, particularly in regard to birth control, divorce, and premarital sex, at considerable cost to the authority of the Catholic hierarchy.

1023. McPherson, M. Peter. "International Family Planning." Department of State Bulletin Mar. 1986: 43-45.

An address given before the American Enterprise Institute (AEI) on November 25, 1985, by the administrator of the Agency for International Development (AID).

1024. McWilliams, Bernard. "The Billings Method Makes Good Sense." Liguorian Sept. 1978: 16-19.

Nontechnical and nonmedical explanation of the Billings ovulation method of natural family planning (NFP).

1025. Mead, Margaret. "Reducing the Need for Abortions." Redbook Sept. 1973: 62+.

Contends that men and women must decide how to use individual freedom with good conscience by developing practices that are consistent with the value they set on individual life and interpersonal relations in families and in the whole community.

1026. Meade, Marion. "Birth Control in the High Schools?" McCall's Jan. 1972: 59.

A report on birth control programs in a New York City school district.

1027. Mears, Judith. The Abortion Controversy: A Doctor's Guide to the Law. New York: ACLU Foundation, 1975.

Deals with the ethical aspects of first trimester abortions as they relate to the Roe v. Wade decision.

1028. Meehan, Francis X. "Social Justice and Abortion." America 17 June 1978: 478-81.

Opposition to abortion has been portrayed as a conservative movement and an insidious example of Catholic politicking. Yet, the pro-life response to a social problem born of rugged individualism is humane and liberal.

1029. Meehan, Francis X., and Charles E. McGroarty. "A Pastoral Approach to the Abortion Dilemma." _Dimension_ 4 (Winter 1972): 131-43.

Discusses counseling, confession practice, and norms for cooperation in abortion situations.

1030. Meehan, Mary. "The Bishops and the Politics of Abortion." _Commonweal_ 23 Mar. 1984: 169.

The popular notion of Catholic bishops as clever politicians is taking something of a beating these days.

1031. _____. "Catholic Liberals and Abortion." _Commonweal_ 20 Nov. 1981: 650-54.

Many pro-abortion victories have been due largely to Catholic leaders in the courts and in Congress. People in the pro-life movement have been surprised, even scandalized, by this state of affairs. Abortion seems such a great wrong that Catholic liberals should oppose it resolutely, whether they approach it as Catholics, as liberals, or simply as humans.

1032. _____. "A Kind Word for Anti-Choice Fanatics." _America_ 7 June 1986: 471-73.

Some march in peace demonstrations; some are handicapped, some are atheists; some oppose the death penalty. Pro-life advocates tend not to fit the stereotypes others have drawn for them.

1033. _____. "The Left and the Right to Life." _Catholic Digest_ Dec. 1980: 36-41.

Liberals who sanction abortion are out of step with their own principles.

1034. _____. "The Other Right-to-Lifers." _Commonweal_ 18 Jan. 1980: 13-16.

The pro-life movement includes in its ranks and among its sympathizers a fair number of liberals and radicals, including Cesar Chavez, Dolores Huerta, Dick Gregory, Jesse Jackson, Daniel Berrigan, Richard Neuhaus, Sens. Harold Hughes, Mark Hatfield, Joseph Biden, Thomas Eagleton, and William Proxmire.

1035. _____. "Seamless Garment? Bernardin's Fresh Start.." _Commonweal_ 23 Mar. 1984: 171.

Conservatives are worried that the "seamless garment" approach could become a way of de-emphasizing the abortion issue and

giving protective cover to liberal politicians who proclaim
their compassion, yet vote to fund abortion and oppose efforts
to save handicapped infants.

1036.   Meikle, Stewart, et al.   "Therapeutic Abortion: A Prospective
Study. Part II." American Journal of Obstetrics and Gynecology 1 Feb. 1973: 339-46.

Reports on the psychosomatic and psychological reactions of
75 women applying for a therapeutic abortion as compared to
those of 33 women in the same stage of pregnancy, but not
requesting an abortion.

1037.   Meilaender, Gilbert. "Abortion: The Right to an Argument."
Hastings Center Report Nov.-Dec. 1989: 13-16.

Moral puzzles about abortion will not be resolved by resort
to compromise positions and adoption of a middle ground, for
abortion concerns how people understand themselves.

1038.   _____. "Against Abortion: A Protestant Proposal."
Linacre Quarterly 45 (1978): 165-78.

Takes a stand against abortion by way of comparing and contrasting Protestant and Catholic thought.

1039.   Melton, Gary B., ed. Adolescent Abortion: Psychological and
Legal Issues. Lincoln: U of Nebraska, 1986.

An American Psychological Association (APA) committee report
concerning the psychological issues that have been central to
the U.S. Supreme Court's analysis of the adolescent abortion
policy.

1040.   Merton, Andrew H. Enemies of Choice: The Right-to-Life Movement and Its Threat to Abortion. Boston: Beacon, 1981.

A history of the anti-abortion movement, with profiles
of some prominent "right-to-lifers"; traces the right-to-life
movement's connections with new-right politicians and its
contributions to the election of Ronald Reagan and other
new-right leaders in 1980.

1041.   Meserve, Harry C. "Pro-Life, Pro-Choice." Editorial. Journal
of Religion and Health 22 (Spring 1983): 3-6.

To be pro-life one must advocate and be willing to support a
broad, consistent life ethic; however, to do so requires an
informed, educated mind and freedom of choice.

1042. Messer, Ellen, and Kathryn May. Back Rooms: Voices from the
       Illegal Abortion Era. New York: St. Martin's, 1988.

       An oral history of how American women dealt with unwanted
       pregnancies in the years before Roe v. Wade.

1043. Miceli, Vincent P. "The Acceptable Holocaust?" Homiletic and
       Pastoral Review Nov. 1984: 56-62.

       Abortionists arouse God's wrath when they reduce live babies
       to cadavers.

1044. Michels, Nancy. Helping Women Recover from Abortion.
       Minneapolis: Bethany, 1988.

       A poignant documentary on how to deal with the guilt, the
       emotional pain, and the emptiness of an abortion.

1045. Milbauer, Barbara, and Bert N. Oberentz. The Law Giveth: Legal
       Aspects of the Abortion Controversy. New York: Atheneum, 1983.

       A summary of the legal history of the abortion struggle with a
       strong pro-choice orientation.

1046. Miles, John A., Jr. "The Wife of Onan and the Sons of Cain."
       National Review 17 Aug. 1973: 891-94.

       The constitutional debate over abortion is being argued under
       the subheading of murder. The wider issue, says the author, is
       the danger inherent in social technology.

1047. Miles, Judith M. Journal from an Obscure Place. Minneapolis:
       Bethany Fellowship, 1978.

       Traces the development of the unborn child from the moment of
       conception.

1048. Mileti, Dennis, and Larry D. Barnett. "Nine Demographic
       Factors and Their Relationship to Attitudes Toward Abortion
       Legalization." Social Biology 19 (1972): 43-50.

       Assesses the structure of American attitudes toward abortion,
       using data from the 1965 National Fertility Study.

1049. Miller, D. D. "The Experience of Abortion." America 23 June
       1979: 510-12.

       Relates physical and emotional details of actual abortion
       procedure.

154

1050.   Miller, E. F.   "'Some' Catholics on Abortion."   Liguorian Oct.
        1972: 8.

        The 1972 Democratic platform committee refuses a proposal to
        put a pro-abortion plank in its platform so as not to offend
        "some" Catholics and lose votes, rather than on the basis of
        right and wrong.   Also criticizes Catholics who have no
        scruples about abortion's being murder.

1051.   Miller, Eva, et al.   "Impact of the Abortion Experience on
        Contraceptive Acceptance."   Advances in Planned Parenthood
        12 (1977): 15-28.

        Reviews patients' contraceptive practices before and after
        abortion.

1052.   Miller, Joanne.   "Hospital Response to the Legalization of
        Abortion in New York State: An Analysis of Program Innovation."
        Journal of Health and Social Behavior 20 (1979): 363-75.

        Investigates the reorientation of hospital services to accom-
        modate women's constitutional right to elective abortion.

1053.   Miller, Louis G.   "Humanae Vitae: Five Years Later."
        Liguorian July 1973: 2-4.

        A status report on American Catholic thought and acceptance of
        the papal encyclical on contraception.

1054.   Miller, Tim.   "Two Competing 'Pro-Life' Measures Split the
        Anti-Abortion Lobby."   National Journal 20 Mar. 1982: 511-13.

        One faction supports an outright ban on abortions, while
        another favors a constitutional amendment that would turn the
        issue largely over to the states.

1055.   Miller, Warren B.   "Psychological Antecedents to Conception
        Among Abortion Seekers."   Western Journal of Medicine 122
        (1975): 12-19.

        Results of a survey of 642 women seeking induced abortion for
        an unwanted pregnancy who were surveyed before the procedure
        regarding their perception of what psychological and behavioral
        factors, if any, played a role in their becoming pregnant.

1056.   Millstein, Beth.   "Dauntless Family Planner."   New Directions
        for Women 7 (Autumn 1978): 19.

        A brief biography of Margaret Sanger, with portrait.

1057.   "A Mistake in San Diego." <u>America</u> 9 Dec. 1989: 416.

A pro-life bishop bans pro-choice politician from communion.

1058.   Mithers, Carol Lynn. "Abortion: The Mourning After."
<u>Mademoiselle</u> Sept. 1983: 66.

Abortion, no matter how antiseptic the conditions under which
it is performed, is an emotionally wrenching experience. A
way needs to be found to acknowledge the feelings of sadness
and loss it brings--to mourn.

1059.   Mitzner, K., et al. "America's War On Life: The Discussion--
Where We Have Been, Where We Go From Here." Symposium.
<u>Triumph</u> Mar. 1973: 17-32.

Addresses the current state of affairs regarding abortion in
America following <u>Roe</u> v. <u>Wade</u>. Discusses the pro-life
movement and its strategies, and the position of the Catholic
church.

1060.   Moczar, Diane. "Why the Pro-Life Battle Is a Catholic Thing."
<u>Triumph</u> May 1974: 24-25.

A general discussion of abortion, the pro-life movement, the
immorality of abortion, and its negative social impact.

1061.   Mohr, James C. <u>Abortion in America: The Origins and Evolution
of National Policy, 1800-1900</u>. New York: Oxford UP, 1978.

Chronicles the nineteenth- and twentieth-century changes in
American attitudes towards abortion.

1062.   Monagle, John F. "The Ethics of Abortion." <u>Social Justice
Review</u> July-Aug. 1972: 112-19.

Discusses ethical and normative models in an attempt to
interpret the complexities woven into the societal practice
of abortion.

1063.   Monahan, William J. "Public Opinion Reflects Secularization,
Rationalization." <u>Hospital Progress</u> Dec. 1982: 65-69.

Gallup polls have indicated that since 1975 a majority of the
U.S. population approves of abortion "under certain circumstances" (if, for example, the mother's health is endangered
or the child is likely to be deformed).

1064.   Monsour, Karem J. "On Abortion and the College Woman."
<u>Mademoiselle</u> Nov. 1973: 64+.

There are approximately 4 million young women in colleges throughout the United States. Despite information about sex, reproduction, and contraception, and the availability of contraceptive services on many campuses, this population remains a high-risk group for unwanted pregnancy.

1065. Monticello, Robert V. "Wade and Bolton: USCC Responses and Plans." Catholic Lawyer 19 (1973): 266-68.

Outlines the U.S. Catholic Conference (USCC) plans and strategies for pro-life activities in progress and stresses the need for them to be both currently effective and long range in their implications.

1066. Moore, Gloria. Margaret Sanger and the Birth Control Movement: A Bibliography, 1911-1984. Metuchen: Scarecrow, 1986.

A bibliography of more than 1,300 items of published materials on the role of Margaret Sanger in the birth control movement.

1067. Morley, Jefferson. "Right-to-Life Porn: The Lurid Logic of 'The Silent Scream.'" New Republic 25 Mar. 1985: 8-10.

The Silent Scream insists that it depicts a murder in order to outrage a public that now tolerates abortion. The unequivocal claim makes the film emotionally powerful, so powerful, in fact, that it undermines the pro-life position it is supposed to advance.

1068. Morrow, Lance. "An Essay on the Unfairness of Life." Horizon 20 Dec. 1977: 34-37.

Two ethical dilemmas--reverse discrimination and free abortion--present the difficulty of seeing justice done.

1069. _____. "Of Abortion and the Unfairness of Life." Time 1 Aug. 1977: 49.

The U.S. Supreme Court decides that the states and localities are free, if they wish, to deny Medicaid money for abortions. The Court made abortion legal; now it has rescinded an important advantage of that legality by making it hard for the poor to obtain abortions.

1070. Morrow, Thomas G. "A Pastoral Application of Natural Family Planning." Homiletic and Pastoral Review June 1981: 54-63.

Not only is natural family planning (NFP) in accord with

1071.   Morton, Bridget Balthrop.   "Abortion: The Modern Temptation."
        St. Anthony's Messenger May 1981: 24-27.

        The mother of two children relates how she and her husband
        agreed to have an abortion if she should conceive a third time
        and how, when she did, she decided otherwise.

1072.   Moser, Susan M.   "A New and Better Birth-Control Method." U.S.
        Catholic Oct. 1975: 16-17.

        Discusses a relatively new method of birth control discovered
        by Drs. Lyn and John Billings in 1968.

1073.   Mowery, Ellen.   "Caring for All the People." Liguorian Nov.
        1976: 34-36.

        The National Conference of Catholic Bishops (NCCB) has express-
        ed the need for respect life programs on a parish level. This
        is the story of how one parish responded to the idea.

1074.   Moynahan, Cornelius.   "On the Subject of Abortion: Massachu-
        setts." Social Justice Review May 1972: 49-53.

        An article by an associate justice of the Massachusetts
        Supreme Court, which consists of the full decision of the court
        in the case of Commonwealth of Massachusetts v. Pierre Victor
        Brunelle.

1075.   Muck, Terry C.   "What If We Win?" Christianity Today 21 Apr.
        1989: 13.

        If the U.S. Supreme Court overturns Roe v. Wade, the fight
        must continue, since the decision would simply hand the
        abortion question back to the states.

1076.   Mudd, Emily H., et al.   "Adolescent Health Services and Contra-
        ceptive Use." American Journal of Orthopsychiatry 48 (1978):
        495-504.

        A study of a health services program for never-pregnant high
        school students, stressing the development of incentives for
        personal involvement in health care, reports a low incidence
        of unintended pregnancy among girls requesting contraceptives.
        The social and emotional characteristics of students continuing
        contraceptive use are compared with those of the small group
        who had unintended pregnancies.

1077.   Muldoon, Maureen.   Abortion: An Annotated Indexed Bibliography.
        Studies in Women and Religion 3. New York: Mellen, 1980.

A compendium of over 3,000 books and periodical articles that deals with the legal, psychological, ethical, and religious problems of abortion.

1078.   Mumford, Stephen D. The Pope and the New Apocalypse: The Holy War Against Family Planning. Research Triangle Park: Center for Research on Population and Security, 1986.

Does not argue the urgency of dealing with the world population dilemma, but provides a schematic view of the problem.

1079.   Murphy, Jamie. "Abortion's Shrinking Majority." Time 23 June 1986: 30-31.

Four U.S. Supreme Court justices sharply questioned the ever-widening scope of Roe and subsequent decisions. If states cannot impose some limits on abortion, the Chief Justice concluded, "I agree we should reexamine Roe."

1080.   Mydans, Seth. "When Is an Abortion Not an Abortion?" Atlantic May 1975: 71-73.

Examines the evidence and conclusions of the manslaughter trial of Dr. Kenneth Edelin.

1081.   "A Mysterious Drop in the Abortion Rate." Newsweek 16 July 1984: 26.

The U.S. Centers for Disease Control (CDC) in Atlanta unable to explain why the abortion rate dropped in 1981, after climbing annually by rates of 4 to 15 percent during the 1970s.

1082.   "NACPA on Abortion." Social Justice Review Sept. 1972: 167-68.

The National Association for Christian Political Action (NACPA) announces its official position on abortion: it is against abortion.

1083.   Nadelson, Carol. "Abortion Counselling: Focus on Adolescent Pregnancy." Pediatrics Dec. 1974: 765-69.

The U.S. Supreme Court decision permitting abortion in the first trimester of pregnancy has resulted in a shift from preabortion psychiatric counseling to quick turnover at the expense of quality care.

1084.   Nadelson, Carol C., Malkah T. Notman, and Jean W. Gillon. "Sexual Knowledge and Attitudes of Adolescents: Relationship to Contraceptive Use." <u>Obstetrics</u> <u>and</u> <u>Gynecology</u> Mar. 1980: 340-45.

Discusses the medical and psychological complications of teenage pregnancy and presents data from a study of 296 adolescents. The areas of inquiry include sexual information, contraceptive practice, the relation of a sex education course to the use of contraceptives, methods of coping, and family relations.

1085. Nardone, Roland M. "The Nexus of Biology and the Abortion Issue." <u>Jurist</u> 33 (1973): 153-61.

A brief summary of the major changes which occur during embryological development and an overview of basic questions about the fetus by a biologist. The intent is to provide the layperson with an appreciation of the nexus between biology and the social-moral issue of abortion. It is not an analysis of the moral and legal aspects of the matter.

1086. Nathanson, Bernard. "Operation Rescue: Domestic Terrorism or Legitimate Civil Rights Protest?" <u>Hastings</u> <u>Center</u> <u>Report</u> Nov.-Dec. 1989: 28-32.

Describes the philosophy and strategy of Operation Rescue.

1087. _____. <u>The</u> <u>Abortion</u> <u>Papers:</u> <u>Inside</u> <u>the</u> <u>Abortion</u> <u>Mentality</u>. New York: Fell, 1983.

Devoted mainly to an analysis of how the press and the electronic media have handled the abortion issue.

1088. Nathanson, Bernard N., and Richard N. Ostling. <u>Aborting</u> <u>America</u>. Garden City: Doubleday, 1979.

The story of the early days of the authors' battle to make abortion legal and safe.

1089. Nathanson, Constance A., and Marshall H. Becker. "Physician Behavior as a Determinant of Utilization Patterns: The Case of Abortion." <u>American</u> <u>Journal</u> <u>of</u> <u>Public</u> <u>Health</u> Nov. 1978: 1104-14.

Health services utilization may be influenced by the structure of the health system and the behavior of health professionals, as well as by the actions of individual patients. The research on which this article is based examines the responses of obstetricians towards women seeking abortion.

1090. _____. "Obstetricians' Attitudes and Hospital Abortion Services." Family Planning Perspectives Jan.-Feb. 1980: 26-32.

Hospitals are much less likely to perform abortions if affiliated physicians dislike performing them or oppose expanding fertility-related services. But doctors' attitudes do not affect the range of abortion-related services offered.

1091. National Conference of Catholic Bishops. Pastoral Plan for Pro-Life Activities. Washington: U.S. Catholic Conference, 1975.

Calls upon all church-sponsored or identifiably Catholic national, regional, diocesan, and parochial organizations and agencies to pursue a three-fold goal.

1092. National Conference on Abortion. Abortion Parley: Papers Delivered at the National Conference on Abortion Held at the University of Notre Dame in October, 1979. Kansas City: Andrews, 1980.

Twelve essays delivered at the National Conference on Abortion (NCA) on topics such as public opinion on abortion, model programs for unmarried pregnant women, and adoption as an alternative to abortion.

1093. "A Natural Way." Time 26 Dec. 1977: 51.

The Department of Health, Education and Welfare (HEW) grants $1.4 million for the study of natural family planning (NFP).

1094. Neary, Kevin. "Pressure Politics Revisited: The Anti-Abortion Campaign." Policy Studies Journal 8 (1980): 698-716.

Focuses on the anti-abortion campaign as an extreme example of pressure group operations. After a review of the history of the abortion controversy, the recent activities of anti-abortion groups in the state of Pennsylvania are assessed. The article concludes with speculations about the probable consequences and future of such closely defined single-interest groups.

1095. Neff, David. "Abortion-Rights Boomerang." Christianity Today 17 Mar. 1989: 16.

Posits that reproductive freedom has turned into "femicide."

1096. Neitz, Mary Jo. "Family, State, and God: Ideologies of the Right-to-Life Movement." Sociological Analysis 42 (1981): 265-76.

Examines the differences between the ideologies of the elite and mass publics on the abortion issue. It argues that within the right-to-life movement there exist two different conceptual frameworks: a "pro-life" framework advocated by the elite and a "pro-family" framework advocated by the mass.

1097. Nelson, J. Robert. "Confusion at the Highest Level." Editorial. Christian Century 28 Feb. 1973: 254-55.

We like to believe in the transcendent wisdom of the U.S. Supreme Court. What Justice Harry Blackmun's opinion conveys is a state of intellectual confusion and shortsightedness.

1098. _____. "Genetic Engineering: Federal Ethics Commission Hears Theologians." Hospital Progress Dec. 1982: 42-47.

In an effort to shape public policy, religious thinkers described their concerns to the President's Commission for the Study of Ethical Problems in Medicine and Biomedical and Behavioral Research.

1099. _____. "What Does Theology Say About Abortion?" Christian Century 31 Jan. 1973: 124-28.

Though Christians disagree on the abortion question, there are enough hopeful signs to justify the pursuit of clearer theological understanding and consequent ethical conviction.

1100. Nelson, James Andrew. "Abortion and the Causal Theory of Names." Diss. State U of New York at Buffalo, 1980.

Concerns two topics of philosophical importance, the theory of reference and the morality of abortion.

1101. Neuhaus, Richard John. "Abortion After Akron: The Contradictions Are Showing." Commonweal 15 July 1983: 388.

Roe v. Wade attempted to settle public policy and offer some protection for the unborn after the first trimester. Akron shattered that and made it clear that the "right to abortion" is unqualified.

1102. _____. "After Roe." National Review 17 Apr. 1989: 38+.

For 16 years, the abortion debate has asked the moral and legal questions: What rights does a woman have? What rights does her unborn child have? Now the debate shifts into the realm of politics, as we contemplate the shape of the battle.

1103.   _____.   "Democratic Morality."   <u>National</u> <u>Review</u> 18 July
         1986: 47.

         Research over the years shows quite clearly that about 20 per-
         cent of the public favors an absolute ban on abortion, another
         50 percent would allow abortion in extreme and rare circum-
         stances, and less than 20 percent supports the current practice
         under <u>Roe</u> v. <u>Wade</u>.

1104.   _____.   "Hyde and Hysteria: The Liberal Banner Has Been
         Planted on the Wrong Side of the Abortion Debate."   <u>Christian</u>
         <u>Century</u> 10-17 Sept. 1980: 849-52.

         The recent ruling on the Hyde amendment, upholding the right
         of Congress to exclude abortion from Medicaid coverage, has
         met with cheers and jeers of equal intensity.   One side sees
         it as a Fascist attack on the pregnant poor, while the other
         lauds it as a critical break in the Communist offensive to
         destroy the family.

1105.   _____.   "Policy by Pathology."   <u>National</u> <u>Review</u> 5 Dec.
         1986: 46.

         Argues against high school sex clinics.

1106.   Neuhaus, Richard John, and John Garvey.   "Two Views on the
         Human Life Amendment."   <u>U.S.</u> <u>Catholic</u> Apr. 1977: 28-31.

         Offers contrasting opinions on the prospect of a human life
         amendment to the U.S. Constitution.

1107.   "The New Abortion Debate."   Editorial.   <u>Commonweal</u> 22 July
         1977: 451-52.

         The recent decision by the U.S. Supreme Court that neither
         the U.S. Constitution nor federal Medicaid legislation requires
         the states to pay for abortions both simplifies and compli-
         cates, for pro- and anti-abortionists alike, the future of the
         abortion debate.

1108.   "A New Attack on Abortion."   <u>Newsweek</u> 11 Nov. 1985: 24.

         Discusses Sen. Orrin Hatch and Rep. Ralph Kemp's latest plan to
         eliminate the use of federal funds to counsel for abortions.

1109.   Newman, James L.   "Fertility in Transition: A World of Fewer
         and Fewer Children."   <u>Focus</u> 36.1 (1986): 2-9.

         To an ever-increasing extent, children--at least in any
         numbers--are taking on a negative connotation, one considered

at odds with the well-being of individuals, couples, and nations.

1110. Newman, Jay. "An Empirical Argument Against Abortion." New Scholasticism 51 (1977): 384-95.

Advances a detailed philosophical argument concluding that if a fetus is not a human being, it becomes one, and that is a close relationship.

1111. "NFP Center Reaches Couples, Teens, Physicians, Parents." Hospital Progress Apr. 1983: 28+.

Natural family planning (NFP) is more than a method to achieve or avoid pregnancy. It teaches couples about the human body, fertility, and the dignity of reproduction and explains how they can use that knowledge to plan their lives together.

1112. Nicholson, Susan Taft. Abortion and the Roman Catholic Church. Knoxville: Religious Ethics, 1979.

A critique of the Roman Catholic church's position on abortion.

1113. Nielson, Harry A. "Toward a Socratic View of Abortion." American Journal of Jurisprudence 18 (1973): 105-13.

The central ethical question as regards abortion concerns making believe one has no moral ties with a fetus, even though it is already on its way to becoming one more like oneself.

1114. Noah, Timothy. "The Right-to-Life Split." New Republic 21 Mar. 1981: 7-9.

Senator Jake Garn and Rep. James Oberstar propose an anti-abortion amendment with an exception for cases in which the mother's life may be endangered. A second constitutional amendment by Sen. Jesse Helms and Rep. Henry Hyde contains no exception. A third proposal, also introduced by Helms and Hyde, attempts to turn the constitutional question into a legislative one by stating in a bill that "human life shall be deemed to exist from conception" and by permitting no federal court to hear abortion cases except the U.S. Supreme Court.

1115. Nolen, William A. The Baby in the Bottle. New York: Coward, 1978.

An investigative review of the Edelin case and its larger meanings for the controversy over abortion reform.

1116. Noonan, John S. "Human Life Federalism Amendment: I. Legal Aspects." Catholic Lawyer 2 (1983): 118-20.

Develops the position that the human life amendment has taken two forms. One is the attempt to amend the meaning of "person" in the Fifth and Fourteenth Amendments. The second form of the human life amendment accords due process to the unborn.

1117. Noonan, John T., Jr. "The Dynamics of Anti-Abortionism." Catholic Mind May 1978: 7-13.

A comparison of the morality and similarity of two famous United States Supreme Court decisions: the Dred Scott case and Roe v. Wade.

1118. _____. "In Re the Human Life Bill." Catholic Mind Nov. 1981: 52-64.

Text of a statement by John T. Noonan, Jr., to the U.S. Senate Judiciary Committee's Subcommittee on the Separation of Powers on a proposed bill to outlaw abortions by providing that "human life shall be deemed to exist from conception."

1119. _____. A Private Choice: Abortion in America in the Seventies. New York: Free, 1979.

A comprehensive study of abortion done through the inquiry process.

1120. _____. "Raw Judicial Power." National Review 2 Mar. 1973: 260-64.

Examines the U.S. Supreme Court's faulty reasoning and urges adoption of a human life amendment to the Constitution.

1121. _____. "Responding to Persons: Methods of Moral Argument in Debate over Abortion." Theological Digest 21 (1973): 291-307.

Contends that moral logic, particularly abortion reasoning, is dead-ended if it centers only on principles like double effect and greater good, or on theories about the relative value of life, fetal viability, exceptions in hard cases, and so forth.

1122. _____. "The Root and Branch of Roe v. Wade." Nebraska Law Review 4 (1984): 668-79.

An explanation of the legal and historical background in American jurisprudence leading to Roe v. Wade.

1123. Noonan, John Thomas. Contraception: A History of Its Treatment
       by the Catholic Theologians and Canonists. Enl. ed.
       Cambridge: Belknap, 1986.

       An investigation of the teaching of the theologians and canon-
       ists of the Catholic church on contraception.

1124. _____. How to Argue About Abortion. New York: Ad Hoc
       Committee in Defense of Life, 1974.

       Proposes a person-to-person approach to the dilemma of when
       humanity exists in a child.

1125. Norback, Judith, ed. Sourcebook of Sex Therapy, Counseling and
       Family Planning. New York: Van Nostrand, 1983.

       Information on family planning, sexuality, and counseling.

1126. "Not a Single-Issue Church, Bishops Say." Origins 20 Sept.
       1984: 217-18.

       New England Catholic bishops state that the enormity of the
       evil of abortion makes it the critical issue of the moment.

1127. "Notes and Comment (The Talk of the Town)." New Yorker 24 Apr.
       1989: 29-30.

       Comments from a woman who, 20 years ago, had an abortion, and
       her thoughts about it and the abortion debate of today.

1128. "Notifying the Parents." Editorial. America 11 Apr. 1981:
       289-90.

       Utah's law requiring parental notification before an abortion
       takes place ruled unconstitutional by the U.S. Supreme Court.

1129. Nourse, Alan Edward. Teen Guide to Birth Control. New York:
       Watts, 1988.

       A birth control guide only, not a substitute for the medical
       advice of a physician.

1130. O'Boyle, Patrick Cardinal. "Death by Abortion Absolutely
       Unacceptable." Social Justice Review Nov. 1972: 234-37.

       Text of a homily given by Patrick Cardinal O'Boyle, archbishop
       of Washington, in Saint Matthew's Cathedral, August 6, 1972.

1131. _____. "The Priceless Value of Every Person." <u>Social Justice Review</u> Dec. 1972: 269-73.

A pastoral letter from Patrick Cardinal O'Boyle of Washington, DC, on inaugurating Respect Life week, stressing the sanctity of human life.

1132. O'Connell, Timothy E. "For American Catholics: End of an Illusion." <u>America</u> 2 June 1973: 514-17.

Brought up short by the U.S. Supreme Court's abortion decision, the Catholic community realizes now that God and country do not always stand together. The myth gone, the government may have lost one of its most stable and politically beneficial allies.

1133. O'Connor, John F. "In Defense of <u>Humanae Vitae</u>." <u>Homiletic and Pastoral Review</u> Oct. 1981: 51-54.

Proposes that contraception is unnatural. In an age that clamors for the natural, it is contradictory to want to introduce the unnatural into the intimate relationship of marriage.

1134. O'Connor, Sandra Day. "Justice O'Connor's Dissent in the <u>Akron</u> Abortion Case." <u>Origins</u> 21 July 1983: 159-64.

Text of Justice Sandra Day O'Connor's dissent in the Akron, Ohio, abortion ordinance case.

1135. O'Donnell, Ann. "Women as Teachers of Violence." <u>Homiletic and Pastoral Review</u> June 1982: 54-58.

Female violence against unborn children by abortion and male aggression towards women signal a full-blown "erotic war."

1136. O'Driscoll, L. H. "Abortion, Property Rights, and the Right to Life." <u>Personalist</u> 58 (1977): 99-114.

The question whether the unborn have the right to life has traditionally been regarded as the critical issue in the abortion controversy, and it has generally been supposed that the inference from "the unborn have the right to life" to "abortion is morally impermissible" is simple and obvious.

1137. O'Hare, Joseph. "Of Many Things." Editorial. <u>America</u> 1 Mar. 1975: Inside front cover+.

At the trial of Dr. Kenneth C. Edelin the crucial questions were: When does a fetus become a person within the meaning of the Fourteenth Amendment? If a woman decides to have an

abortion, is her doctor entitled to make certain that the
fetus dies, regardless of the viability of the fetus after
separation from the mother? Until the U.S. Supreme Court
makes the law much clearer than it did in 1973, cases like
Dr. Edelin's will recur.

1138.   _____. "Of Many Things." Editorial. America 23 Apr.
1977: Inside front cover.

Argues that efforts at population control should be encouraged,
but only as part of a comprehensive development plan that does
not attempt to manage human beings by the dogmas of
technology.

1139.   _____. "Of Many Things." Editorial. America 18 Feb.
1978: Inside front cover.

The president-designate of the Planned Parenthood Federation
of America (PPFA), Faye Wattleton, calls for a more aggressive
campaign to secure government funding for abortions.

1140.   O'Reilly, Jane. "Twenty-Four Brave Nuns, Who Believe That
Lives Are as Important as Souls, Have Confronted the Catholic
Church's Position on Abortion." Vogue Apr. 1985: 182+.

Recounts the Vatican's reaction to an ad in the New York Times,
signed by 24 Catholic nuns, saying that they are only part of
a growing movement among religious women demanding a moral
vote.

1141.   O'Reilly, Tom. "Pro-Life: Not a Catholic Monopoly." Liguorian
Jan. 1980: 11-13.

Points out that many of the pro-life supporting groups and
individuals are not Catholic, but include, for example,
Lutherans for Life, Baptists for Life, and Sens. Orrin Hatch,
Mark Hatfield, and Jesse Helms.

1142.   O'Rourke, Kevin D. "Because the Lord Loved You." Hospital
Progress Aug. 1973: 73-77.

Discusses the theological reasons for the sanctity of life
and the conviction of Catholic health care leaders against
abortion.

1143.   _____. "The Right of Privacy: What Next?" Hospital
Progress Apr. 1975: 58-63.

Concerns the values and principles associated with the slogan
"Respect for Human Life." It considers the ideas and principles behind the U.S. Supreme Court decision to legalize

abortion on demand, the decisions that may result if these
ideas and principles are applied to other antisocial
behavioral patterns, and the steps that might be taken to
prevent such an application.

1144. O'Steen, David N. "Neither Incompetent nor Indifferent."
        Commonweal 23 Mar. 1984: 179-82.

        Explains the various decisions of American bishops not to
        get involved in procedural or constitutional issues regarding
        abortion leglislation, on the grounds that their primary
        function is the teaching of moral principles.

1145. Odell, Catherine M., and William Odell. The First Human Right:
        A Pro-Life Primer. Huntington: Sunday Visitor, 1983.

        Provides information needed for a fundamental grasp of the
        abortion controversy from a moral and ethical view of the
        issue.

1146. "Of Laws, Not Men." Editorial. Nation 1 Feb. 1986: 100-01.

        Argues that the right to legal abortion must be upheld, and
        that President Reagan is mollifying his right wing and John
        Cardinal O'Connor is only advancing his career.

1147. Oliker, Stacey. "Abortion and the Left: The Limits of 'Pro-
        Family' Politics." Socialist Review Mar.-Apr. 1981:
        71-95.

        The anti-abortion movement and the proposed human life
        amendment are explained in terms of feminism, female sexual
        liberation, and women's equality.

1148. Olmstead, Frank H. "Abortion Choice and the Law in Vermont:
        A Recent Study." Vermont Law Review 7 (1982): 281-313.

        A two-part study: Part 1 reviews and summarizes the U.S.
        Supreme Court cases on abortion, 1972-82; Part 2 explores the
        legal status of abortion in Vermont during the four- to five-
        year period preceding Roe v. Wade.

1149. Omran, Abdel Rahim, ed. Liberalization of Abortion Laws:
        Implications. Chapel Hill: Carolina Population Center, 1976.

        A collection of essays outlining what is presently known and
        might be expected under varying degrees of liberalized
        abortion.

1150. "On the Abortion Front..." <u>National</u> <u>Review</u> 14 Feb. 1975: 147-
       48.

       A potpourri of information: the second anniversary of <u>Roe</u>
       v. <u>Wade</u>, the Edelin lawsuit, the New York Court of Appeals,
       and the first issue of the <u>Human</u> <u>Life</u> <u>Review</u>.

1151. Oomas, Theodora, ed. <u>Teenage</u> <u>Pregnancy</u> <u>in</u> <u>a</u> <u>Family</u> <u>Context</u>:
       <u>Implications</u> <u>for</u> <u>Policy</u>. Family Impact Seminar Series.
       Philadelphia: Temple UP, 1981.

       The first book published in the United States which applies
       a family impact perspective to an examination of how teenage
       pregnancy policies affect families.

1152. Orenstein, Peggy. "The Politics of Abortion." <u>Vogue</u> June
       1989: 250-51.

       Right-to-lifers have extended their reach to other reproductive
       issues.

1153. Orloski, Richard J. "Abortion: A Deeper Look at the Legal
       Aspects." <u>U.S.</u> <u>Catholic</u> Sept. 1973: 39-40.

       <u>Roe</u> v. <u>Wade</u> and <u>Doe</u> v. <u>Bolton</u> point to the need for a reexam-
       ination by the Catholic hierarchy of its role in the political
       and legal affairs of man, and the need for a reemphasis upon
       the spiritual leadership of the church through the teachings of
       the church, not through the influence of civil and criminal
       law.

1154. _____. "Abortion: Legal Questions and Legislative Alter-
       natives." <u>America</u> 10 Aug. 1974: 50-51.

       Recent U.S. Supreme Court decisions on abortion suggest two
       possible strategies: one, a constitutional amendment, would
       be impossible; the alternative is to obtain state
       legislation.

1155. Osofsky, Howard J., and Joy Osofsky, eds. <u>The</u> <u>Abortion</u>
       <u>Experience</u>: <u>Psychological</u> <u>and</u> <u>Medical</u> <u>Impact</u>. Hagerstown:
       Harper, 1973.

       A compilation of considerable data on the history of abortion
       in the United States.

1156. Osofsky, Joy D., et al. "Psychosocial Aspects of Abortion
       in the United States." <u>Mount</u> <u>Sinai</u> <u>Journal</u> <u>of</u> <u>Medicine</u> Sept.-
       Oct. 1975: 456-68.

Reviews some of the literature on the psychological effects
of abortion both before and after legalization and shares the
results of the authors' research.

1157. Ostling, Richard N. "A Bold Stand on Birth Control: John Paul
Insists That Catholics Must Shun Contraception." _Time_ 3 Dec.
1984: 66.

Pope John Paul II says that the practice and attitude of
contraception are "harmful to man's interior spiritual
culture."

1158. _____. "Church and State: A Judge Fines the Catholic
Bishops." _Time_ 19 May 1986: 19.

A New York judge fines the Catholic bishops $100,000 per day
for failing to turn over church documents.

1159. Ostrander, Sheila, and Lynn Schroeder. "Birth Control by
Astrology?" _McCall's_ May 1972: 84+.

A European doctor's controversial theory about fertility in
women.

1160. Overduin, Daniel Ch, and John I. Fleming. "The Prevention of
Procreation: Contraception." _International Review of Natural
Family Planning_ 8 (1984): 131-44.

Argues that there is a growing disillusionment with contraceptives on medical, moral, and social grounds and stresses that
there is a distinction between contraception and family
planning. Family planning has as its focus loving and
responsible parenthood; contraception is by its very nature
divorced from a couple's anticipation of becoming parents.

1161. "Overkill on Abortion." Editorial. _America_ 12 July 1986:
1-2.

An analysis of the reasoning and the decision in the U.S.
Supreme Court's case of _Thornburgh_ v. _American College of
Obstetricians and Gynecologists_.

1162. Pable, Martin W. "Pastoral Counseling and Abortion." _Priest_
Oct. 1975: 15+.

Discusses the moral responsibilities of Catholic priests to
provide counseling to women considering abortion.

1163. Paganelli, Vitale. "_Humanae Vitae_ Revisited." _Linacre
Quarterly_ 41 (1974): 33-40.

Aims to contribute positively to a fuller understanding and acceptance of the teachings of Humanae Vitae.

1164. Paige, Connie. The Right to Lifers: Who They Are, How They Operate, Where They Get Their Money. New York: Summit, 1983.

Traces the internal politics of the anti-abortion movement since the U.S. Supreme Court decision of 1973.

1165. Palmer, Nancy Sigrest. "Knowledge of Contraception and Use of Contraceptive Methods Among College Students in a Major Southeastern Public University." Diss. U of Alabama, 1984.

Investigates the relationship between a knowledge of contraception and the use of contraceptive methods by college students.

1166. Palmer, Paul F. "A Pastoral Problem." Priest Oct. 1972: 63-67.

Discusses the various pastoral responses to Humanae Vitae visa-vis the concepts of assent and dissent.

1167. Panuthos, Claudia, and Catherine Romen. Ended Beginnings: Healing Childbearing Losses. South Hadley: Bergin, 1984.

Tries to provide readers with a new understanding of childbearing loss.

1168. "Papa Don't Preach." Nation 25 Oct. 1986: 396-97.

Discusses the dispensing of contraceptives by school districts as part of a social program for students. Refers to New York City and Chicago.

1169. Papa, Mary Bader. "Stressing the Natural in Natural Family Planning." Columbia Dec. 1976: 6-17.

A wide-ranging article which claims that natural family planning (NFP) is getting a second and closer look for new and important reasons as the birth control pill's side effects begin to surface.

1170. "Parental Rights." America 27 Feb. 1982: 143-44.

The Reagan administration's move to require federally funded birth control clinics to notify parents whose children are supplied with contraceptives is a proposal that should be supported.

1171. Parness, Jeffrey A. "Social Commentary: Values and Legal Personhood." West Virginia Law Review 3 (1981): 487-503.

Discusses legal personhood vis-a-vis the Roe v. Wade decision on abortion.

1172. Parness, Jeffrey A., and Susan K. Pritchard. "To Be or Not to Be: Protecting the Unborn's Potentiality of Life." University of Cincinnati Law Review 2 (1982): 257-98.

After delineating the misunderstanding of Roe v. Wade, this article examines the exercise of discretion in characterizations of personhood outside the context of Roe.

1173. Partie, Dianne. "Contraceptives: Your Questions Answered." Mademoiselle Aug. 1979: 85+.

Just how effective are the barrier contraceptives--the diaphragm, condoms, foams, jellies, and suppositories?

1174. "Pastoral Message on Abortion." Catholic Mind Sept. 1973: 7-9.

Text of the February 13, 1973, statement by the 37-member Administrative Committee of the National Conference of Catholic Bishops (NCCB), prompted by the decision of the U.S. Supreme Court in Roe v. Wade, January 22, 1973.

1175. "A Pastoral Plan for Pro-Life Activities." Catholic Mind Mar. 1976: 55-64.

A statement issued by the National Conference of Catholic Bishops (NCCB), outlining a plan for pro-life activities.

1176. "Pastors Across the Country March Against Abortion." Christianity Today 8 Nov. 1985: 64-65.

Two thousand pastors in 300 cities march in silence near hospitals that perform abortions, saying, "We can no longer tolerate institutions of healing serving as institutions of death."

1177. Patterson, Janet M., and R. C. Patterson, Jr. Abortion: The Trojan Horse. Nashville: Nelson, 1974.

Deals with the human problems of birth control, methods of abortion, and alternatives to abortion.

1178. Paul, Eve W., and Paula Schaap. "Abortion and the Law in 1980." New York Law School Law Review 3 (1980): 497-525.

Discusses the U.S. Supreme Court and lower court decisions
before and after the Roe and Doe decisions.

1179. Paulshock, Bernadine Z. "Birth Control: What I Want My
Daughter to Know." Today's Health Feb. 1975: 20+.

A physician combines motherly concern with medical expertise
in this message about contraception.

1180. Payne, Edmund C., et al. "Outcome Following Therapeutic
Abortion." Archives of General Psychiatry June 1976:
725-33.

Studies show that the resolution of the dilemma of unwanted
pregnancy by means of induced abortion is not, for most women,
a psychologically damaging procedure.

1181. Pearson, Albert M., and Paul M. Kurtz. "The Abortion Controversy: A Study in Law and Politics." Symposium: The 1984
Federalist Society National Meeting. Harvard Journal of Law
and Public Policy 2 (1985): 427-64.

Explores the evolution of the U.S. Supreme Court's 1973
decision on abortion and looks at the controversy in terms
of the political reaction it engendered.

1182. Pedersen, Daniel. "The 'A-Word' in Ireland." Newsweek
31 July 1989: 45.

The U.S. Supreme Court abortion ruling sends ripples
overseas.

1183. Pennsylvania Abortion Law Commission. Report of the Pennsylvania Abortion Law Commission Appointed by the Governor to
Review Pennsylvania's Abortion Law. Harrisburg: The Commission,
1972.

A majority report of the commission appointed by Gov. Richard
Thornburgh to review Pennsylvania's abortion law.

1184. Pennsylvania Department of Health. State Health Data Center.
Pregnancies by Women's Age Groups: Live Births, Fetal Deaths
and Induced Abortions--Pennsylvania Residents, 1976-1980.
Harrisburg: The Center, 1983.

A statistical report on the pregnancy rates, live birth rates,
out-of-wedlock births, and proportion of abortions for all
childbearing females from 1976 to 1980 in Pennsylvania.

1185. "People Like Us." National Review 22 Feb. 1985: 18.

Portrays the 71,000 pro-life marchers not as the "alienated" types, or mad clinic bombers, or urban rioters of the 1960s, but rather as patriotic "people like us."

1186. Perkins, Robert L., ed. Abortion, Pro and Con. Cambridge: Schenkman, 1974.

Does not attempt to pass judgment upon those who seek or avoid abortion for any reason whatsoever, but states the arguments, pro and con, and examines their logic.

1187. Personal Decisions. Videocassette. Dirs. Tom Goodwin and Geraldine Wurzburg. Cinema Guild, 1988. 30 min.

Examines the reasons for abortions and shows real-life stories dealing with why some women choose to have them.

1188. Petchesky, Rosalind Pollock. Abortion and Woman's Choice: The State, Sexuality, and Reproductive Freedom. New York: Longman, 1984.

A feminist view of the historical, legal, economic, and cultural aspects of abortion.

1189. Peters, Ed. "Is It Really Abortion?" Social Justice Review Jan.-Feb. 1982: 24-25.

Argues that what the plaintiffs in Roe v. Wade sought was not the right to abortion, but permission to commit a direct attack on the fetus. Thus, what the Court actually legalized was not abortion, but feticide. The distinction is crucial; the Court sanctioned not an event of nature, but an assault on nature.

1190. Petersen, Larry R., and Armand L. Mauss. "Religion and the 'Right to Life': Correlates of Opposition to Abortion." Sociological Analysis 37 (1976): 243-54.

Shows that religious conservatism is indeed positively related to opposition to abortion. Education, church attendance, and religious liberalism/conservatism were found to be the most important predictors of abortion attitudes.

1191. "Pills from the Bishops." Newsweek 30 July 1973: 40-41.

Discusses the expansion of a state-sponsored program of family planning fully backed by the country's powerful Catholic hierarchy.

1192. Pilpel, Harriet F. *Abortion: Public Issue, Private Decision.* Public Affairs Pamphlet 527. New York: Public Affairs Committee, 1975.

Deals with the legal aspects of the abortion controversy that the U.S. Supreme Court was called upon to settle.

1193. Pine, Rachael. "*Roe* on the Brink." *Nation* 24 July 1989: 112.

In a decision foretelling the demise of procreative choice, particularly for the poor, the U.S. Supreme Court shook the constitutional foundation of women's liberty and equality.

1194. Pipes, Mary. *Understanding Abortion.* Topsfield: Salem, 1987.

Personal accounts of 30 women who have experienced an abortion.

1195. Planned Parenthood Federation of America. *Considering What to Do.* Rev. ed. New York: Planned Parenthood Federation of America, 1984.

Deals with the importance of early pregnancy detection and discusses some decision-making considerations and possible options.

1196. Planned Parenthood Federation of America. *Deciding on Abortion.* New York: Planned Parenthood Federation of America, 1984.

Discusses abortion procedures, aftercare, and costs, and provides information on finding services.

1197. Planned Parenthood of New York City. *Abortion: A Woman's Guide.* New York: Abelard, 1973.

Discusses how pregnancy occurs, various methods of abortion, and alternative methods of birth control.

1198. Pohlman, Edward Wendell, comp. *Population: A Clash of Prophets.* New York: New American Library, 1973.

The topics discussed in the articles by sincere prophets of deep conviction deserve careful and even solemn consideration.

1199. Polenberg, Richard. "The Second Victory of Anthony Comstock?" *Society* May-June 1982: 32-38.

Discusses the "Comstockian denial" that there is any difference

between the ending of a pregnancy and the prevention of one.
The author presents Margaret Sanger's stand on abortion.

1200. Polgar, Steven. "Introductory Statement: The Objectives and
History of Birth Planning." International Journal of Health
Services 3 (1973): 557-60.

A review of the history of birth control which attempts to
introduce the "goals and ideologies" that have been part of
the movement. Margaret Sanger is seen as having linked birth
control with "the emancipation of women."

1201. "Political Responsibility and Abortion." Editorial. America
6 Mar. 1976: 173.

The significance of abortion as a campaign issue is discussed.
To give it exclusive importance so that candidates are
supported or "disqualified" on this one issue alone is clearly
a violation of principle and a failure of Christian political
responsibility.

1202. "Politics and Abortion." Editorial. Commonweal 27 Feb.
1976: 131-32.

Abortion has become an issue in the 1976 presidential campaign
in a manner that, in the long run, will add little substance
and considerable bitterness to the discussion of one of the
most critical moral problems of our time.

1203. Polk, Glenda Chitwood. "A Comparison of Crisis Variables
Among Groups of Women Experiencing Induced Abortion." Diss.
U of Alabama, 1983.

Describes the crisis-related variables of self-concept and
identifies the crisis variables which are predictive of repeat
abortions.

1204. Pollitt, Katha. "Hentoff, Are You Listening?" Mother Jones
Feb.-Mar. 1985: 60.

The views of Nat Hentoff on abortion are exposed as irresponsible and illogical.

1205. "The Pols and the Bishops." National Review 5 Oct. 1984: 18-
19.

The current phase of the abortion controversy has seen Mondale,
Cuomo, and Kennedy taking their cracks at moral theology and at
the Catholic bishops. Meanwhile, the Catholic bishops have
entered the debate with enough force to make the Democrats
swallow hard. Archbishop O'Connor went further: he publicly

accused Geraldine Ferraro of misrepresenting Catholic teaching on abortion.

1206.   Poma, Pedro A. "Contraceptive and Sexual Knowledge in Abortion Clients." Advances in Planned Parenthood 14 (1979): 123-29.

Health care workers feel frustrated that their clients use abortions to terminate pregnancies that could easily have been prevented by available contraceptive methods.

1207.   Poole, Carol. "Contraception and the Adolescent Female." Journal of School Health Oct. 1976: 475-79.

Discusses the sexual attitudes prevalent in America today, the implications of making contraceptives more available to teenagers, the various methods teenagers use for contraception, and the advantages and disadvantages of each method. Also examines the role clinics can play in administering birth control to adolescents in an effective manner.

1208.   Population Control: For and Against. New York: Hart, 1973.

A pro-birth control essay.

1209.   Potts, Malcolm. "Abortion: The New Civil War." World Press Review Apr. 1985: 44.

A civil war is taking place in the United States. It is a war about whether abortion should be legal. The U.S. Supreme Court ruling commands respect as an ambitious attempt to deal with an intractable problem.

1210.   Potts, Malcolm, and Peter Diggory. Textbook of Contraceptive Practice. 2nd ed. New York: Cambridge UP, 1983.

An attempt to take a global view of contraceptive practices, while still placing emphasis on the everyday problems, primarily encountered in the United States and Great Britain.

1211.   Potts, Malcolm, Peter Diggory, and John Peel. Abortion. Cambridge: Cambridge UP, 1977.

Traces the history of abortion and discusses the techniques associated with it.

1212.   Powell, John Joseph. Abortion: The Silent Holocaust. Allen: Argus, 1981.

Analyzes pro-abortion arguments in an attempt to dispose of them.

1213. Powell, Lewis Franklin, Jr. "Supreme Court Strikes <u>Akron</u> Abortion Provisions." <u>Origins</u> 21 July 1983: 149+.

In a 6-3 decision, June 15, 1983, the U.S. Supreme Court struck down major provisions of the Akron, Ohio, abortion ordinance that had become a model for numerous other local ordinances in the United States.

1214. Pratt, Gail L., Meni Koslowsky, and Ronald M. Wintrob. "Connecticut Physicians' Attitudes Toward Abortion." <u>American Journal</u> <u>of</u> <u>Public</u> <u>Health</u> Mar. 1976: 288-90.

Reports on a study of all Connecticut-licensed specialists in obstetrics and gynecology and a small sample of family physicians invited to participate in the study investigating several aspects of the cognitive, emotional, and behavioral components of attitudes toward abortion.

1215. Prebil, Thomas J. "Legal Issues in NFP." <u>International</u> <u>Review</u> <u>of</u> <u>Natural</u> <u>Family</u> <u>Planning</u> 7 (1983): 318-25.

Addresses several topics that have been identified by natural family planning (NFP) teachers as areas of concern in their practice. Three areas are discussed: malpractice, consent forms, and ownership of records.

1216. "Presbyterians Meet." <u>Christian</u> <u>Century</u> 3 July 1985: 64.

The Presbyterian church in the United States reaffirms its pro-choice decision (1983) in its 197th General Assembly.

1217. Prescott, James. "The Abortion of <u>The</u> <u>Silent</u> <u>Scream</u>." <u>Humanist</u> Sept.-Oct. 1986: 10+.

The film <u>The</u> <u>Silent</u> <u>Scream</u> is attacked as a false and wrongful cry for human pain, suffering, and violence.

1218. Prescott, James W. "Abortion and the 'Right-to-Life': Facts, Fallacies, and Fraud." <u>Humanist</u> July-Aug. 1978: 18-24.

Claims that the anti-abortion movement as a "right-to-life" movement, which purports to respect the dignity, quality, and equality of human life, is one of the greatest frauds ever perpetrated upon the American public. Part 1 of a two-part series.

1219. Prescott, James W., and Douglas Wallace. "Abortion and the 'Right-to-Life': Facts, Fallacies, and Fraud." <u>Humanist</u> Nov.-Dec. 1978: 36-42.

The major hidden currents in the anti-abortion movement are the negative moral values associated with sexual pleasure and the accompanying authoritarian values to limit and suppress the expression of sexual pleasure. Part 2 of a series begun in July-August 1978.

1220. "President Reagan Authors Anti-Abortion Article." Christianity Today 17 June 1983: 42-43.

A 10-page essay by Ronald Reagan for the spring issue of the Human Life Review in which he urges Americans to oppose abortion on demand. In his essay, Reagan emphasizes the value of human life.

1221. "President Reagan Won't Pursue Contraception Squeal Rule." Jet 19 Dec. 1983: 5.

The Reagan administration recently gave up its attempt to force federally aided birth control clinics to tell parents before prescribing contraception for unmarried teenagers.

1222. "Presidential Pen: Reagan Writes on Abortion." Time 9 May 1983: 36.

Reagan's byline appears over a pro-life article called "Abortion and the Conscience of the Nation." The 10-page, 3,000-word essay graphically expresses Reagan's strong views.

1223 Press, Aric, and Ann McDaniel. "A Court in Collision." Newsweek 14 Jan. 1985: 28.

Is medical technology moving faster than the law?

1224. Press, Aric, and Diane Camper. "The Court Stands by Abortion." Newsweek 27 June 1983: 62-63.

Justice Lewis F. Powell, Jr., indicated that the meaning of the Constitution cannot change every 10 years, although in abortion cases, at least, it may be fine-tuned by advances in medical technology.

1225. Press, Aric, et al. "Abortion Storm." Newsweek 23 June 1986: 26-27.

The U.S. Supreme Court vote of 5-4 in Pennsylvania case heats up a highly divisive political issue.

1226. Preston, Willard F. "The Unborn Child." Linacre Quarterly 46 (1979): 50-54.

Testimony of a pro-life physician to members of the Delaware General Assembly.

1227. Price, Elizabeth. "Sexual Misunderstanding: The True Cause of the Magisterium's Ban on Contraception." Cross Currents 30 (1980): 27-37.

Concludes that the debate would be greatly assisted or even resolved if the Catholic church's teaching on sex in marriage were examined in depth to decide whether that teaching could be said to show the guidance of the Holy Spirit--the claim made by those who support the Catholic church's teaching on contraception--or not.

1228. Pro-Life Catechism: Abortion, Genetics, Euthanasia, Suicide, Child-Abuse. Boston: Daughters of St. Paul, 1984.

Contends that respect for human life at all stages of development should be fostered through education and through laws that teach respect for life.

1229. "Prochoice Forces Claim Momentum in Washington." Christianity Today 12 May 1989: 59.

Advocates of legalized abortion buoyed by an unprecedented turnout for their march on Washington, DC, but pro-life forces are claiming that the momentum of the abortion debate is still on their side.

1230. "Prolifers Gear Up for Election-Year Battles." Christianity Today 7 Sept. 1984: 65-66.

Anti-abortionists are monitoring efforts in four states to pass constitutional amendments that would prohibit public funding for abortions.

1231. "Prostitutes and Contraceptives." Society May-June 1983: 2.

Street prostitutes use contraceptives less often than sexually active women of the same age in the general population, according to a study conducted in San Francisco.

1232. "Pulpit, Press, Polling Booth." Editorial. America 16 Oct. 1976: 223.

Argues that the results of a pro-life-sponsored signature campaign should not be announced until after the election to avoid embarrassment.

1233. "Punitive and Tragic." <u>Nation</u> 2 July 1977: 3-4.

The Burger Supreme Court shows its insensitivity to individual rights in its 6-3 decision allowing states to deny public funds for abortion, except in cases of medical necessity.

1234. Putnam, Ruth Anna. "Current Debate: Abortion." <u>Tikkun</u> Sept.-Oct. 1989: 81.

Holds that abortions must remain legal, but that many, perhaps a majority, of the 15 million abortions performed are morally indefensible.

1235. Quinn, John. "A Broader Perspective on <u>Humanae Vitae</u>." <u>Origins</u> 25 May 1978: 10-12.

<u>Humanae Vitae</u> portrays a sublime vision of Christian marriage and married love.

1236. Quinn, John R. "Abortion: A Clear and Constant Teaching." <u>Origins</u> 6 Dec. 1984: 413-14.

Abortion never represents a "legitimate moral choice," says Archbishop John R. Quinn. "The assertions contained in the statement of the Committee on Pluralism and Abortion which imply that church teaching about abortion has not always been clear and constant are not correct."

1237. _____. "Abortion: The Axe at the Root of Human Rights." <u>America</u> 1 Apr. 1989: 284-85.

Argues that abortion is the destruction of unborn human life. That is the real and most fundamental problem and constitutes the most pernicious danger to the whole edifice of human rights.

1238. _____. "Contraception: A Proposal for the Synod." <u>Catholic Mind</u> Feb. 1981: 25-34.

Text of a speech by Archbishop John R. Quinn presented to the synod on behalf of the National Conference of Catholic Bishops (NCCB).

1239. Quist, Allen. <u>The Abortion Revolution and the Sanctity of Human Life</u>. Milwaukee: Northwestern, 1980.

Explores the U.S. Supreme Court's <u>Roe</u> v. <u>Wade</u> decision and its impact on the human development field.

1240. Railsback, Celeste Michelle Condit. "The Contemporary American Abortion Controversy: A Study of Public Argumentation." Diss. U of Iowa, 1982.

Discusses the crucial public argument that raged over the place abortion held in the American public consciousness from 1960 through 1980.

1241. Ramsey, Paul. "Protecting the Unborn." Commonweal 31 May 1974: 308-14.

An adaptation of written testimony presented to a subcommittee of the Senate Judiciary Committee holding hearings on abortion amendments.

1242. Ranieri, Ralph F. "The Unwed Mother: A Parish Approach to the Abortion Problem." Today's Parish Oct. 1978: 11-12.

If the unwed mother had all the resources she needed at her disposal--from conception until after birth--perhaps an alternative to abortion would appear more feasible.

1243. Reagan, Patricia A. "In Search of Health History, Margaret Sanger: Health Educator." Health Education July-Aug. 1982: 5-7.

A brief biography and an assessment of Margaret Sanger.

1244. Reagan, Ronald. Abortion and the Conscience of the Nation. Nashville: Nelson, 1984.

Urges the nation to choose the sanctity of life over the quality of life.

1245. _____. "Fifteen Million Lives Snuffed Out: President Ronald Reagan Reports." Columbia Aug. 1983: 4-9.

Spells out President Reagan's opposition to abortion as a means of birth control.

1246. _____. Proposed Legislation--President's Pro-Life Act of 1988. Washington: GPO, 1988.

A message from President Reagan transmitting a draft of proposed legislation to prohibit the use of federal funds for abortion except where the life of the mother would be endangered.

1247.   "Real Dialogue in Los Angeles." America 12 Nov. 1977: 324.

        Highlights a joint document, "Respect for Life: Jewish and
        Roman Catholic Reflections on Abortion and Related Issues,"
        which indicates where Jewish and Catholic views converge and
        diverge.

1248.   Reardon, David C. Aborted Women: Silent No More. Chicago:
        Loyola UP, 1987.

        Builds on a survey the author conducted with 252 women who
        have had abortions and who are members of a national support
        group known as Women Exploited by Abortion (WEBA).

1249.   Redford, Myron H. Legal Abortion in Washington State: An
        Analysis of the First Year's Experience. Seattle: Population
        Study Center, 1973.

        Describes how Washington State's abortion law came about,
        compares that law with abortion laws in other states, and
        examines the state's first year's experience with legal
        abortion.

1250.   Reed, Evelyn, and Claire Moriarity. Abortion and the Catholic
        Church: Two Feminists Defend Women's Rights. New York: Path-
        finder, 1973.

        Discusses why the Catholic church hierarchy opposes women's
        right to an abortion and the meaning of the Catholic church's
        position on abortion.

1251.   Reed, George E. "Civil Rights Commission Issues Biased Pro-
        Abortion Report." Hospital Progress June 1975: 24+.

        Characterizes the 1975 Report of the U.S. Commission on Civil
        Rights, entitled Constitutional Aspects of the Right to Limit
        Childbearing, as "one of the most disturbing and biased reports
        ever promulgated by a federal agency."

1252.   Reed, James. From Private Vice to Public Virtue: The Birth
        Control Movement and American Society Since 1830. New York:
        Basic, 1978.

        Focuses on those individuals whose actions represent innovation
        or change in the birth control movement.

1253.   Reed, Susan. "The Abortion Clinic: What Goes On." People
        Weekly 26 Aug. 1985: 103-06.

        A recounting by a number of women of their inner thoughts
        regarding the pros and cons of abortion.

1254. Reeder, Ann. "Abortion--Have We Gone Too Far?" Mademoiselle Jan. 1975: 66+.

Contends abortion should be available, but does not agree with those who suggest that the abortion of a fetus has no more serious implications than the extraction of a tooth.

1255. Rees, Grover, III. "State Protection of the Viable Unborn Child After Roe v. Wade: How Little, How Late?" Louisiana Law Review 37 (1976): 270-82.

Discusses the extent of legal protection available for the unborn.

1256. _____. "The True Confession of One One-Issue Voter." National Review 25 May 1979: 669+.

Not an essay on abortion, but an effort to explain how one-issue voters think. However, the article builds its case on the issue of abortion.

1257. "Regain the Body Politic." Editorial. Nation 13 Feb. 1989: 181.

Politics, rather than reason or religion, is at the heart of the struggle over abortion rights, and it is only through political action that women's reproductive rights will be confirmed.

1258. Reiss, Ira, Albert Banwart, and Harry Foreman. "Premarital Contraceptive Usage: A Study and Some Theoretical Explorations." Journal of Marriage and the Family 37 (1975): 619-30.

A group of 482 females from a large midwestern university is examined in terms of attendance at a contraceptive clinic. Females who do and do not attend the clinic and females who have sought contraceptive advice from a private physician are compared.

1259. Reisser, Teri K., and Paul C. Reisser. Help for the Post-abortal Woman. Pomona: Focus on the Family, 1988.

Offers help and hope to women who now regret having had an abortion.

1260. Remsberg, Charles, and Bonnie Remsberg. "Abortion." Seventeen Sept. 1972: 140+.

Two views of one of the most perplexing ethical and practical problems a young woman can face.

1261. _____. "Second Thoughts on Abortion: From the Doctor Who Led the Crusade for It." _Good Housekeeping_ Mar. 1976: 69+.

Bernard Nathanson, M.D., was once head of New York's first and busiest abortion clinic. Now he feels that the removal of a fetus is the taking of human life.

1262. "Respect for Life." Editorial. _Columbia_ Sept. 1972: 6-7.

An overview article for Respect Life Week, discussing abortion, the aged, poor, young, war-afflicted, and the family, as a totality of persons touched by this movement.

1263. "Respect for Life: Jewish and Roman Catholic Reflections on Abortion and Related Issues." _Catholic Mind_ Feb. 1978: 54-64.

Consists of the Jewish and Catholic views on abortion, as well as a joint expression of goals.

1264. Reynolds, Brenda M. _Human Abortion: Guide for Medicine, Science and Research with Bibliography_. Washington: ABBE, 1984.

A textbook for students and researchers looking for current and progressive research material on human abortion.

1265. Rhoden, Nancy K. "A Compromise on Abortion?" _Hastings Center Report_ July-Aug. 1989: 32-37.

Discusses why the abortion issue remains so intractable, what aspects of _Roe_ v. _Wade_ are most vulnerable, and whether compromise is possible.

1266. _____. "Should Medical Technology Dictate a Woman's Right to Choose?" _Technology Review_ Apr. 1986: 21-22.

If viability remains the cutoff point for elective abortion, and medical technology allows earlier viability, such developments could render _Roe_ v. _Wade_ an anti-abortion decision.

1267. Rice, Charles E. _Beyond Abortion: The Origin and Future of the Secular State_. Chicago: Franciscan Herald, 1978.

Contends that the intellectual triumph of philosophical positivism has undermined the assumptions upon which our founding fathers developed the Constitution.

1268. Rice, Dabney. "Abortion: Rights and Risks." _Harper's Bazaar_ June 1976: 71+.

Presents facts about abortion centering on these questions:
1) What are your rights? 2) Whose decision is it? 3) How long
can you wait?

1269.   Riga, P. J. "Equal Protection of the Laws and the Fourteenth
Amendment: Value or Humanity?" Linacre Quarterly 51 (1984):
176-80.

Opponents of the constitutional human life amendment sidestep
issues and say that what really matters is not whether the
unborn is a human being, but whether it is a human being
valuable enough to protect.

1270.   Riga, Peter J. "Byrn and Roe: The Threshold Question and
Juridical Review." Catholic Lawyer 23 (1978): 309-31.

Claims that the U.S. Supreme Court failed to consider the fundamental issue concerning the humanness of the unborn fetus in
the Roe v. Wade decision.

1271.   _____. "Let's Break the Law to Stop Abortions." U.S.
Catholic Sept. 1975: 13-14.

Discusses abortion, public taxes, and civil disobedience,
saying it is time for Catholics to take a long, hard look at
this question as it concerns the taxes they pay and the kind
of public programs for which their taxes are paying.

1272.   _____. "Roe vs. Wade: The New Class Warfare." Priest
Sept. 1973: 13-18.

The war on the unborn has been consistently urged by a diver-
sified group of ecologists, demographers, doctors, crusading
clergy, and women libbers versus the Catholic hierarchy and
its assorted minions.

1273.   Rigali, Norbert. "Dialogue with Richard McCormick." Chicago
Studies 16.3 (1977): 299-308.

Argues that Humanae Vitae was a fitting response to its
historical situation and replies to some questions raised by
a distinguished moral theologian.

1274.   _____. "The Historical Meaning of the Humanae Vitae
Controversy." Chicago Studies 15.2 (1976): 127-38.

A well-known moralist maintains that Humanae Vitae was a
fitting response in the historical situation in which it
originated. The challenges made to the traditional position
on birth control failed to prove their point, however.

1275. _____. "Theologians and Abortion." <u>Priest</u> June 1974: 22-25.

Urges Catholic theologians and the laity to realize that two issues must be distinguished from one another: the question of the morality of abortion and the matter of its legality.

1276. Right-to-Choose Education Fund. <u>New Jersey Women Speak Out!</u> New Brunswick: Right-to-Choose Educ. Fund, 1986.

Samples of letters collected in New Jersey in the spring of 1985 from women who have had abortions, illegal or legal, as part of the "Silent No More" campaign.

1277. "Right-to-Life: New Strategy Needed." <u>Triumph</u> Apr. 1972: 46.

If the right-to-life movement is to exist, its new strategy must be to acquaint Americans with the absolutely clear evidence that a distinct human life begins at the moment of conception. To date it has not done so.

1278. Roach, John. "Bishops Support Hatch Amendment: Capitol Hill Testimony." <u>Origins</u> 19 Nov. 1981: 359+.

The National Conference of Catholic Bishops (NCCB) and the U.S. bishops' Committee for Pro-Life Activities (CPLA) say, "There should be no misinterpretation about our own position on the abortion issue. We are committed to full legal recognition of the right to life of the unborn child and will not rest in our efforts until society respects the inherent worth and dignity of every member of the human race."

1279. Roach, John R. "Choices That Make Us What We Are: Abortion and the Bomb." <u>Origins</u> 25 Nov. 1982: 377+.

Offers that, historically, a commitment to the sanctity of life has led Catholic bishops to be advocates of the unborn. Now it involves the bishops also "in the difficult but necessary task of assessing defense policy in the age of nuclear weapons by the light of moral doctrine."

1280. Robbins, James M. "Out-of-Wedlock Abortion and Delivery: The Importance of the Male Partner." <u>Social Problems</u> 31 (1984): 334-50.

Compares the relationships of 139 single women who had abortions with those of 109 single women who chose to have their babies.

1281. Roberts, Edwin A., Jr. "Thoughts After Viewing an Abortion." <u>Catholic Digest</u> Apr. 1972: 6-8.

Maintains that, however simple the abortion procedure, it is
still a killing.

1282. Roberts, John I., ed. _Beyond Intellectual Sexism: A New Woman,
a New Reality_. New York: McKay, 1976.

A scholarly essay which carries the struggle for reproductive
control from the past to the issues of today, including
abortion.

1283. Robins, Joel. "Failures of Contraceptive Practice." _New York
State Journal of Medicine_ Mar. 1976: 361-65.

Among 310 consecutive patients applying for elective abortion,
100 women with a history of having previously requested termination of an unwanted pregnancy were identified and interviewed
about their knowledge and practice of contraception. Inadequa-
cies in the delivery of contraceptive services were thereby
identified, leading to a series of recommendations for the
improvement of contraceptive practice.

1284. Robinson, Donald B. _The Miracle Finders: The Stories Behind
the Most Important Breakthroughs of Modern Medicine_. New
York: McKay, 1976.

In this history of medical researchers, Margaret Sanger's role
in the development of the birth control pill is detailed.

1285. Robinson, James. "Human Life Federalism Amendment: II.
Legislative Update." _Catholic Lawyer_ 2 (1983): 127-28.

Provides a legislative update and a state-of-the-art report
on Hatch's human life amendment.

1286. Robinson, James L. "Political Developments in the Abortion
Area." _Catholic Lawyer_ 25 (1980): 319-26.

Categorizes the congressional reaction to the U.S. Supreme
Court decisions on abortion.

1287. Rockefeller, John D. "No Retreat on Abortion." _Newsweek_
21 June 1976: 11.

The chairman of the Population Council and head of the Presidential Commission on Population Growth and the American
Future, maintains that when you combine the religious, moral,
and social issues with the fact that women need and will seek
abortions even if they are illegal, the case for legalized
abortion is overwhelming.

1288. Rockmore, Milton, comp. "Are You Sorry You Had an Abortion?" _Good Housekeeping_ July 1977: 120+.

Seven women answer the question, "Are you sorry you had an abortion?" Some say, "I'd do it again"; others are haunted by the baby they never had.

1289. Rodgers-Melnick, Ann. "After Abortion: No Need for Faith to Die." _U.S. Catholic_ Dec. 1985: 29-35.

Contends that priests, counselors, liturgy planners, and parish volunteers should spearhead post-abortion counseling and reconciliation programs to counsel women who have had abortions.

1290. _____. "Prolife Parishes Should Love Unwed Mothers." _U.S. Catholic_ Apr. 1985: 13-18.

Contends that parishes need to give out messages of love and help before pregnancy occurs and to demonstrate their support publicly in the form of material assistance, and that parishes must not neglect the fathers of these children.

1291. Rodman, Hyman. "The Abortion Quiz." _Nation_ 2 Aug. 1975: 70.

Poses questions on abortions and warns respondents to be careful how they answer, for the more confident they are, the more prejudiced they may show themselves to be.

1292. _____. "Controlling Adolescent Fertility." _Society_ Nov.-Dec. 1985: 35-37.

Advocates a wide variety of policy decisions for limiting teenage fertility, both for those under and those over age 15.

1293. Rodman, Hyman, et al. _The Abortion Question_. New York: Columbia UP, 1987.

Focuses on the history of the abortion controversy in the United States.

1294. Rodman, Hyman, Susan H. Lewis, and Saralyn B. Griffith. _The Sexual Rights of Adolescents: Competence, Vulnerability, and Parental Control_. New York: Columbia UP, 1984.

Purports to present sufficient information on the legal, social, and psychological aspects of adolescents' sexual rights to enable readers to come to their own conclusions about desirable social policies.

1295. "Roe vs. Wade Came Late for the Real Jane Roe." People Weekly
       5 Aug. 1985: 72.

       The real story of Norma McCorvey, also known as Jane Roe, the
       woman of the Roe v. Wade court case.

1296. Rogers, Everett M. Communication Strategies for Family
       Planning. New York: Free, 1973.

       Attempts to apply relevant social research findings to
       practical programs in family planning.

1297. Rosen, R. A. Hudson, et al. "Health Professionals' Attitudes
       Toward Abortion." Public Opinion Quarterly 38 (1974):
       159-73.

       Attitudes toward abortion as obtained in a 1971 nationwide
       survey of students and faculty in nursing, medicine, and
       social work are compared to abortion attitudes of the
       general population.

1298. Rosen, Raye Hudson. "Adolescent Pregnancy Decision-Making:
       Are Parents Important?" Adolescence 15 (1980): 43-54.

       Examines the extent to which teenagers involve parents in
       decision making on the resolution of unwanted conceptions,
       even though legalization of abortion allows them to terminate
       pregnancies without parental knowledge.

1299. Rosen, Ruth. "Historically Compromised." Tikkun July-Aug.
       1989: 20-21.

       Argues that the right to abortion is integral to the entire
       complex of women's rights and that women should maintain the
       right to make this personal decision.

1300. Rosenblatt, Roger. "Welcome to Uncomfortable Times." U.S.
       News and World Report 17 July 1989: 8-9.

       With the Webster decision, it appears that the U.S. Supreme
       Court wishes to return the issue to the American public again.

1301. Rosenblum, Art. Natural Birth Control Book. 5th ed.
       Philadelphia: Aquarian Research Foundation, 1982.

       Presents some suggested natural methods of birth control.

1302. Rosenblum, Victor G. "Letting the States Set Abortion Policy."
       The Christian Century 8 Mar. 1989: 252-53.

Both sides of the abortion debate agree that <u>Webster</u> v. <u>Reproductive Health Services</u> may be the most consequential case since <u>Roe</u> v. <u>Wade</u> made the right to have an abortion a component of the right to privacy in 1973.

1303.   Ross, John A.   <u>Family Planning and Child Survival: 100 Developing Countries</u>. New York: Columbia UP, 1988.

A reference for anyone seeking information in the fields of family planning and child survival in the developing world.

1304.   Ross, John A., and W. Parker Mauldin, eds.   <u>Berelson on Population</u>. New York: Springer, 1988.

Bernard Berelson's writings on population as they developed in his thoughts and career.

1305.   Rossi, Alice S., ed.   <u>The Feminist Papers: From Adams to de Beauvoir</u>. New York: Columbia UP, 1973.

An anthology of abridged feminist writings.

1306.   Rossi, Philip J.   "Rights Are Not Enough: Prospects for a New Approach to the Morality of Abortion." <u>Linacre Quarterly</u> 46 (1979): 109-17.

Approaches the moral issues involved in abortion from the proposition that a particularly frustrating impasse has been reached both in scholarly discussion of and public debate about abortion.

1307.   Rothman, Sheila M.   <u>Woman's Proper Place: A History of Changing Ideals and Practices, 1870 to the Present</u>. New York: Basic, 1978.

Discusses Margaret Sanger's problems with the progressives and sees Sanger's reliance on physicians and her support of "doctors only" bills as leading to the failure of the clinic movement.

1308.   Rousseau, Mary F.   "Abortion and Intimacy." <u>America</u> 26 May 1979: 429-32.

As a social structure, abortion on demand produces a barrier to intimacy. Its evil is not that it prevents birth, but that it does it so casually.

1309.   Rovner, Julie.   "Congress Puts Bush on Spot over Funding of Abortion." <u>Congressional Quarterly Weekly Report</u> 14 Oct. 1989: 2708-10.

A surprise House vote eases curbs in place since 1981, as members respond to a shift in the political winds.

1310. _____. "Veto over Abortion Funding Pains Some in the GOP." Congressional Quarterly Weekly Report 21 Oct. 1989: 2789-92.

Despite a shift in the political winds, Bush is moving on a broad front to enforce anti-abortion views.

1311. Rubin, Eva R. Abortion, Politics and the Courts: Roe vs. Wade and Its Aftermath. Rev. ed. Contributions in American Studies 89. New York: Greenwood, 1987.

Provides an overview of the abortion reform efforts of the 1950s and the legislative initiatives of the 1960s.

1312. Rudel, Harry Wendell, et al. Birth Control: Contraception and Abortion. New York: Macmillan, 1973.

Designed as a textbook for medical students and as a reference for practicing physicians.

1313. Ruether, Rosemary R. "Catholics and Abortion: Authority vs. Dissent." Christian Century 2 Oct. 1985: 859-62.

A New York Times ad explicitly asked for the cessation of institutional sanctions against those with dissenting positions on abortion.

1314. Ruf, Benjamin A. "The Constitutionality of the Human Life Bill." Washington University Law Quarterly 1 (1983): 219-52.

Evaluates the extent of congressional power to enact the human life bill despite the U.S. Supreme Court's rulings in Roe v. Wade and concludes that the human life bill is a valid exercise of the congressional enforcement power entitled to judicial deference under either theory.

1315. Rush, Curt S. "Genetic Screening, Eugenic Abortion, and Roe vs. Wade: How Viable Is Roe's Viability Standard?" Brooklyn Law Review 50 (1983): 113-42.

Discusses the rights of women with regard to abortion in terms of trimesters, fetal viability, rights of privacy, and "compelling" state interests.

1316. Russell, Joyce Markes. "Contraception in a New Context." America 3 Oct. 1981: 182-83.

Contends that the church's stand against artificial contraception is idealistic if presented apart from the whole vision of holiness.

1317.   Ryan, Barbara, and Eric Plutzer. "When Married Women Have Abortions: Spousal Notification and Marital Interaction." *Journal of Marriage and the Family* 51 (1989): 41-50.

Data indicate that the assumption that notification and discussion of intent to abort a fetus promote marital harmony is plausible for only a circumscribed subset of women whose marriages are already harmonious.

1318.   Ryan, George M., and Patrick J. Sweeny. "Attitudes of Adolescents Toward Pregnancy and Contraception." *American Journal of Obstetrics and Gynecology* I June 1980: 358-66.

A study, based in Tennessee, with statistical charts, regarding attitudes towards, and knowledge levels of, contraception, abortion, pregnancy, career plans, and parenting.

1319.   Ryle, Edward J. "Pregnancy Counseling and the Request for Abortion: Tentative Suggestions for Catholic Charities." *Catholic Charities Review* June 1973: 8-15.

Attempts to provide some guidelines for counseling; discusses the principle of self-determination as it is verified in counseling women seeking abortion assistance, and considers some of the ethical factors that might determine the stance of the caseworker in a Catholic agency.

1320.   _____. "Some Sociologicical and Psychological Reflections on the Abortion Decisions." *Jurist* 33 (1973): 218-29.

Considers some of the social and psychological data related to the U.S. Supreme Court's decisions. It discusses 1) American attitudes towards and assumptions about abortion prior to the decisions; 2) the American experience of legal abortion; 3) some of the psychological aspects of pregnancy and induced abortion.

1321.   Sachdev, Paul, ed. *International Handbook on Abortion.* New York: Greenwood, 1988.

A collection of data from all continents on the general pattern of the legal status of abortions, indications for abortion, and fertility trends.

1322.   _____. *Perspectives on Abortion.* Metuchen: Scarecrow, 1985.

194

Essays on the contemporary arguments of pro-life and pro-choice advocates.

1323. Sachdev, Satya Paul. "Factors Relating to the Abortion Decision Among Premaritally Pregnant Females." Diss. U of Wisconsin at Madison, 1975.

Examines the sexual and contraceptive behaviors that led to unintended pregnancies among never-married women and their decision to seek termination preterm.

1324. Sachs, Andrea. "Abortion on the Ropes: Is the Historic Roe v. Wade Ruling about to Be Overturned?" Time 5 Dec. 1988: 58-59.

The battle over Roe v. Wade will not be won or lost in the Oval Office or in state legislatures. The showdown will take place where the struggle began: in the U.S. Supreme Court.

1325. _____. "Reining In Abortions for Minors." Time 22 Aug. 1988: 62.

Two courts issue conflicting decisions on parental notification.

1326. Sackett, Victoria A. "Between Pro-Life and Pro-Choice." Public Opinion 8.2 (1985): 53-55.

Discusses the degree of public support and acceptance of abortion since the 1973 U.S. Supreme Court decision on abortion. Based on National Opinion Research Center (NORC) and other surveys.

1327. Safran, Verna. "Caught in the Abortion Backlash." Progressive May 1985: 16.

Sees the present backlash on abortion tied to the wedding of the monied Right with the religious Right and the failure of nerve on the part of liberals and the religious Left.

1328. Salholz, Eloise. "Pro-Choice: 'A Sleeping Giant' Awakes: A Shift in Tactics." Newsweek 24 Apr. 1989: 39-40.

Details a shift in pro-choice tactics.

1329. Salholz, Eloise, et al. "The Battle over Abortion." Newsweek 1 May 1989: 28-32.

Reviews the status of abortion legislation and comments on possible rulings of the U.S. Supreme Court in pending cases.

1330. _____. "Voting In Curbs and Confusion: How Five Likely State Restrictions Might Work." Newsweek 17 July 1989: 16-20.

With the U.S. Supreme Court's ruling in Webster v. Reproductive Health Services, the battlefield shifts to the fine print of state regulatory codes.

1331. Saltenberger, Ann. Every Woman Has a Right to Know the Dangers of Legal Abortion. 3d ed. Glassboro: Air-Plus Enterprises, 1982.

Aims to lay to rest some of the myths about abortion and to bring forward previously published, but little known, information on the legal aspects of the abortion issue.

1332. San Jenko, Grace Loretta. "Physicians' Attitudes Toward Abortion Patient Care." Thesis (MS). Northridge: California State U, 1973.

Attitudes of general practitioners and obstetrician-gynecologists toward abortion patient care in Los Angeles County, California, were investigated. The statistical data revealed that the quality of care received by abortion patients can be affected by the attitudes of medical personnel.

1333. Sanders, Marion K. "Enemies of Abortion." Harper's Mar. 1974: 26-30.

The Catholic hierarchy rejects a woman's "right" to govern her own body and it will not rest until that "right" is abolished.

1334. Santamaria, J. N. "The Social Effects of Contraception." Linacre Quarterly 51 (1984): 114-27.

Recounts the positive and negative effects of contraception following the introduction of the birth control pill in the early 1960s in the Western world.

1335. Sarvis, Betty, and Hyman Rodman. The Abortion Controversy. New York: Columbia UP, 1973.

Makes no attempt to hide a commitment to the liberalized abortion laws, yet makes it clear that the authors are not paralyzed by monolithic perceptions.

1336. _____. Abortion Controversy. 2nd ed. New York: Columbia UP, 1974.

Deals with the moral issue of the abortion controversy, especially in the Western nations.

1337. Sass, Lauren R., ed. _Abortion: Freedom of Choice and the Right to Life_. New York: Facts on File, 1978.

A compilation of reprints of more than 300 newspaper editorials that were published between 1973 and 1978 on the reaction to the abortion issue.

1338. "Saying No to NOW." _Time_ 28 Apr. 1975: 75-76.

Discusses restrictions placed on Catholic members of the National Organization for Women (NOW) by San Diego's Bishop Leo T. Maher.

1339. Scanlan, Alfred. "Recent Developments in the Abortion Area." _Catholic Lawyer_ 21 (1975): 315-21.

A review of recent abortion cases in the United States from the perspective of spousal consent, state regulation, and public assistance.

1340. Schaller, Warren A. "Slavery and Abortion." _Catholic Digest_ Dec. 1972: 24-26.

The analogy of abortion to slavery is a good analogy: both deny basic human rights.

1341. Scharf, Kathleen Rudd. "Abortion and the Body Politic: An Anthropological Analysis of Legislative Activity in Massachusetts." Diss. Boston U, 1981.

Indicates that abortion is, in Massachusetts, a symbolic issue through which the workers and the professional-managerial class express their status concerns.

1342. Scheidler, Joseph M. _Closed: Ninety-Nine Ways to Stop Abortion_. San Francisco: Ignatius, 1985.

Essentially a how-to book in support of the pro-life movement.

1343. Schmidt, Stanley. "The Right to What?" Editorial. _Analog Science Fiction/Science Fact_ May 1983: 6+.

Examines the logical consistency of opposing abortion on the grounds of right to life and debating the issue in terms of when life begins. Concludes that when life begins is not the issue: the issue is when humanity begins.

1344. Schmude, Richard W. "Law, Abortion and Rights." _Linacre Quarterly_ 49 (1982): 215-21.

Shares some thoughts concerning the <u>Roe</u> v. <u>Wade</u> decision and contends that the U.S. Supreme Court, in deciding that case, turned its collective back on the U.S. Constitution, the principles on which this nation was founded, and its own constitutional teachings.

1345. Schneider, Carl E., and Maris A. Vinoriskis, eds. <u>The Law and Politics of Abortion</u>. Lexington: Lexington, 1980.

Presents a variety of views on abortion and the law.

1346. Schneider, Sandra M., and Douglass S. Thompson. "Repeat Aborters." <u>American Journal of Obstetrics and Gynecology</u> 1 Oct. 1976: 316-20.

In an attempt to learn more about the phenomenon of repeat abortions, 116 women seeking a repeat abortion are compared in various ways with three groups of women not seeking a repeat abortion but otherwise similar.

1347. Schulte, Eugene J. "Tax-Supported Abortions: The Legal Issues." <u>Catholic Lawyer</u> 21 (1975): 1-7.

Suggests that the most meaningful abortion-related legal battle being waged is the one over the question of who is to pay for abortions and sterilizations. The particular legal arguments advanced by these abortion proponents rely on three concepts: due process, equal protection, and statutory claims to abortion.

1348. Schwartz, Amy E. "Bitter Pill." <u>New Republic</u> 18 Feb. 1985: 10.

Why pro-lifers cannot swallow birth control.

1349. Schwartz, Michael. "Pro-Life Doesn't Stop at Birth." <u>Liguorian</u> Jan. 1981: 7-11.

Points out that there are other pro-life issues besides abortion. For example, what about people who are already born? What about the environment? What about poverty and racism? What about capital punishment and war? It encourages the pro-life movement not to be single-issue oriented.

1350. Schwartz, Michael C. "Bringing the Sexual Revolution Home: Planned Parenthood's 'Five-Year Plan.'" <u>America</u> 18 Feb. 1976: 114-16.

Showering young people with contraceptives and provocative literature results in tremendous peer pressure that makes teenagers who do not engage in sex feel abnormal. Through these tactics Planned Parenthood is creating a demand for its own services.

1351. Schwartz, Michael, and James H. Ford. "Family Planning Clinics: Cure or Cause of Teenage Pregnancy?" Linacre Quarterly 49 (1982): 143-64.

Attacks the general philosophy and positions of the Planned Parenthood Federation.

1352. Scientists for Life, Inc. The Position of Modern Science on the Beginning of Human Life. Thaxton: Sun Life, 1975.

A collection of ideas from a number of scientists on the subject of when human life begins.

1353. Seaman, Barbara, and Gideon Seaman. Women and the Crisis in Sex Hormones. New York: Rawson, 1977.

Outlines the dangers of hormone therapy, suggests nutritional alternatives during menopause, and recommends that the birth control pill be replaced by other methods of birth control.

1354. "Second Thoughts About Abortions." U.S. News and World Report 3 Mar. 1975: 78.

Medical leaders in many parts of the United States are reviewing their position on abortion as the troublesome issue heads for another showdown in the courts. What they are studying closely are the implications of the manslaughter conviction of the Boston surgeon, Dr. Kenneth Edelin.

1355. Segers, Mary C. "Abortion: The Last Resort." America 27 Dec. 1975: 456-58.

One Catholic mother, also a political scientist, wrestles with the moral, social, political, and religious issues associated with abortion and her church's teaching.

1356. Seims, Sara. "Abortion Availability in the United States." Family Planning Perspectives Mar.-Apr. 1980: 88+.

Eight in 10 counties in the United States had no doctor, clinic, or hospital in 1977 that provided any abortions. As a result, over 1 million women were unable to obtain the abortion services they needed in their home counties. Most seriously disadvantaged were poor women and teenagers.

1357. Seligmann, Jean, et al. "The Medical Quandary." Newsweek 14 Jan. 1985: 26-27.

Neonatology and other technological changes raise new policy questions.

1358.   "Setback for Abortion." _Time_ 24 Feb. 1975: 67.

No one questioned the legality of the abortion which Edelin performed. At issue were Edelin's actions during and imme- diately after the operation.

1359.   "Sex Education Best Way to Curb Teen Pregnancy." _Jet_ 25 Nov. 1985: 27.

Americans agree that the best way to stem the tide of teen pregnancy is through communication and education.

1360.   Shaffer, Thomas, et al.   "The Abortion Rulings: Analysis and Prognosis." Symposium: CHA to Conduct Anti-Abortion Campaign. _Hospital Progress_ Mar. 1973: 81-96b.

A series of commentaries by religious, legal, and medical personnel, all of whom take issue with _Roe_ v. _Wade_.

1361.   Shalaby, Lisa.   "How Women Feel About Abortion: Psychological, Attitudinal, and Physical Effects of Legal Abortion." Diss. U of Iowa, 1975.

Emphasizes the post-abortion experiences of over 100 women who had abortions during 1973 and 1974 at the Emma Goldman Clinic for Women and at the University Hospital of Iowa City.

1362.   Shannon, Thomas A.   "Sterlization Can Be Moral." _U.S. Catholic_ May 1978: 11-12.

Traditionally, the reasons of maternal health, economic situation, and the ability to provide for other family members are given as justifications for using the rhythm method. These serious reasons can also be used to justify other means of contraception, including sterilization.

1363.   Shapiro, Constance Hoenk.   _Adolescent Pregnancy Prevention: School-Community Cooperation_.   Springfield: Thomas, 1981.

Highlights for concerned parents, teachers, religious leaders, and family planners the dimensions and ramifications of ado- lescent sexual activity and suggests broad-based school and community response to the prevention of adolescent pregnancy.

1364.   Shapiro, Howard I.   _The Birth Control Book_.   New York: St. Martin's, 1977.

Looks at contraception, sterilization, and abortion in a
question-and-answer format.

1365.   Shapiro, Laura. "Abortion: Back to Square One." <u>Mother</u> <u>Jones</u>
        Sept.-Oct. 1977: 13-14.

        Details the regression of public opinion and practice in
        regard to abortion and buttresses its views by detailing
        recent legal rulings and interpretations.

1366.   Shapiro, Thomas M. <u>Population</u> <u>Control</u> <u>Politics:</u> <u>Women,</u>
        <u>Sterilization</u> <u>and</u> <u>Reproductive</u> <u>Choice</u>. Philadelphia: Temple
        UP, 1985.

        Covers the issues of population control, sterilization, and
        reproductive freedom.

1367.   Shapiro, Walter, et al. "An Abortion Anniversary." <u>Newsweek</u>
        Feb. 1985: 22.

        A review of the annual march on Washington on the anniversary
        date of <u>Roe</u> v. <u>Wade</u>.

1368.   Sharkey, Nora C. "A New Yorker Looks at Abortion." <u>St.</u>
        <u>Anthony's</u> <u>Messenger</u> Feb. 1972: 10-14.

        A state resident discusses her feelings on the permissive law
        on abortions in New York State, and comments on the effects of
        the abortion clinic business.

1369.   Sharkey, Nora Clare. "Birthright New York." <u>Catholic</u> <u>Digest</u>
        Feb. 1972: 100-03.

        Birthright is an abortion-alternative service offered by the
        archdiocese of New York to any woman who asks for help, regard-
        less of her religion or financial situation.

1370.   Sharma, Pra Rash C. <u>Population</u> <u>Policy:</u> <u>A</u> <u>Select</u> <u>Research</u>
        <u>Bibliography</u>. Monticello: Council of Planning Librarians,
        1974.

        A compilation of materials from local, regional, national, and
        international journals and books reporting research findings on
        the subject matter of population policy.

1371.   Sharma, Prakash. <u>Family</u> <u>Planning</u> <u>Programs:</u> <u>A</u> <u>Selected</u>
        <u>International</u> <u>Research</u> <u>Bibliography</u>. Monticello: Council of
        Planning Librarians, 1974.

A compilation of some 250 selected references on birth control published chiefly between 1968 and 1973.

1372. Shaw, Margery W., and A. Edward Doudera, eds. Defining Human Life: Medical, Legal and Ethical Implications. Ann Arbor: AUPHA, 1983.

Papers presented at a conference cosponsored by the American Society of Law and Medicine (ASLM) and the Institute for the Interprofessional Study of Health Law (IISHL) which explored the societal attitudes toward the regulation of abortion.

1373. Shaw, Russell. "What Chance Do Prolife Amendments Have?" Columbia Oct. 1973: 10.

Discusses the realistic probability of a pro-life amendment to the U.S. Constitution.

1374. _____. "Will Congress Be Allowed to Dodge the Abortion Issue?" Columbia July 1975: 38.

Questions how the U.S. Congress will handle the abortion issue.

1375. Sheeran, Patrick J. Women, Society, the State and Abortion: A Structural Analysis. New York: Praeger, 1987.

Reviews the present legal policies on abortion, analyzes the consequences of those policies, and presents a global history of abortion over the centuries.

1376. Shehan, Lawrence Cardinal. "Humanae Vitae: 1968-1973." Homiletic and Pastoral Review Nov. 1973: 14+; Dec. 1973: 20+.

A three-part article by Lawrence Cardinal Shehan explaining the Catholic church's theological teaching on contraception.

1377. Shepard, Mary Jo, and Michael B. Bracken. "Contraceptive Practice and Repeat Induced Abortion: An Epidemiological Investigation." Journal of Biosocial Science 11 (1979): 289-302.

The relationship between abortion experience and contraceptive practice is examined among women having a first or a repeat induced abortion at the same clinic.

1378. Sherman, Carl. "Can the Condom Make Sex Safe Again?" Mademoiselle Dec. 1986: 120.

The condom protects against herpes and acquired immune

deficiency syndrome (AIDS). But how effective is it in
preventing pregnancy?

1379. Shettles, Landrum Brewer. Rites of Life: The Scientific
Evidence for Life Before Birth. Grand Rapids: Zondervan, 1983.

About human life from conception to birth. Intended as a guide
to the biological requisites of human life, the fascinating
complexities of its emergence, and the purposeful progress
of its development in the womb.

1380. Shivanandan, Mary. "Contemporary Attitudes Toward Sex."
Marriage and Family Living Nov. 1981: 18+.

Couples of all different faiths and backgrounds are experiencing, through natural family planning (NFP), a progressive
transformation of love in every area of their lives.

1381. _____. Natural Sex. New York: Rawson, 1979.

Covers the author's psychological, emotional, and spiritual
concepts of natural family planning (NFP).

1382. Shoemaker, Donald P. Abortion, the Bible and the Christian.
Grand Rapids: Baker, 1976.

Discusses the legal and ethical developments involving unborn
life which have created today's abortion issue and climate.

1383. Short, John. "The Pro-Life Agenda." Triumph Jan. 1974:
17-19.

Claims that as long as the anti-life movement is a government
project, the pro-life movement's job is much broader than
amending the Constitution.

1384. Shostak, Arthur B., and Gary McLough. Men and Abortion:
Losses, Lessons and Love. New York: Praeger, 1984.

A collection of over 1,000 interviews with men who have been
partners to women who have experienced an abortion.

1385. Showalter, J. Stuart, and Brian L. Andrew. "State Statutes
Regulating Abortion Leave Unresolved Issues." Hospital Progress Dec. 1982: 60-64.

States have dealt with parental consent and notice, spousal
consent and notice, waiting periods, fetal descriptions, regulation of facilities, and other aspects of abortion.

1386. _____. "Three Supreme Court Rulings Nullify Several
Abortion Restrictions." <u>Hospital</u> <u>Progress</u> July 1983: 20-21.

The U.S. Supreme Court strikes down several restrictive
statutes and local ordinances in Missouri, Ohio, and Virginia.
These invalid provisions include 24-hour waiting periods, fetal
description rules, and second-trimester hospitalization
requirements. On the other hand, the Court upholds regulations that require pathology reports, a second physician
during certain abortions, and parental or judicial consent
before a minor may secure an abortion.

1387. Siegel, Mark A., et al., eds. <u>Abortion:</u> <u>An</u> <u>Eternal</u> <u>Social</u> <u>and</u>
<u>Moral</u> <u>Issue</u>. Plano: Information Aids, 1986.

Deals with the social history of abortion from ancient times
to the <u>Roe</u> v. <u>Wade</u> U.S. Supreme Court decision.

1388. Silberner, Joanne. "When the Law and Medicine Collide." <u>U.S.</u>
<u>News</u> <u>and</u> <u>World</u> <u>Report</u> 17 July 1989: 23.

The legal and political debate cannot change the age when a
fetus is viable.

1389. "Silent Majority for Choice." <u>Progressive</u> Dec. 1989: 9.

The silent, complacent majority was content with the post-<u>Roe</u>
v. <u>Wade</u> status quo; however, with the <u>Webster</u> decision the
silent majority has begun to murmur.

1390. <u>The</u> <u>Silent</u> <u>Scream</u>. Videocassette. Keep the Faith, 1977. 30
min.

A graphic anti-abortion film which presents actual footage of
an abortion as if it were a spoken narration by the infant
being aborted.

1391. <u>The</u> <u>Silent</u> <u>Scream</u>. Anaheim: American Portrait Films, 1985.

A complete text of <u>The</u> <u>Silent</u> <u>Scream</u> documentary film, with an
authoritative response to the critics.

1392. "<u>The</u> <u>Silent</u> <u>Scream</u> in Britain." <u>America</u> 15 June 1985: 484.

Presents some British reaction to the American-made film.

1393. "<u>The</u> <u>Silent</u> <u>Scream</u>: Seeking an Audience." <u>Newsweek</u> 25 Feb.
1985: 37.

The White House encourages an anti-abortion campaign to distribute hundreds of copies of <u>The</u> <u>Silent</u> <u>Scream</u> film to every senator, representative, and U.S. Supreme Court justice.

1394. Silverstein, Elliot M. "A Legal and Psychological Study of Pro-and Anti-Abortion Groups." Diss. U of North Carolina at Chapel Hill, 1977.

Results of a questionnaire sent out by several groups to measure certain legal and psychological hypotheses relative to the abortion issue.

1395. Simpson, Peggy. "The Political Arena." <u>Ms</u>. Aug. 1989: 46-47.

A battle over abortion in New Hampshire previews what could happen if the U.S. Supreme Court weakens <u>Roe</u> v. <u>Wade</u>.

1396. _____. "Politics." <u>Ms</u>. Apr. 1989: 88-89.

Discusses the need for an organized political strategy to protect abortion rights in the United States.

1397. Sinclair-Faulkner, Tom. "Abortion in Canada: A New Phase in the Conflict." <u>Christian</u> <u>Century</u> 16 Oct. 1985: 923-26.

The Catholic hierarchy has perceptibly shifted from its conciliatory role to line up with pro-life activists in order to confront a society in which most people and every political party apparently favor easier access to abortion.

1398. Singh, B. Krishna, and Peter J. Leahy. "Contextual and Ideological Dimensions of Attitudes Toward Discretionary Abortion." <u>Demography</u> 15 (1978): 381-88.

Examines the contextual and ideological dimensions of attitudes toward discretionary abortion, using two national surveys.

1399. Skerry, Peter. "The Class Conflict over Abortion." <u>Public</u> <u>Interest</u> 52 (1978): 69-84.

Discusses the relationship between social class and opinion about abortion. Notes differences among the upper middle class and the working and lower middle class.

1400. Sklar, June, and Beth Berkov. "Abortion, Illegitimacy, and the American Birth Rate." <u>Science</u> 13 Sept. 1974: 909-15.

Legalized abortion had a dramatic effect on the number of

illegitimate babies born during 1971, a study in all states reveals.

1401. Skowronski, Marjory. _Abortion and Alternatives_. Millbrae: Femmes, 1977.

Includes the medical, legal, moral, religious, historical, philosophical, and psychological aspects of abortion as they relate to a woman facing the option.

1402. Slesinski, Robert. "Contraception and the Christian Institution." _Linacre Quarterly_ 46 (1979): 264-78.

Aims to help dissipate the confusion and uncertainties surrounding the Catholic position as promulgated in _Humanae Vitae_ and to allay misgivings about it.

1403. _____. "Created in the Image of God: Man and Abortion." _Linacre Quarterly_ 43 (1976): 36-48.

A theologically based argument against abortion.

1404. Sloane, R. Bruce, and Diana Frank Horvitz. _A General Guide to Abortion_. Chicago: Nelson, 1973.

Provides some guidelines and facts about therapeutic abortion.

1405. Smedes, Lewis B. "The Arguments in Favor of Abortion Are Strong...If You Accept One All-Important Assumption." _Christianity Today_ 15 July 1983: 62.

Poses a list of questions to determine whether any one or all of them makes a clear case for the freedom of abortion.

1406. Smetana, Judith G. _Concepts of Self and Morality: Women's Reasoning About Abortion_. New York: Praeger, 1982.

Shows that the U.S. Supreme Court decisions will not go far in quieting the abortion debate.

1407. Smith, Alphonsus Philip. "The _Roe_ vs. _Wade_ and _Doe_ vs. _Bolton_ Decisions on Abortion: An Analysis, Critique and Examination of Related Issues." Diss. Drew U, 1981.

Presents an historical analysis of the key legal concepts the U.S. Supreme Court employed in making its _Roe_ v. _Wade_ and _Doe_ v. _Bolton_ decisions.

1408. Smith, Anita. "Ancient and Modern: A Brief History of Contraception." _Nursing Mirror_ Feb. 1976: 55-56.

A history of contraception from 1850 B.C. in Egypt through 1970. Discusses pessaries, various acids, applications, and applicators, sheaths, intrauterine devices (IUDs), spermicides, ovulation suppressants, and surgical procedures.

1409. Smith, Elizabeth Dorsey. _Abortion: Health Care Perspectives_. Norwalk: Appleton, 1982.

Discusses the social context in which abortion care has developed, the physiological basis for abortion procedures, the psychological implications of abortion, and the roles of various members of the health care team.

1410. Smith, Elizabeth M. "Counseling for Women Who Seek Abortion." _Social Work_ Mar. 1972: 62-68.

Presents information obtained from a sample of women seeking abortions.

1411. _____. "A Follow-up Study of Women Who Request Abortion." _American Journal of Orthopsychiatry_ 43 (1973): 574-85.

Reviews the literature on the psychological effects of induced abortion and reports on the characteristics of an unselected sample of 154 women who contacted a problem-pregnancy counseling service, and on the subsequent adjustment of 80 of the 125 who obtained abortions.

1412. Smith, Philip A. "The Right to Privacy: _Roe_ v. _Wade_ Revisited." _Jurist_ 2 (1983): 289-317.

Since _Roe_ v. _Wade_, the U.S. Supreme Court has expanded the parameters of abortion in some areas and refused to expand them in others; but it has consistently and repeatedly reaffirmed a woman's constitutional right to terminate her pregnancy.

1413. Smith, Rachel Richardson. "Abortion, Right and Wrong." _Newsweek_ 25 Mar. 1985: 16.

Why can we not view abortion as one of those anguished decisions in which human beings struggle to do the best they can in trying circumstances? Why is abortion viewed so coldly and factually on the one hand and so judgmentally on the other?

1414. Sobran, M. J., Jr. "Abortion: The Class Religion." _National Review_ 23 Jan. 1976: 28-31.

"Abortionism" is rhetorically portrayed as a tenet of those secularist and anti-traditional creeds that are usually grouped together under the heading "liberalism."

1415. Soloway, Richard Allen. Birth Control and the Population Question in England, 1877-1930. Chapel Hill: U of North Carolina P, 1982.

Concerns itself with the origins and evolution of the birth control movement in England between the year 1877, when the decline in population growth attracted popular attention, and the year 1930, when the long decline ended.

1416. Sorrentino, Mary Ann, and Maureen Orth. "My Church Threw Me Out." Redbook June 1986: 14+.

Mary Ann Sorrentino reveals her story, claiming she was the first Catholic ever to be publicly excommunicated for helping other women obtain abortions.

1417. South, Julia. "To the Backstreet by the Backdoor." New Statesman 22 Nov. 1985: 14-15.

The second and concluding article in a survey of changing tactics over the abortion issue tackles the ambivalence that even radicals can now feel.

1418. Spake, Amanda. "The Propaganda War over Abortion." Ms. 14 July 1985: 88+.

Details the pro and con propaganda employed by opposing camps in the abortion debate.

1419. Spalding, Denise. "Abortions: Legal but How Available?" Ms. 4 Sept. 1975: 103-05.

Taking stock--clinics, laws, and quality care.

1420. Span, Paula. "Why Smart Women Are Stupid About Birth Control." Glamour Nov. 1986: 252+.

Claims that some women, old enough and educated enough to know better, "are behaving in a very irrational way."

1421. Speckhard, Anne. The Psycho-Social Aspects of Stress Following Abortion. New York: Sheed, 1979.

Contends that women who have risked irresponsible pregnancy and abortion have tended to be too weak either to confront their sexual partners or to reveal themselves in crisis to their families and friends.

1422. Spencer, Patricia. "Thanks for Humanae Vitae." Homiletic and Pastoral Review Mar. 1979: 25+.

A mother of eight from Chicago expresses her gratitude to Pope Paul VI for his prophetic gift of Humanae Vitae.

1423. Spitzer, Robert J. The Right-to-Life Movement and Third-Party Politics. Contributions in Political Science 160. New York: Greenwood, 1987.

Well written, carefully researched, original in its treatment of third-party problems, and significant in its subject matter.

1424. "Splintered High Court Rules on Major Abortion Case." Congressional Quarterly Weekly Report 8 July 1989: 1717-24.

Roe v. Wade is scaled back as a Missouri statute is upheld. Rehnquist writes fragmented bench's opinion (article includes excerpts from all justices' opinions).

1425. Spring, Beth. "Feminists Against Abortion? The ProLife Movement Is Broadening." Christianity Today 22 Apr. 1983: 35-36.

For years, the pro-life movement was stereotyped as a Catholic endeavor. Now that it is recognized as spanning all faiths, there are efforts to put it into political, instead of religious, pigeonholes.

1426. _____. "Harsh Days at the High Court." Christianity Today 15 July 1983: 30-31.

The Bob Jones ruling strikes against religious freedom, and the abortion decision devastates the right-to-life movement.

1427. _____. "A New Political Group Will Oppose Abortion, Poverty, and Nuclear Arms." Christianity Today 13 June 1986: 36-37.

An organization representing both Protestants and Catholics will endorse candidates who hold a consistent pro-life ethic.

1428. _____. "New Problems in Congress for the Antiabortionists." Christianity Today 4 Feb. 1983: 60+.

The U.S. House of Representatives changed its rules, with the likely effect of blocking debate on abortion funding.

1429. _____. "Prolife and Prochoice Activists Renew the Battle." Christianity Today 20 Feb. 1987: 48-50.

Both sides claim to be making significant headway in three important arenas of activity: public opinion, courts and legislatures, and services to women.

1430. _____. "Proposed Prolife Bill Goes for the Jugular." Christianity Today 12 June 1987: 48-49.

A proposed pro-life bill states that the U.S. Supreme Court "erred" and that "a right to abortion is not secured by the Constitution." It prohibits the federal government from paying for an abortion unless the mother's life is endangered. Finally, the bill would bar federal family-planning dollars from groups that provide abortion procedures or referrals.

1431. _____. "White House Files Prolife Court Brief." Christianity Today 3 Sept. 1982: 66+.

The Reagan administration suggests that the U.S. Supreme Court might have been wrong in 1973 when it struck down all state laws restricting abortions, and administration lawyers made their arguments in a friend-of-the-court brief filed late in July.

1432. "The Squeal Rule: Halt!" Newsweek 28 Feb. 1983: 17.

Henry F. Werker and Thomas A. Flannery, U.S. district judges in New York and Washington, respectively, ban the U.S. Department of Health and Human Services from enforcing the "squeal rule," an impending federal regulation that would require some 5,000 federally subsidized health clinics nationwide to notify the parents of any girl who applied for prescription contraceptives until a full-scale trial on its legality could be held.

1433. Stafford, Geraldine. "Humanae Vitae and the Catholic Priest." Homiletic and Pastoral Review Dec. 1980: 30+.

Discusses the moral and religious dilemmas many priests--present and former--face in dealing with Humanae Vitae.

1434. Stafford, Tim. "The Abortion Wars: What Most Christians Don't Know." Christianity Today 6 Oct. 1989: 16-20.

Ours is not the first abortion war: two previous periods saw protracted contests over whether abortion would be accepted or proscribed.

1435. Stahel, Thomas H. "Abortion, Lies and Videotape." America 11 Nov. 1989: 313-14.

Describes the Florida pro-life movement and Gov. Bob Martinez's failure to get more restrictive abortion laws in Florida.

1436. Stan, Adelle-Marie. "Abortion Rights Alert." Ms. May 1985: 24.

National Abortion Rights Action League (NARAL) and other pro-choice groups hope to mobilize new activists in what they see as the battle to keep abortion legal and accessible.

1437. Stanford-Rue, Susan M., and David Hazard. Will I Cry Tomorrow? Healing Post-Abortion Trauma. Old Tappan: Revell, 1986.

A book for women who need to be healed of post-abortion trauma.

1438. Starr, Mark, et al. "Meese Weighs in on Abortion." Newsweek 29 July 1985: 60-61.

Edwin Meese, U.S. attorney general, urges the U.S. Supreme Court to reverse itself on its 1973 abortion ruling.

1439. "Statement on Pluralism and Abortion." Origins 6 Dec. 1984: 414.

Contends that the position of the Catholic hierarchy in opposing abortion is not "the only legitimate Catholic position."

1440. "Statements of National Conference of Catholic Bishops." Catholic Lawyer 19 (1973): 29-35.

Official statements by various bishops, a cardinal, and priests on the pro-abortion decision of the U.S. Supreme Court.

1441. Steinem, Gloria. "Abortion Alert." Ms. Nov. 1977: 118.

The demand for reproductive freedom as an inalienable human right has become the bottom line for women throughout the world and is chief among the issues exploding feminism into a populist movement.

1442. _____. "A Basic Human Right." Ms. Aug. 1989: 38+.

The right to choose whether, when, and with whom to have children is as fundamental as freedom of speech.

1443. Steiner, Gilbert Yale, ed. The Abortion Dispute and the American System. Washington: Brookings, 1983.

Evaluates how the U.S. abortion policy affects the governmental system.

1444. Steinfels, Peter. "The Politics of Abortion." Commonweal 22 July 1977: 456.

A common policy now emerging from the U.S. Supreme Court, Congress, and the Department of Health, Education and Welfare (HEW) is that abortions should not be paid for by public funds.

1445. _____. "The Search for an Alternative." Commonweal 20 Nov. 1981: 660-64.

Alternatives for liberal Catholics: Take every opportunity to voice disagreement with Roe v. Wade. If Democrats, lobby for the repeal of the Democratic party's platform support for abortion and its funding. Finally, find a way to articulate the kind of prohibition suggested here in legal form and have it entered into the lists of Congress.

1446. Steinhoff, Patricia C. Abortion Politics: The Hawaii Experience. Honolulu: UP of Hawaii, 1977.

Both a history of the repeal of Hawaii's criminal abortion law and an analysis of the processes by which the repeal came about.

1447. Stengel, Elizabeth Bell. "Abortion: The Battle's Not Over." Ms. Feb. 1975: 98-99.

Points out that despite the Roe v. Wade decision, the U.S. Supreme Court ruling has not "settled the matter" once and for all: a large number of Americans are strongly lobbying for a constitutional amendment.

1448. Stephen, Beverly. "Moment of Truth: Having a Second Child." Working Woman Apr. 1986: 131+.

For a working mother, the real career crisis may come not with the birth of her first child but with the birth of her second. What do mothers do? That depends.

1449. Stettner, Allison G., and Anita P. Cowan. Health Aspects of Family Planning: A Guide to Resources in the United States. New York: Humanities Sciences, 1982.

A list of technical and nontechnical resources for use in patient education and professional education and training relative to family planning.

1450.   "Stifled Squeal." *Time* 28 Feb. 1983: 24.

Two federal district judges issue temporary injunctions blocking the Department of Health and Human Services (HHS) from
requiring that some 5,000 federally funded family-planning
clinics notify parents within 10 working days of the time that
their children (age 17 or under) receive prescription contraceptives.

1451.   Stith, Richard. "The World as Reality, as Resource, and as
Pretense." *American Journal of Jurisprudence* 20 (1975):
141-53.

Argues that by ignoring the child prior to the moment it
happens to emerge from the womb, the U.S. Supreme Court in
Roe v. *Wade* has indicated that it does not find an inherent
value in an infant even after birth.

1452.   Stokes, Bruce. "U.S. Switch on Family Planning Raises Fear
About Economic Development." *National Journal* 4 Aug. 1984:
1476-79.

The new limits on the use of U.S. funds by international groups
that support abortions have buoyed right-to-life groups and
worried population experts.

1453.   Storer, Horatio Robinson, and Franklin Fiske Heard. *Criminal
Abortion: Its Nature, Its Evidence and Its Law*. New York:
Arno, 1974.

Deals with the legal aspects of the abortion question and cites
specific laws to support the authors' beliefs.

1454.   "Strange Bedfellows." Editorial. *Christianity Today* 10 May
1974: 33-34.

Contends that the Religious Coalition for Abortion Rights
(RCAR) uses deceptive rhetoric to substantiate its position of
total support for the present U.S. Supreme Court-imposed status
quo on abortion (that is, abortion on demand). It is also
deceptive in attempting to give the impression that major
Protestant bodies endorse its position.

1455.   "Strategy on Abortion." *Time* 1 Dec. 1975: 59.

The nation's Roman Catholic bishops approve a new anti-
abortion strategy, a "Pastoral Plan for Pro-Life Activities."
The bishops not only called for a parish- to national-level
effort by Catholics, but proposed the formation of inter-
denominational pro-life groups in all 435 congressional
districts to fight for an amendment overturning the U.S.
Supreme Court's 1973 decision.

1456.   Stratton, Robert W.   "State Legislation Can Lessen Impact
        of Court's Abortion Decision."   Hospital Progress Oct. 1973:
        8-9.

        Explores how state legislation and regulations, by seizing
        upon the U.S. Supreme Court's own language, can significantly
        lessen the impact of "abortion on demand."

1457.   Stucky, Mary.   "Abortion Harassment."   McCall's Mar. 1979:
        52.

        Despite their disparate positions, both anti-abortion and pro-
        choice groups are distressed at what seems to be a disturbing
        trend: the harassing of women who do get abortions.

1458.   Stukane, Eileen.   "The Trauma of Abortion."   Cosmopolitan
        Nov. 1984: 166+.

        Contends that a woman's decision to end her pregnancy is
        never trivial.   The emotional impact can be staggering,
        especially when the man involved is absent and uncaring.

1459.   "Stunning Approval for Abortion: Decision Blow by Blow."
        Time 5 Feb. 1973: 50-51.

        Every woman in the United States now has the same right to
        an abortion during the first six months of pregnancy as she
        has to any other minor surgery.   So bold and uncompromising
        is the ruling that no state is unaffected.

1460.   "Subsidized Birth Control: Controversial but Spreading."
        U.S. News and World Report 10 Sept. 1973: 33-35.

        Coming: Another big boost for nationwide birth control--at
        government expense.   It is sure to add to a storm that started
        brewing a decade ago.

1461.   Suh, Mary, and Lydia Denworth.   "Operation Rescue."   Ms. Apr.
        1989: 92-94.

        Details Operation Rescue and the tactics of its leader,
        Randall Terry.

1462.   Sullivan, Thomas D.   "The Right to Life and Self-Conscious-
        ness."   America 7 Oct. 1978: 222-24.

        One current argument supporting policies of permissive abortion
        is based on the theory that human life must be aware of its
        own self before it has rights.   The unborn fail this test.

1463. Summerhill, Louise. The Story of Birthright: The Alternative
       to Abortion. Kenosha: Prow, 1973.

       Details the work of Birthright volunteers with unwed mothers.

1464. Sumner, L. W. Abortion and Moral Theory. Princeton:
       Princeton UP, 1981.

       An elegant statement holding that the sooner one has an
       abortion, the lesser the consequences. Connects practical
       issues of abortion with moral theory.

1465. Sundstrom, Colleen. "A Bookshelf on Family Planning."
       American Journal of Public Health July 1974: 666-73.

       A comprehensive guide to family-planning resources, including
       publications and periodicals, organizations, and libraries.

1466. "The Supreme Court and Abortion." Society Mar.-Apr. 1976:
       6-9.

       A study reports that the year following the 1973 U.S. Supreme
       Court decision on abortion saw varied responses on the part
       of U.S. health institutions and professionals in different
       areas of the country. As a result, the provision of abortion
       services remained highly concentrated geographically, and the
       availability and accessibility of abortion services remained
       uneven a year after the Court's rulings.

1467. "Supreme Court Eases Rules on Abortion." U.S. News and World
       Report 5 Feb. 1973: 36.

       Outlines when and for what reasons abortion, in each of the
       trimesters of gestation, is permissible in the United States.

1468. "Supreme Court Ignites a Fiery Abortion Debate. Time 4 July
       1977: 6-8.

       State and local governments, said the U.S. Supreme Court, can
       choose whether or not to finance the abortions of needy women
       for nontherapeutic reasons (conditions that do not endanger
       their health).

1469. "Supreme Court on Abortion." Editorial. America 3 Feb.
       1973: 81.

       Claims that the Roe v. Wade decision is long on history
       but short on science, and that certain matters, such as statu-
       tory protection for the right of all organizations and indi-
       viduals not to participate in abortions against their own
       consciences and traditional values, should receive immediate

attention. The constitutional right of women to choose to have an abortion must not be extended to the right to compel others to participate against their will.

1470. "Supreme Court on Medicare and Abortion." Origins 30 June 1977: 86-90.

A state participating in the Medicaid program is not constitutionally required to pay for nontherapeutic abortions for poor women, even though that state pays for expenses related to childbirth, the U.S. Supreme Court ruled.

1471. "Supreme Court to Consider Woman's Right to Abortion." Hospital Progress Mar. 1972: 10+.

The National Right to Life Committee (NRLC) filed an amicus curiae brief in the U.S. Supreme Court of the United States in cases involving the abortion laws of Texas and Georgia. The brief defends the constitutional right of the states to impose sanctions against abortion on the grounds of their overwhelming interest in safeguarding human life from unwarranted destruction.

1472. "Supreme Court Upholds Ruling Against a Law Restricting Abortion." Christianity Today 13 June 1986: 43.

Nine justices refuse--on procedural grounds--to decide in favor of an Illinois statute that restricts abortion.

1473. Swan, George S. "The Thirteenth Amendment Dimensions of Roe vs. Wade." Journal of Juvenile Law 4 (1980): 1-33.

Explores the possibility of protecting the unborn under the Thirteenth Amendment of the Constitution. It is particularly noted that Roe v. Wade dealt with Fourteenth Amendment issues only.

1474. Swyhart, Barbara Ann DeMartino. Bioethical Decision-Making: Releasing Religion from the Spiritual. Philadelphia: Fortress, 1975.

Attempts to relate religious and ethical concepts to provide a guide to contemporary bioethical problems.

1475. Symonds, Richard, and Michael Carder. The United Nations and the Population Question, 1945-1970. New York: McGraw, 1973.

Considers the role of the League of Nations and the agencies of the United Nations in regard to the population question.

1476. Symposium on Reproductive Rights. Fort Lauderdale: Nova U
Center for the Study of Law, 1989.

Attempts to bring reproductive rights issues into perspective.

1477. Szumski, Bonnie, ed. Abortion: Opposing Viewpoints. St.
Paul: Greenhaven, 1986.

A collection of essays to help the reader consider opposing
viewpoints of the abortion question and to critically
analyze those viewpoints.

1478. Tagg, John. "Understanding Mario Cuomo." National Review
8 Feb. 1985: 25+.

An analysis of Gov. Mario Cuomo's speech at Notre Dame University, a speech which dealt with abortion and the response to
it in a pluralistic society and which is described as a
"potential" earthshaker.

1479. Tatalovich, Raymond, and Byron W. Daynes. "The Limits of
Judicial Intervention in Abortion Politics." Christian
Century 6-13 Jan. 1982: 16-20.

The U.S. Supreme Court's landmark 1973 rulings in Roe v.
Wade and Doe v. Bolton did not resolve the abortion
controversy but rather aggravated it to the point where the
very fabric of democratic politics is threatened.

1480. _____. Politics of Abortion: A Study of Community
Conflict in Public Policy-Making. New York: Praeger, 1981.

Contends that abortion politics is best analyzed when viewed
as a sequential process of agenda setting, community conflict,
and consensus building.

1481. _____. "The Trauma of Abortion Politics." Commonweal
20 Nov. 1981: 644-49.

The debate over abortion today is a contest between divergent
values, and the dispute is so combative that the antagonists
cannot even "agree to disagree."

1482. Tax, Meredith. "March to a Crossroads on Abortion." Nation
8 May 1989: 613+.

Recounts the details and personal perspective of the pro-
choice April 9, 1989, march on Washington, DC.

1483. "Teen-Agers and Abortion." Origins 2 Apr. 1981: 657+.

The text of the 6-3 decision, March 23, 1981, of the U.S.
Supreme Court upholding a Utah law requiring that parents be
notified when their unmarried, minor, and dependent daughter
seeks an abortion.

1484. "Teenage Birth Control." Society Mar.-Apr. 1979: 3.

Teenagers who do not use birth control can be divided into
three groups: 1) those who lack information about, or access
to, contraception; 2) those who are not motivated to contracept because they feel it is not worth dealing with a doctor
or pharmacist, that it makes sex seem too planned; 3) those
who want to have babies because they feel they have no other,
more attractive options.

1485. "Teenagers and Prescription Contraceptives: Parental Notification Urged." Origins 2 Apr. 1982: 719-21.

The U.S. Catholic Conference (USCC) supports proposed regulation requiring notification of parents within 10 days after
a contraceptive drug or device is prescribed for a teenager
and urges that the proposal be amended to require notification of parents before prescription contraceptives are
dispensed or used.

1486. Teresa, Mother. " A Nobel Laureate Speaks in Defense of Unborn
Life." Christianity Today 6 Sept. 1985: 62-63.

Mother Teresa of Calcutta, awarded the Nobel Peace Prize in
1979, identified abortion as "the greatest destroyer of peace"
in the world.

1487. Teresa, Mother, et al. Who Is for Life? Westchester:
Crossway, 1984.

A series of essays affirming the value of human life, of
compassionate action, and of standing against evil wherever
it is to be found.

1488. Terkel, Susan Neiburg. Abortion: Facing the Issues. New
York: Watts, 1988.

Describes the history and current status of the abortion laws;
the medical procedures involved in abortion; and the religious,
ethical, and political viewpoints that contribute to the controversy.

1489. Tetlow, Joseph A. "Grievous Moral Mischief." America 19 Nov.
1977: 359.

The National Abortion Rights Action League (NARAL) statement:
"Abortion is now the central issue in a momentous struggle
which will determine the fate of many of the basic rights and
liberties that protect us all."

1490. Thimmesch, Nick. "Abortion Culture." Newsweek 9 July
        1983: 7.

        Claims that the U.S. abortion culture is reminiscent of
        Germany's faulted medical utilitarian philosophy of the
        1930s: What is useful is good.

1491. Thomas-Baily, Jane. "How to Keep the Pro-Life Movement Small."
        Commonweal 22 May 1987: 308-09.

        Shares insights which, if practiced, will diminish the size
        of the pro-life movement.

1492. Thompson, Dick. "A Setback for Pro-Life Forces." Time 27 Mar.
        1989: 82.

        New studies find abortions pose little danger to women.

1493. "The Thread and the Cloth: Arguments in the Supreme Court's
        Abortion Case." Newsweek 8 May 1989: 19.

        Excerpts from the U.S. Supreme Court testimony in the Webster
        v. Reproductive Health Services case.

1494. Tierney, Barbara. "Planned Parenthood Didn't Plan on This."
        Business Week 3 July 1989: 34.

        Details how abortion foes are attacking Planned Parenthood's
        corporate sponsors.

1495. Tietze, Christopher. Fertility Regulation and the Public
        Health: Selected Papers of Christopher Tietze. New York:
        Springer, 1987.

        An objective analysis and presentation of the public health
        aspects of human fertility and its regulation.

1496. _____. Induced Abortion: A World Review, 1983. 5th ed.
        New York: Population Council Fast Book, 1983.

        Presents an overview of current international data on induced
        abortion, primarily from the public health, demographic, and
        policy points of view.

1497. _____. "Repeat Abortions--Why More?" Family Planning Perspectives Sept.-Oct. 1978: 286-88.

The increasing number of repeat abortions reflects the growing number of women who, having had first abortions, are therefore at risk of having a subsequent procedure.

1498. _____. "Teenage Pregnancies: Looking Ahead to 1984." Family Planning Perspectives July-Aug. 1978: 205-07.

Seeks to estimate how many of today's 14-year-olds are likely to experience one or more pregnancies, births, abortions, and miscarriages before they reach age 20, assuming that there is no change in the level or timing of sexual activity among teenagers, or in their use of contraception or abortion.

1499. Tietze, Christopher, and Sarah Lewit. "Legal Abortion." Scientific American Jan. 1977: 21-27.

The 10-year trend in many parts of the world towards the legalization of induced abortion has led to new studies of the practice, more open release of data, better medical procedures, and lower mortality rates.

1500. Tietze, Christoper, et al. Birth Control and Abortion. New York: MSS Information, 1972.

Papers discussing the various effects of oral contraceptives.

1501. Tkac, Debora. "Birth Control After 35." Prevention Aug. 1985: 57-61.

Holds that any method of birth control is safer than no birth control at all, and recommends that older women examine the options.

1502. "Too Many Abortions." Editorial. Commonweal 11 Aug. 1989: 419-20.

Argues that 1.5 million abortions a year is a national scandal and that abortion, while legal, is not moral.

1503. Tooley, Michael. Abortion and Infanticide. New York: Oxford UP, 1983.

Supports several positions on abortion with interesting and challenging arguments and illustrations.

1504. Topalian, Elyse. <u>Margaret Sanger: A Biography of the Feminist Who Brought Safe and Legal Birth Control to the Women of America</u>. New York: Watts, 1984.

Traces Margaret Sanger's personal and professional life from childhood through her nursing career years in New York.

1505. Torres, Aida, Jacqueline Darroch Forrest, and Susan Eisman. "Telling Parents: Clinic Policies and Adolescents' Use of Family Planning and Abortion Services." <u>Family Planning Perspectives</u> Nov.-Dec. 1980: 284-92.

Contends that if all family-planning and abortion facilities had to notify parents, some 33,000 more unwanted pregnancies would occur among teens now practicing effective contraception; and that 42,000 now obtaining legal abortions would turn to illegal practitioners or have unwanted births.

1506. Toufexis, Anastasia. "Birth Control: Vanishing Options." <u>Time</u> 1 Sept. 1986: 78.

Lawsuits and other safety concerns mean new worries.

1507. "Toward Moderation of Abortion Law." <u>America</u> 4 Feb. 1989: 75.

The morality of abortion is the most intensely debated ethical question in American public life today.

1508. Traugott, Michael W., and Maris A. Vinovskis. "Abortion and the 1978 Congressional Elections." <u>Family Planning Perspectives</u> Sept.-Oct. 1980: 238-46.

Contends that recent shifts towards more restrictive abortion policies reflect an increasingly conservative House membership rather than any broad change in public attitudes toward abortion.

1509. Trotter, Robert J. "Abortion Laws Still in Ferment." <u>Science News</u> 29 Jan. 1972: 75.

States are rewriting and liberalizing antiquated abortion laws, but they will be subject to attack until the U.S. Supreme Court rules on their constitutionality.

1510. Trudeau, Garry. "Silent Scream II: The Prequel." <u>New Republic</u> 10 June 1985: 8.

The complete six strips of the cartoon "Doonesbury" which cartoonist Garry Trudeau withdrew from publication.

1511. Trussell, James, et al. "The Impact of Restricting Medical
       Financing for Abortion." Family Planning Perspectives
       May-June 1980: 120+.

       If all states observed the Hyde amendment restrictions, many
       thousands of Medicaid-eligible women who would have obtained
       abortions under the 1977 funding policy would not receive them.

1512. "Truth in Advertising, Please." Editorial. America 4-11 Jan.
       1986: 1.

       Attacks Planned Parenthood's ads, charging that the promoters
       and writers of those ads claim the moral high ground, but
       that in such presentations there is deplorable blindness or,
       more likely, dishonesty.

1513. Tunnadine, David, and Roger Green. Unwanted Pregnancy--Acci-
       dent or Illness? New York: Oxford UP, 1978.

       A work based on interviews with 147 women and intended for
       those women who must make a decision about an abortion.

1514. "Turning Back Webster." Editorial. Nation 30 Oct.
       1989: 477.

       Since the Webster v. Reproductive Health Services decision
       on abortion, a new wave of activisim is challenging the
       hegemony of the Republican anti-abortion axis at every level.

1515. "Twisted Logic." Editorial. Christianity Today 22 Dec.
       1972: 24-25.

       Decries that today the churches themselves, or at least many
       of them, are working to bring the laws of society back into
       conformity with pre-Christian paganism, against the now clear
       wishes of the majority of church members.

1516. "U.S. Bucks the Tide on Birth Control." U.S. News and World
       Report 20 Aug. 1984: 8.

       The Reagan administration says that, from now on, internation-
       al organizations must pledge not to promote abortions before
       the U.S. government will grant family-planning money.

1517. "U.S. Supreme Court on Abortion." Editorial. Social Justice
       Review Feb. 1973: 359+.

       Lists, in synopsis form, the findings of the U.S. Supreme
       Court in the Roe v. Wade decision, and also notes the
       major provisions of the Hogan human life amendment to the
       Constitution.

1518. Uddo, Basile J. "The Human Life Bill: Protecting the Unborn Through Congressional Enforcement of the Fourteenth Amendment." Loyola Law Review 4 (1981): 1079-97.

An article adapted from the testimony of Professor Uddo (professor of law at Loyola University School of Law in New Orleans, Louisiana) in favor of the Helms-Hyde human life bill before the Senate Judiciary Committee, Subcommittee on Separation of Powers.

1519. _____. "Manipulating 'The Choice' on CBS." America 21 Mar. 1981: 230-32.

Alleges that CBS aired on national television a show that was pro-abortion propaganda.

1520. Uehling, Mark D., et al. "Clinics of Deception: Pro-Lifers Set Up Shop." Newsweek 1 Sept. 1986: 20.

Radical pro-lifers have opened 2,000 free "clinics" which give pregnancy tests and outwardly appear to offer abortion.

1521. Ullman, Alice. "Social Work Service to Abortion Patients." Social Casework Oct. 1972: 481-87.

Reports that debates about abortion continue among the health professions, religious groups, and the general public as to how the women who are undergoing abortions are affected; what the psychological implications of having an abortion are; why women make that decision; whether they need help in coping with their decision.

1522. Ullyot, Joan. "Birth Control and Performance." Runner's World Nov. 1986: 78-79.

Most scientific studies to date have failed to show any adverse effect on athletic performance due to the use of oral contraceptives.

1523. "The Unborn and the Born Again." New Republic 2 July 1977: 5+.

Discusses the U.S. Supreme Court decision on the use of state funds to cover abortion costs.

1524. Underhill, Merrilee. "The Long Arm of Planned Parenthood." Liguorian Oct. 1984: 40-44.

Discusses the modus operandi of the Planned Parenthood Foundation (PPF).

1525. United Nations. Department of International Economic and Social Affairs. Population Division. Adolescent Reproductive Behaviour: An Annotated Bibliography. New York: United Nations, 1988.

An annotated bibliography which attempts to provide a general overview of the literature on adolescent fertility and closely related issues.

1526. United States. Commission on Civil Rights. Constitutional Aspects of the Right to Limit Childbearing. Washington: Commission, 1975.

Analyzes the manner in which the constitutional amendments designed to nullify the right to limit childbearing would undermine the First, Ninth, and Fourteenth Amendments.

1527. United States. Cong. Senate. Committee on Labor and Human Resources. Family Planning Amendments of 1986, Report Together with Additional Views. Washington: GPO, 1986.

S 881 amended the existing authority of the Public Health Services Act to extend Title X for four years.

1528. United States. Cong. Senate. Subcommittee on Constitutional Amendments of the Committee on the Judiciary. Hearings on Abortion. 93rd Cong., 2nd sess. [94th Cong., 1st sess.] S. J. Res. 119 and S. J. Res. 130. 4 vols. Washington: GPO, 1974-76.

Hearings on S. J. Res. 119 and S. J. Res. 130 proposing an amendment to the Constitution of the United States for the protection of unborn children and other purposes.

1529. United States. Cong. Senate. Subcommittee on Separation of Powers of the Committee on the Judiciary. Hearings on the "Human Life" Bill. 97th Cong., 1st sess. S 158. 2 vols. Washington: GPO, 1982.

Hearings on S 158, which contend that human life shall be deemed to exist from conception.

1530. United States. Cong. Senate. Subcommittee on the Constitution of the Committee on the Judiciary. Hearings on Constitutional Amendments Relating to Abortion. 97th Cong., 1st sess. S. J. Res. 17, 18, and 19. 2 vols. Washington: GPO, 1983.

A series of hearings by the Subcommittee on the Constitution on the subject of proposed amendments to the Constitution in regard to abortion.

1531. United States. Cong. Senate. Subcommittee on the Constitution of the Committee on the Judiciary. Hearings on the
Legal Ramifications of the Human Life Amendments. 98th Cong.,
1st sess. S. J. Res. 3. Washington: GPO, 1983.

Hearings which considered the legal ramifications of constitutional amendment proposals with the specific goal of
revising Roe v. Wade.

1532. United States. Cong. Senate. Subcommittee on the Constitu-
tion of the Committee on the Judiciary. Hearings on the
Abortion Funding Restriction Act. 99th Cong., 1st sess.
S 522. Washington: GPO, 1986.

Hearings on S 522, which takes the initial step of ensuring
that federal tax dollars are not used to terminate fetal
lives.

1533. United States. Cong. Senate. Subcommittee on the Constitu-
tion of the Committee on the Judiciary. Hearings on the
Medical Evidence on Fetal Pain. 99th Cong., 1st sess.
Washington: GPO, 1986.

Committee hearings focusing upon the current state of the
medical evidence concerning fetal pain.

1534. United States. Cong. Senate. Committee on Labor and Human
Resources. Hearings on Family Planning Amendments of 1987.
100th Cong., 1st sess. S 1366. Washington: GPO, 1988.   #6.
Testimony to reaffirm the participants' support for family-
planning programs and to strengthen the existing programs.

1535. United States. Cong. House. Human Resources and Inter-
governmental Relations Subcommittee of the Committee on
Government Operations. Hearings on the Medical and Psychological Impact of Abortion. Washington: GPO, 1989.

Hearings focus on the impact of abortion on the physical
health and mental well-being of the 1.5 million American
women who have abortions every year.

1536. "Unsocial Issues." New Republic 27 Feb. 1984: 9-10.

Despite the fact that President Reagan launched his reelection
bid discussing abortion, the author argues that "social"
issues, abortion in particular, are best left to the conscience of individual citizens. What he objects to most is
that these issues should become political footballs in the
first place.

1537.   "Untidiness Revisited." Editorial. <u>Commonweal</u> 8 Feb. 1985:
        69-70.

        Compares two schools of thought on abortion and its legality,
        one Rabbi Hertzberg's and the other <u>Commonweal</u>'s.

1538.   Urberg, Kathryn A. "A Theoretical Framework for Studying
        Adolescent Contraceptive Use." <u>Adolescence</u> 17 (1982):
        528-40.

        Presents a theoretical framework for viewing adolescent
        contraceptive usage. Specifically, the five major aspects
        of problems in this area are problem recognition, motivation,
        generation of alternatives, decision making, and implementa-
        tion.

1539.   Vacek, Edward. "Contraception and Responsibility." <u>Catholic
        Charismatic</u> June-July 1980: 14-17.

        Discusses the "responsible use" of human sexuality, along
        with the agony and distress that this one issue has brought
        to the Catholic church, with references to <u>Humanae</u> <u>Vitae</u>
        throughout.

1540.   Van den Haag, Ernest. "Is There a Middle Ground?" <u>National
        Review</u> 22 Dec. 1989: 29-31.

        Discusses the morality and/or immorality of abortion.

1541.   Van den Haag, Ernest, and John T. Noonan, Jr. "Abortion: A
        Civilized Exchange." <u>National Review</u> 6 Sept. 1985: 37-39.

        A proponent and an opponent of abortion debate whether a
        fetus is a human being and whether a presentient fetus is
        an actual versus a potential human being.

1542.   Van der Tak, Jean. <u>Abortion, Fertility, and Changing Legisla-
        tion: An International Review</u>. Lexington: Lexington, 1974.

        Represents the first attempt to review, consolidate, and
        interpret, on a worldwide basis, the findings of many workers
        in the expanding field of abortion research.

1543.   Van Gelder, Lindsay, and Pam Brandt. "Beyond Sex Ed: School
        Clinics Tackle the Teen-Pregnancy Epidemic." <u>McCall's</u> May
        1987: 89+.

        A parent's reflections on her daughter's family-planning
        involvement in a school-based clinic in St. Paul, Minnesota.

1544. Van Vleck, David B. _How and Why Not to Have That Baby_. Charlotte: Optimum Population, 1972.

Discusses some of the alternatives to abortion that are available and recommends people who can help a woman make a decision.

1545. Van Winden, Lori. _The Case Against Abortion: A Logical Argument for Life_. Ligouri: Ligouri, 1988.

The main thrust is towards all those who share in the concept that being pro-life is a sociocultural issue.

1546. Vanderford, Marsha L. "Vilification and Social Movements: A Case Study of Pro-Life and Pro-Choice Rhetoric." _Quarterly Journal of Speech_ 75 (1989): 166-82.

Both pro-lifers and pro-choicers see abortion as an important social, political, and moral issue that should be regulated by legislation; both expect that their views should be upheld in court; and both engage in extensive vilification of their opponents.

1547. Vaux, Kenneth. "After 'Edelin': The Abortion Debate Goes On." _Christian Century_ 5 Mar. 1975: 213-14.

A guilty verdict in _Massachusetts_ v. _Edelin_ is character- ized as every bit as much a shock to the progressive vanguard as _Roe_ v. _Wade_ was to conservative traditionalists.

1548. Verhey, Allen. "Learning from _Roe_ v. _Wade_." Editorial. _Reformed Journal_ Apr. 1983: 3-5.

Contends that _Roe_ v. _Wade_ can remind us that the most important opposition to the outcome of its findings will be moral, ethical, and religious, not legal.

1549. Verkamp, Bernard J. "Personhood, Abortion and the Law." _America_ 23 Jan. 1982: 46-48.

As the controversy continues, both liberals and conservatives must distinguish the juridical concept of legal personhood from the philosophic definition of the human person.

1550. Visentin, Charles A. _A Message to an Aborted Baby Killed by the Cowardice of Its Mother and the Venal Complicity of the Attending Physician_. Albuquerque: American Classical College P, 1976.

Deals with the moral and religious aspects of the abortion controversy.

1551. "Vocal Prochoice Activists Launch Nationwide Offensive."
       Christianity Today 12 July 1985: 42+.

       Pro-life groups fight back in an escalating battle over
       legalized abortion.

1552. Voegeli, William J., Jr. "A Critique of the Pro-Choice
       Argument." _Review of Politics_ 43 (1981): 560-71.

       Contends that the pro-choice argument is but a component in
       the case for legalized abortions, not the whole of it.

1553. Vogel, Morris J., and Charles E. Rosenberg, eds. _The Thera-
       peutic Revolution: Essays in the Social History of American
       Medicine_. Philadelphia: U of Pennsylvania, 1979.

       Details to some extent the positions of doctors confronted
       with the necessity of defending the moral standards of the
       community and cites why the author considers Margaret Sanger's
       fight for birth control a necessity.

1554. Von Feldt, Elmer. "Clear Answer to a Political Dilemma."
       Columbia Feb. 1975: 4.

       The Vatican's Sacred Congregation for Catholic Doctrine
       issues a ruling with special application to Catholic jurists,
       political leaders, doctors, nurses, social workers, lawyers,
       and others whose professions bring them in contact with the
       consequences of the U.S. Supreme Court's decision establishing
       a "right" to kill the unborn.

1555. Von Stamwitz, Alicia. "My Visit to an Abortion Clinic."
       Liguorian Aug. 1983: 26-31.

       A woman recounts her experiences as a "prospective client"
       at an abortion clinic.

1556. Wahlberg, Rachel Conrad. "Abortion: Decisions to Live With:
       Conference at Southern Methodist University." _Christian
       Century_ 27 June 1973: 691-93.

       A report on a conference designed to explore various view-
       points and to help people "make decisions they can live with."

1557. Walbert, David F. _Abortion, Society and the Law_. Cleveland:
       Western Reserve UP, 1973.

       A series of scholarly articles on abortion published in the
       Case Western Law Review.

1558. Walker, Marlan C., and Andrew F. Puzder. "State Protection of the Unborn After Roe vs. Wade: A Legislative Proposal." Stetson Law Review 13 (1984): 237-66.

Suggests legislation, reviews Roe v. Wade's progeny, and demonstrates that states may constitutionally declare that life begins at conception if done in connection with a statute which attempts to protect the unborn in areas other than abortion.

1559. Walker, Vern R. "Presumptive Personhood." Linacre Quarterly 45 (1978): 179-86.

Claims that the fetal right to life is an important assertion concerning fundamental morality.

1560. Wall, James M. "Birth Control Clinic Controversy." Editorial. Christian Century 16 Oct. 1985: 907-08.

Defends the appropriateness of a birth control clinic on public school property as a pragmatic attempt to curb the serious social problem of teenage pregnancy.

1561. _____. "Options in the Abortion Debate." Editorial. Christian Century 18 Feb. 1976: 139-40.

Outlines possible options in the abortion debate, vis-a-vis the politics of the presidential race.

1562. _____. "Right-to-Life Activists Split on Federal Tactics." Editorial. Christian Century 23 Dec. 1981: 1332-33.

Offers contrasting views on two strategies: the Hatch amendment (a states' rights approach to abortion) versus the Hyde amendment (human life bill).

1563. Wallerstein, Judith S., Peter Kurtz, and Marion Bar-Din. "Psychosocial Sequelae of Therapeutic Abortion in Young Unmarried Women." Archives of General Psychiatry Dec. 1972: 828-32.

Presents post-abortion courses of 22 unmarried pregnant women in middle and late adolescence who successfully obtained therapeutic abortions under recently liberalized abortion statutes and practices.

1564. Walling, Regis. When Pregnancy Is a Problem. St. Meinrad: Abbey, 1980.

Raises issues and questions that must be answered when a woman is deciding on what to do about an unexpected, unplanned, or unwanted pregnancy.

1565.   Wallis, Claudia. "Abortion, Ethics and the Law." _Time_
        6 July 1987: 82-83.

        Advancing technology further complicates a national dilemma:
        society's obligation to protect a newly independent life and
        the mother's right to privacy.

1566.   _____. "_Silent Scream_: Outcry over Antiabortion Film."
        Time 25 Mar. 1985: 62.

        Documents reactions from medical personnel, pro-choice and pro-
        life proponents over the film's release.

1567.   Walsh, Mary Ann. "Forgiveness for Abortion." _Catholic Digest_
        July 1983: 83-84.

        Those who have had abortions also suffer from the fact that the
        same church that has told them abortion is sinful has not told
        them as vociferously that God is merciful.

1568.   _____. "Pro-Life Is a Very Pregnant Issue." _U.S._
        Catholic Dec. 1981: 13-14.

        Argues that to be pro-life in action is to take so strong a
        stand that obstacles such as cost, human respect, changing
        standards, anger, and fear are surmounted.

1569.   Walsh, Michael J. "What the Bishops Say." _Month_ May 1973:
        172-75.

        Gives insight into the magisterium of the Catholic church as
        it relates to abortion and presents the role of bishops and
        their responsibility.

1570.   Wardell, Dorothy. "Margaret Sanger: Birth Control's Success-
        ful Revolutionary." _American Journal of Public Health_ July
        1980: 736-42.

        A biographical sketch of Margaret Sanger which includes some
        brief assessments by her major biographers.

1571.   Wardle, Lynn D. _The Abortion Privacy Doctrine: A Compendium_
        and Critique of Federal Court Abortion Cases. Buffalo: Hein,
        1981.

        Aims to provide a reference for students, scholars, and prac-
        ticing lawyers who are interested in examining specific issues
        of abortion privacy.

230

1572. _____. "Human Life Federalism Amendment: I. Legal
Aspects." Catholic Lawyer 2 (1983): 121-26.

A constitutional amendment is not the be-all and end-all of
the pro-life movement. A constitutional change, similar to
the Hatch amendment, is necessary, as is the enactment of
concomitant enforcing legislation.

1573. Wardle, Lynn D., and Mary A. Wood. A Lawyer Looks at Abortion.
Provo: Brigham Young UP, 1982.

The result of considerable individual and collaborative
research on the legal aspects of the abortion controversy.

1574. "Wattleton Blasts Reagan on Harsh Abortion Stand." Jet 6 Aug.
1984: 39.

The president of Planned Parenthood Federation of America
(PPFA) accuses the federal government of subverting abortion
funding.

1575. Wattleton, Faye. "Our World Needs Family Planning." Cosmopolitan Jan. 1987: 54.

Claims that a study of worldwide social statistics indicates
the imperative of family planning.

1576. _____. "Repro Woman." With Marcia Ann Gillespie. Ms.
Oct. 1989: 50-53.

Articulates Planned Parenthood Federation of America's (PPFA)
position and passionately defends reproductive freedom.

1577. _____. "Reproductive Rights for a More Humane World."
Humanist July-Aug. 1986: 5+.

The text of a speech by Faye Wattleton, president of Planned
Parenthood Federation of America (PPFA), on being named 1986
Humanist of the Year by the American Humanist Association
(AHA).

1578. Wax, Judith. "Abortion Controversy: What's It All About?"
Seventeen Nov. 1975: 118+.

Discusses the questions: 1) When does life begin? 2) What are
a woman's rights to control of her own body? 3) Do the unborn
have rights, too?

1579. "Ways to Cut U.S. Birth Rate--Findings of an Official Study."
U.S. News and World Report 27 Mar. 1972: 64.

Relaxed rules on abortion, contraceptives, and sterilization
are urged by a federal commission over the objections of a
number of its members.

1580. Weber, Paul J. "Bishops in Politics: The Big Plunge." America
       20 Mar. 1976: 220+.

       The abortion issue has evoked a new political activism among
       American Catholics and a different kind of leadership from the
       bishops.

1581. Weinberg, Roy David. Family Planning and the Law. 2nd ed.
       Dobbs Ferry: Oceana, 1979.

       Considers the legal aspects of state and federal laws estab-
       lished up to 1979 on the abortion issue.

1582. Weinstein, Bette. "Birth-Control Pill for Men." McCall's
       July 1974: 34-35.

       Men are reported to be eager for the development of a male
       contraceptive pill, reinforcing the opinion that many men feel
       that contraception is every bit as much a male problem as a
       female one.

1583. Weisbord, Robert G. "Birth Control and the Black American: A
       Matter of Genocide." Demography 10 (1973): 571-90.

       Examines the roots and rationale of the genocide notion of the
       1960s and 1970s, charging that birth control and abortion are
       integral elements of a white genocidal conspiracy directed
       against Afro-Americans.

1584. _____. Genocide? Birth control and the Black American.
       Westport: Greenwood, 1975.

       Examines the question of genocide as it relates to birth
       control.

1585. Weisheit, Eldon. Abortion? Resources for Pastoral Counseling.
       St. Louis: Concordia, 1976.

       Deals with the process of reaching a decision on whether to
       have an abortion.

1586. Weisman, Adam Paul. "Clinical Examination." New Republic
       16 Mar. 1987: 15-16.

       The practice of dispensing contraceptives to teenagers in

school is reflected upon in the two-year study report, "Risking the Future," by the National Academy of Sciences (NAS).

1587. Welton, K. B. Abortion Is Not a Sin. Costa Mesa: Pandit, 1987.

A new age looks at an age-old problem.

1588. Wendel, George D., and John E. Dunsford. "Sustaining the Prolife Momentum: Legal and Political Strategies." Hospital Progress Dec. 1982: 70-83.

Abortion, like slavery, has divided the nation deeply. Although ending legalized abortion may be as difficult as ending slavery, prolife advocates are convinced they will alter the course of society.

1589. Wennberg, Robert N. Life in the Balance: Exploring the Abortion Controversy. Grand Rapids: Eerdmans, 1985.

Attempts a systematic moral evaluation of the abortion controversy.

1590. _____. "The Right to Life: Three Theories." Christian Scholar's Review 13.4 (1984): 315-32.

Distinguishes and evaluates three answers to the question: Whose life is to be respected?

1591. Wessling, Frank. "Let's Quit Pretending about Birth Control." U.S. Catholic Aug. 1977: 29-31.

Discusses the possibility of being Catholic while at the same time working for a change in the way the church officially talks about birth control.

1592. Western Regional Conference on Abortion. Abortion in the Seventies: Proceedings of the Western Regional Conference on Abortion, Denver, Colorado, February 27-29, 1976. New York: Natl. Abortion Federation, 1977.

Presents the intent of conference participants' thoughts and concerns on some questions relating to abortion.

1593. Westley, Richard J. "Abortion Debate: Finding a True Pro-Life Stance." America 5 June 1976: 489-92.

Claims that a true pro-life stance requires that anti-abortionists put aside their personal anger and frustration and look at pro-abortionists as their brothers and sisters.

1594. _____. "Some Reflections on Birth Control." Listening
       12.2 (1977): 43-61.

       Discusses the five basic principles of the Catholic church's
       tradition regarding conception.

1595. Westoff, Charles F., and Larry Bumpass. "The Revolution in
       Birth Control Practices of U.S. Roman Catholics." Science
       5 Jan. 1973: 41-44.

       Reports on the convergence of Catholic and non-Catholic con-
       traceptive practices over the past two decades.

1596. Westoff, Charles F., and Norman B. Ryder. The Contraceptive
       Revolution. Princeton: Princeton UP, 1977.

       Detailed interviews with numerous women assessing the growth
       of, and reliance on, contraceptive activity.

1597. Westoff, Charles F., et al. Toward the End of Growth: Popula-
       tion in America. Englewood Cliffs: Prentice, 1973.

       A collection of essays on current patterns of fertility
       control and their implications for future trends of population
       growth in the United States.

1598. Whelan, C. M. "Of Many Things." Editorial. America 10 Feb.
       1973: Inside front cover.

       Argues against the constitutional right to abortion legisla-
       tion in the U.S. Congress and state legislatures and suggests
       three possible courses of action, now that the U.S. Supreme
       Court has legalized abortion.

1599. Whelan, Charles M. "Religious Belief and Public Morality."
       America 29 Sept. 1984: 159-63.

       Mario M. Cuomo, governor of New York, delivers an address
       at Notre Dame University defending his policies on abortion
       legislation.

1600. White, Byron. "Roe v. Wade--The Abortion Case." Catholic
       Mind Apr. 1973: 11-12.

       The text of Justice Byron R. White's dissenting opinion when,
       on January 22, 1973, the U.S. Supreme Court, by a vote of 7 to
       2, ruled that laws in Texas and Georgia restricting the
       practice of abortion were unconstitutional.

1601. White, Byron, et al. "The Court's Dissenters: Abortion Control
Law." Origins 25 Jan. 1979: 506-09.

The U.S. Supreme Court issues a warning to the states that they
should not attempt to forbid or regulate abortions when there
is a chance for survival of the fetus.

1602. Whitehead, John W., ed. Arresting Abortion: Practical Ways to
Save Unborn Children. Westchester: Crossway, 1985.

Outlines ways in which the abortion issue can be addressed
at all levels of society.

1603. Whitehead, K. D. "From Abortion to Sex Education." Homiletic
and Pastoral Review Nov. 1973: 60-69.

Addresses the question: Are pro-abortionists laying the
groundwork for a new paganism by urging widespread acceptance
of an amoral sex education?"

1604. _____. Respectable Killing: The New Abortion Imperative.
New Rochelle: Catholics United for the Faith, 1972.

Explores population explosion as it relates to legalization of
abortion.

1605. "Why We Can't Be Silent About Anti-Abortion Tactics."
Editorial. Glamour June 1985: 52.

Refutes information presented in The Silent Scream.

1606. Wilber, George L. Childbearing and Family Planning.
Lexington: Social Welfare Research Institute, U of Kentucky,
1972.

Contains programmatic and policy implications based on an
improved understanding of factors that help determine the
acceptance and practice of family planning and childbearing
itself.

1607. Wilbur, Amy E. "The Contraceptive Crisis." Science Digest
Sept. 1986: 55+.

Fears, lawsuits, and red tape have sharply reduced America's
birth control choices. What is left? What is reliable? What
is ahead?

1608. Will, George F. "America Gets 'Condomized.'" Newsweek 16
Feb. 1987: 82.

Relates how society becomes desensitized to previous taboo
subjects once the media promotes new products--in this case,
condoms.

1609.   _____. "Discretionary Killing." Newsweek 20 Sept.
         1976: 96.

         Contends that life beginning at conception is not disputable.
         The dispute concerns when, if ever, abortion is a victimless
         act.

1610.   _____. "Splitting Differences." Newsweek 13 Feb.
         1989: 86.

         Holds that this democratic nation needs a vigorous argument,
         not judicial fiat, about abortion.

1611.   _____. "Teen-Agers and Birth Control." Newsweek 28 Feb.
         1983: 80.

         Adolescents have a third choice between contraception and
         pregnancy: continence.

1612.   Williams, Doone, and Greer Williams. Every Child a Wanted
         Child: Clarence James Gamble, M.D., and His Work in the Birth
         Control Movement. Boston: Francis A. Countway Library of
         Medicine, 1978.

         Tells of Dr. Gamble's sincere belief in Christian giving and
         relates how he gave money to the cause of birth control.

1613.   Williams, Elisa, et al. "Adoption Vs. Abortion: Some Pro-
         Choice Forces Embrace a New Option." Newsweek 28 Apr. 1986:
         39.

         Pro-life and pro-choice forces agree that there is a need to
         better inform pregnant women about the option of putting
         unwanted babies up for adoption.

1614.   Williams, Mary Kay. Abortion: A Collision of Rights. n.p.:
         NC News Publ., 1972.

         Draws on the evidence from medical science, law, and other
         disciplines in confronting pro-abortion arguments. Written
         in popular style.

1615.   Williams, Roger M. "The Power of Fetal Politics." Saturday
         Review 9 June 1979: 12-15.

Claims that the anti-abortion movement is a cause that refuses to yield and that opposition to abortion has become implacable, and perhaps the nastiest public-issue campaign in at least a half century.

1616. Willis, Judith. "Comparing Contraceptives." FDA Consumer May 1985: 28-35.

Discusses pros and cons of various types of contraceptives and provides comparative charts.

1617. Willke, J. C. Abortion: Questions and Answers. Rev. ed. Cincinnati: Hayes, 1988.

Using a question-and-answer format, covers the right-to-life movement.

1618. Willke, Jack C. Handbook on Abortion. Rev. ed. Cincinnati: Hayes, 1979.

Condensation of the world's scientific literature pertaining to the unborn.

1619. _____. How to Teach the Pro-Life Story. Cincinnati: Hayes, 1973.

Reviews the methodology, rationale, techniques, action programs, and materials which help teach the pro-life story.

1620. _____. Slavery and Abortion: History Repeats. Cincinnati: Hayes, 1984.

Willke's views on the quality of life as it relates to the poor, blacks, and the oppressed and their roles in the abortion issue.

1621. Willke, Jack C., and Karen Mulhouser. "Abortion: Pro and Con." Encyclopedia Americana/CBS News Audio Resource Library, 1981.

Interviews with Dr. Jack C. Willke, president of the National Right-to-Life Committee (NRLC), and Karen Mulhouser, president of the National Abortion Rights League (NARL).

1622. Willke, John C., and Mrs. John C. Willke. "Abortion Is Killing." Columbia Apr. 1973: 10-19.

Concludes that proponents of abortion can try to tell women that what is growing inside them is only a fetus, when in reality it is human life.

1623. Willke, John C., and Nanette Falkenberg.   "Should Abortion
       Be Legal?" _Seventeen_ Jan. 1986: 86+.

       Two contrasting views on abortion: one, pro-life; the other,
       pro-choice.

1624. Willoughby, William F.   "Catholic Bishops: Abortion the
       Issue." _Christianity Today_ 19 Dec. 1975: 35.

       Two hundred Catholic bishops declare an all-out war against
       permissive abortion.

1625. Wills, Garry.   "'Save the Babies': Operation Rescue." _Time_
       1 May 1989: 26-28.

       Operation Rescue, a case study in galvanizing the anti-
       abortion movement.

1626. Wilson, Robert R., ed. _Problem Pregnancy and Abortion Counsel-
       ing._ Saluda: Family Life, 1973.

       Meant to help counselors of women to impart guidance on abor-
       tion practices.

1627. Winter, Eugenia B. _Psychological and Medical Aspects of
       Induced Abortion: A Selective Annotated Bibliography, 1970-
       1986._ Bibliographies and Indexes in Women's Studies 7.
       New York: Greenwood, 1988.

       An annotated list of 500 books, periodical articles, and
       audiovisuals on the psychological and medical aspects of
       abortion.

1628. "The Wire Next Time?" _Progressive_ Sept. 1985: 9-10.

       Takes issue with President Reagan's request to the U.S.
       Supreme Court to reverse _Roe_ v. _Wade_, categorizing it as an
       utterly cynical and hypocritical maneuver.

1629. Wissler, Steven Paul.   "Church-Based Clinic Gives Contracep-
       tives to Teens." _Christianity Today_ 20 Feb. 1987: 50+.

       Claims that the action of the Fairlington United Methodist
       Church-based clinic is a meaningful, Christian outreach to
       kids.

1630. Withers, Kay. "Pope John Paul I and Birth Control." _America_
       24 Mar. 1979: 233-34.

Documents and the testimony of close friends and aides
of the late Pope John Paul I reveal that he disagreed with
the traditional church teaching on birth control.

1631. Witherspoon, Joseph Parker. "Impact of the Abortion Decisions
upon the Father's Role." Jurist 35 (1975): 32-65.

Discusses federal and state decisions in regard to the father's
role in an abortion.

1632. Wogaman, J. Philip, ed. The Population Crisis and Moral
Responsibility. Washington: Public Affairs, 1973.

Original essays by leading ethicists, theologians, and population experts seeking to clarify fundamental problems posed by
the present rapid growth rate of the world population.

1633. Wohl, Lisa Cronin. "Antiabortion Violence on the Rise." Ms.
Oct. 1984: 135-40.

Reports on selected incidences of anti-abortion violence,
chiefly at clinic locations throughout the United States and
emphasizes that physical harm to innocent people is wrong.

1634. Wolfe, Ronald. "The Abortion Question and the Evangelical
Tradition." Dimension 5 (Summer 1973): 84-89.

Discusses abortion as a moral and religious issue.

1635. Womran, Abdel R., ed. Liberalization of Abortion Laws:
Implications. Chapel Hill: Carolina Population Center,
U of North Carolina, 1976.

A collection of essays outlining what is presently known
and what might be expected under varying degrees of liberalized abortion.

1636. Woodward, Kenneth L. "Birth-Control Factor." Newsweek
5 Apr. 1976: 57.

Father Andrew Greeley and his colleagues at the National
Opinion Research Center (NORC) claim that many Catholics
reject the church's encyclical Humanae Vitae.

1637. _____. "Politics and Abortion." Newsweek 20 Aug.
1984: 66-67.

Family issues play a role in the race for the White House.

1638.   Woodward, Kenneth L., with Alden Cohen. "Abortion and the
        Churches." Newsweek 24 July 1989: 45-46.

        Describes how some Protestants wrestle with their consciences
        regarding abortion.

1639.   Woodward, Kenneth L., and Mark D. Uehling. "The Hardest
        Question." Newsweek 14 Jan. 1985: 29.

        Abortion remains an intractable issue because it is not just
        a conflict between ethical theories or choices, but is pri-
        marily a clash between radically different understandings
        of the self and of the world, shaped by divergent social and
        economic expectations.

1640.   Woodworth, Karen Lohela. "It Takes Two--A Planned Parenthood
        Focus on Teen-Age Boys." Ms. Dec. 1979: 35.

        Highlights a series of advertisements (posters) and radio and
        television spot announcements directed at teenage boys, rather
        than girls.

1641.   Worden, Portia. "Current Opinion on Abortion." PTA Magazine
        May 1972: 12-14.

        Concludes that abortion in America is becoming more widely
        practiced each year. Will our society one day accept it as
        easily as it now accepts divorce? Certainly, much further
        research, much additional debate, will have to take place
        before that decision can be made.

1642.   Wright, John H. "The Birth Control Controversy, Continued."
        America 22 Aug. 1981: 66-68.

        Attempts a move toward healing the division in the Catholic
        church on the subject of contraception by suggesting that we
        understand Pope Paul VI's teaching in Humanae Vitae as an
        obligatory ideal.

1643.   _____. "An End to the Birth Control Controversy."
        America 7 Mar. 1981: 175-78.

        Many Catholic couples are still uneasy both with Pope Paul's
        Humanae Vitae and the many interpretations that seem to
        compromise the church's teaching authority.

1644.   Wroblewski, Sergius. "John Paul II and Humanae Vitae."
        Homiletic and Pastoral Review Oct. 1984: 52-55.

        Pope John Paul II offers a philosophical and Christian frame-

work for an understanding of the Catholic church's ban on
artificial birth control.

1645.   Wylie, Pete. "U.S. Supreme Court Prepares to Hear Right-to-
        Life and Religious Freedom Cases." Christianity Today
        4 Oct. 1985: 64+.

        Reviews the fall 1985 case docket of the U.S. Supreme Court,
        in which, in at least four cases, the justices will reexamine
        the rights of handicapped newborns and the unborn.

1646.   Yarbrough, Tinsley E.   "The Abortion-Funding Issue: A Study in
        Mixed Constitutional Cues."   North Carolina Law Review Mar.
        1981: 611-27.

        Examines the McRae case and related abortion-
        funding decisions in the light of relevant earlier cases.

1647.   Young, Alma T., Barbara Berkman, and Helen Rehr.   "Women Who
        Seek Abortions: A Study."   Social Work May 1973: 60-65.

        A study conducted by social workers at Mount Sinai Medical
        Center to determine which abortion patients needed intensive
        counseling by social workers.

1648.   Young, Curt.   The Least of These: What Everyone Should Know
        About Abortion. Chicago: Moody, 1983.

        Aims to help Christians realize the scope of the abortion
        problem and understand how it can be resolved through the
        efforts of ordinary people.

1649.   Zabin, Laurie, and Leo Maher.   "Birth-Control Clinics in
        Schools?" U.S. News and World Report 29 Sept. 1986: 82.

        Pro and con arguments on birth control clinics in schools.

1650.   Zabin, Laurie S., and Samuel D. Clark, Jr.   "Why They Delay:
        A Study of Teenage Family Planning Clinic Patients." Family
        Planning Perspectives Sept.-Oct. 1981: 205+.

        Fear that their parents will find out is a major reason most
        teens delay the visit to a family-planning clinic until a year
        or more after starting intercourse.

1651.   Zagano, Phyllis. "The Church and Abortion, Perception and
        Reality." Commonweal 23 Mar. 1984: 173-75.

        Discusses an anti-abortion strategy being considered by
        Catholic bishops and selected members of Congress.

1652. Zahn, Gordon C. "Casting a Vote for Life." *America* 24 Nov. 1984: 337-39.

The debate during the recent election showed that single-issue voting has its place in American democracy.

1653. Zaphiris, Chrysostom. "The Morality of Contraception: An Eastern Orthodox Opinion." *Journal of Ecumenical Studies* 11 (1974): 677-90.

Discusses the morality of contraception, emphasizing four basic points: the purpose of marriage as viewed scripturally and patristically; the official teachings of the Orthodoxy concerning contraception; the moral issue from an Orthodox perspective; and "the Orthodox notion of synergism and its implications for the moral question of contraception."

1654. Zelnik, Melvin, and John F. Kantner. "Attitudes of American Teenagers Toward Abortion." *Family Planning Perspectives* Mar.-Apr. 1975: 89-91.

Teenagers are reported to be more conservative in their attitudes towards abortion than adults; however, the never married, sexually experienced, and older teenagers show greatest approvals of abortion.

1655. _____. "Contraceptive Patterns and Pregnancy Among Women Aged 15-19 in 1976." *Family Planning Perspectives* May-June 1978: 135-44.

Premaritally sexually active teenagers are classified by contraceptive-use status as "always-users," "never-users," or "sometimes-users" of contraception.

1656. _____. "Sexual Activity, Contraceptive Use and Pregnancy Among Metropolitan-Area Teenagers: 1971-1979." *Family Planning Perspectives* Sept.-Oct. 1980: 230-37.

Reports that although more teens are practicing contraception and doing so earlier and consistently, pre-marital pregnancies continue to rise, partly because contraceptors are using ineffective methods.

1657. Zimmerman, Mary K. *Passage Through Abortion: The Personal and Social Reality of Women's Experiences*. Praeger Special Studies in U.S. Economic, Social, and Political Issues. New York: Praeger, 1977.

Holds that abortion is a personal, subjective experience and decision.

242

1658.   _____. "Passage Through Abortion: A Sociological
          Analysis." Diss. U of Minnesota, 1976.

          Examines the experience of having an abortion in contemporary
          American society.

1659.   Zintl, Robert T. "New Heat over an Old Issue: Renewing the
          Abortion Fight." Time 4 Feb. 1985: 17.

          Renewing the abortion fight, thousands of demonstrators gather
          on the Ellipse south of the White House on the twelfth anni-
          versary of Roe v. Wade.

1660.   Zuckerman, Ruth Jane. Abortion and the Constitutional Rights
          of Minors. New York: ACLU, 1973.

          Contends that a state-imposed requirement of parental consent
          for an abortion is unconstitutional.

SUBJECT INDEX

References are to item numbers, not to page numbers.

Abortion (general), 3, 4, 10, 42, 43, 46, 49, 55, 83, 131, 147, 153, 182, 190, 205, 208, 224, 234, 239, 282, 300, 303, 309, 314, 334, 381, 396, 403, 415, 418, 419, 420, 441, 447, 453, 455, 480, 497, 514, 544, 549, 597, 617, 639, 647, 651, 664, 693, 716, 734, 762, 785, 797, 803, 816, 823, 831, 834, 835, 838, 846, 858, 860, 869, 881, 883, 896, 904, 923, 926, 946, 950, 960, 964, 987, 988, 991, 997, 1007, 1068, 1069, 1124, 1186, 1188, 1194, 1196, 1197, 1212, 1254, 1259, 1268, 1280, 1281, 1291, 1312, 1317, 1323, 1327, 1331, 1332, 1340, 1346, 1357, 1367, 1404, 1405, 1409, 1418, 1434, 1446, 1453, 1492, 1496, 1497, 1500, 1510, 1542, 1556, 1563, 1564, 1585, 1592, 1605, 1610, 1618, 1620, 1626, 1635, 1641; California, 944; Canada, 1397; Europe, 574; Great Britain, 574, 575, 835, 1392; Pennsylvania, 19, 176, 485, 621, 974, 1006, 1094, 1183, 1184, 1225; United States, 69, 75, 96, 211, 218, 236, 250, 265, 321, 383, 386, 413, 497, 498, 518, 535, 574, 575, 610, 631, 690, 704, 713, 757, 771, 773, 777, 786, 828, 830, 939, 943, 965, 986, 1027, 1087, 1088, 1119, 1145, 1164, 1177, 1192, 1239, 1244, 1248, 1267, 1276, 1293, 1335, 1336, 1337, 1356, 1375, 1401, 1463, 1477, 1544, 1550, 1557, 1604, 1648, 1657; Washington (state), 1249
-addresses, essays, lectures (general), 314, 726, 1149, 1322; Canada, 1322; United States, 532, 725, 1156, 1322
-bibliographies, 1077, 1264, 1627
-biographies: United States, 1437, 1657

-canon law, 276, 349, 408, 672, 1236, 1439, 1554, 1569, 1624
-case studies (general: developing countries, 778; Minnesota, 464; United States, 120, 122, 192, 273, 284, 435, 439, 543, 573, 629, 660, 661, 682, 687, 711, 756, 798, 836, 969, 1020, 1042, 1081, 1103, 1398, 1400, 1563, 1625
-congresses (general), 1092; government policy, 1443; United States, 1092, 1152, 1372
-criminal procedure, 576, 875, 984
-handbooks, manuals, etc. (general), 74, 351, 461, 475, 487, 1618; cross-cultural studies, 475, 1321; government policy, 1321
-history, 206, 574, 1155, 1211, 1297, 1387; New York (city): 19th century, 825
-law and legislation (general), 14, 118, 159, 178, 460, 509, 681, 744, 781, 795, 856, 1048, 1107, 1146, 1178, 1181, 1182, 1223, 1224, 1234, 1241, 1302, 1347, 1419, 1428, 1462, 1468, 1485, 1509, 1530, 1533, 1549, 1579, 1598, 1601, 1631, 1646; addresses, essays, lectures, 540, 726, 1571; Catholic church, 345, 444, 626, 745, 1153; Colorado, 323, 324; congresses: United States, 1372, 1440, 1443; Europe, 632; Florida, 507, 1435; France, 40; Georgia, 788, 1471; Germany, 965; handbooks, manuals, etc., 1321; Hawaii,

1466; history: United States, 25, 34, 70, 1061, 1488; Illinois, 1472; Italy, 685; Massachusetts, 882, 1115, 1341; Michigan, 845; Missouri, 204, 318, 339, 442, 463, 653, 655, 656, 657; Montana, 352; New Hampshire, 1395; New Jersey, 776; New York (state), 27, 114, 177, 732, 919, 920, 1052, 1368; Pennsylvania, 19, 621; Texas, 8, 516, 788, 1471; United States, 8, 12, 116, 149, 221, 232, 278, 317, 320, 321, 391, 393, 497, 506, 510, 527, 535, 574, 583, 599, 606, 607, 611, 632, 640, 672, 678, 704, 723, 743, 749, 750, 751, 779, 872, 875, 876, 890, 891, 905, 918, 965, 1004, 1005, 1039, 1045, 1046, 1088, 1119, 1154, 1244, 1267, 1293, 1311, 1329, 1337, 1339, 1386, 1438, 1456, 1467, 1526, 1573, 1648, 1660; Utah, 612, 1128, 1483; Vermont, 1148
-legal procedures, 362, 695, 875, 903, 1542
-legal trends (general), 231, 283, 398, 494, 523, 574, 589, 599, 1209, 1385, 1499, 1537; Great Britian, 575; United States, 139, 140, 214, 404, 575, 667, 780, 820, 1271, 1287, 1300, 1325, 1374
-moral and ethical aspects (general), 13, 95, 108, 118, 119, 137, 141, 156, 189, 202, 213, 218, 383, 394, 417, 446, 454, 530, 533, 535, 550, 552, 581, 583, 590, 599, 616, 643, 650, 671, 680, 692, 696, 701, 704, 727, 734, 752, 761, 767, 770, 773, 818, 824, 826, 835, 855, 879, 899, 908, 909, 951, 957,

962, 996, 1033, 1100,
1110, 1113, 1121, 1143,
1145, 1199, 1204, 1217,
1220, 1237, 1244, 1260,
1306, 1379, 1390, 1391,
1406, 1413, 1464, 1477,
1481, 1486, 1503, 1507,
1540, 1541, 1559, 1566,
1578, 1589, 1609, 1615,
1622, 1648, 1652, 1654;
case studies, 284, 545,
546, 1011, 1037, 1042,
1071; Catholic church,
110, 371, 372, 603, 759,
922, 1050, 1130, 1140,
1580; congresses, 832,
1443; United States, 33,
58, 84, 101, 107, 115,
143, 209, 230, 261, 313,
599, 686, 763, 851, 990,
1043, 1049, 1099, 1144,
1150, 1187, 1189, 1293,
1502, 1634
-political aspects
(general), 41, 57, 99,
117, 196, 244, 257, 259,
260, 277, 302, 400, 457,
645, 654, 677, 841, 862,
921, 946, 947, 977,
1010, 1030, 1188, 1201,
1202, 1256, 1257, 1388,
1396, 1480, 1561, 1580;
Catholic church, 728;
congresses, 941; Mass-
achusetts, 301; United
States, 72, 73, 99, 161,
172, 174, 184, 388, 390,
515, 619, 696, 703, 705,
801, 868, 943, 1019,
1035, 1164, 1286, 1479,
1637
-psychological aspects
(general), 52, 131, 183,
375, 412, 424, 440, 777,
784, 949, 1058, 1167,
1177, 1180, 1203, 1214,
1288, 1320, 1361, 1411,
1414, 1458, 1515, 1535;
addresses, essays,
lectures, 1156; biblio-
graphy, 1627; case
studies, 573, 1036,
1055, 1127, 1384, 1421,

1513; congresses, 963;
United States, 771, 854,
1039, 1044, 1248, 1259,
1406
-public opinion (general),
39, 322, 327, 433, 434, 462,
577, 634, 658, 683, 702,
730, 733, 853, 912, 973,
1132, 1417, 1508; United
States, 311, 801, 965, 1322
-religious aspects (general),
6, 50, 96, 181, 217, 233,
303, 354, 393, 395, 567,
602, 671, 713, 718, 1013,
1047, 1112, 1126, 1142,
1190, 1192, 1239, 1244,
1313, 1352, 1355, 1382,
1403, 1463, 1550, 1587,
1634, 1638, 1651; addresses,
essays, lectures, 596, 844;
case studies (general), 308;
Catholic church, 60, 233,
266, 275, 278, 289, 290,
335, 343, 452, 535. 722,
770, 801, 939, 948, 953,
967, 968, 994, 1014, 1087,
1176, 1205, 1228, 1263,
1275, 1279, 1416, 1567;
Christianity, 11, 106,
120, 127, 128, 137, 216,
218, 383, 387, 449, 470,
472, 478, 518, 562, 563,
609, 648, 696, 830, 859,
1038, 1044, 1212, 1437,
1474, 1585, 1589, 1602,
1648; congresses, 1092;
history, 54, 458, 766;
Judaism, 160, 252, 578,
648, 1263; Protestant
churches, 582, 961
-social aspects (general),
5, 36, 37, 51, 63, 66, 67,
98, 104, 109, 144, 185,
248, 251, 254, 285, 293,
346, 415, 423, 430, 479,
598, 605, 618, 624, 643,
715, 731, 774, 871, 897,
982, 998, 1028, 1046,
1085, 1240, 1308, 1490,
1536, 1639, 1658; case
studies, 307, 1421; United
States, 340, 511, 1495
-statistics: United States,

709, 712, 937
Abortion clinics, 17, 18,
  325, 471, 570, 588, 867,
  878, 954, 955, 1105,
  1253, 1258, 1521, 1555
Abortion counseling (gen-
  eral), 792, 794, 804,
  907, 966; case studies,
  193, 625, 807, 1089,
  1410, 1513, 1647; United
  States, 5, 18, 124, 191,
  226, 329, 382, 411, 572,
  628, 967, 1029, 1039,
  1044, 1076, 1083, 1108,
  1162, 1259, 1289, 1319,
  1410, 1626
Abortion funding, 26,
  467, 529, 537, 553, 594,
  600, 710, 735, 911, 1523,
  1532
Abortion services: direct-
  ories, 461; Illinois, 821;
  United States, 708, 1090,
  1294, 1444, 1466

Bernardin, Joseph Cardinal,
  397
Birth control (general),
  85, 133, 146, 150, 167,
  200, 294, 295, 410, 419,
  477, 525, 549, 555, 670,
  679, 684, 697, 758, 928,
  979, 1002, 1003, 1072,
  1109, 1125, 1129, 1138,
  1179, 1188, 1200, 1245,
  1296, 1301, 1304, 1348,
  1378, 1420, 1501, 1522,
  1542, 1582, 1606, 1608,
  1611, 1632, 1636; Cali-
  fornia, 944; developing
  countries, 68, 356, 410,
  717, 1303, 1475; Europe,
  1159; Great Britain, 575;
  New York (city), 1026;
  United States, 136, 150,
  565, 575, 822, 839, 916,
  924, 927, 1003, 1192,
  1195, 1334, 1363, 1505,
  1544, 1553, 1585, 1597,
  1607
-addresses, essays, lec-
  tures (general), 528,
  993, 1008, 1198, 1208;

United States, 547
-bibliographies, 1370, 1449;
  United States, 385
-case studies: developing
  countries, 356, 358;
  United States, 188, 755,
  817
-government policy, 536,
  1460
-handbooks, manuals, etc.,
  1129
-history (general), 574, 1200,
  1612; bibliography, 1066;
  England, 1415; France, 1018;
  United States, 468, 646,
  1252
-law and legislation: United
  States, 1506, 1581; history,
  427
-moral and religious aspects,
  15, 294, 765, 1583, 1632
-political aspects: United
  States, 1366
-psychological aspects, 68
-public opinion, 742
-religious aspects, 272, 294;
  Catholic church, 414, 582,
  1591, 1594, 1595, 1630,
  1643, 1644; Christianity,
  1078; history of doctrines,
  1123
-research, 166, 742
-violence, 138
Birth control clinics: United
  States, 164, 165, 631, 1170,
  1221, 1520, 1543, 1560,
  1629, 1633, 1649
Birthright (organization),
  1369, 1463
Blackmun, Harry Andrew, 47,
  585, 970, 1097
Bradlaugh, Charles, 294
Bradlaugh-Besant trial, 294
Burger, Justice Warren, 225,
  1233
Bush, Pres. George, 130, 469,
  1309, 1310

Catholic church doctrines,
  493, 535, 819, 967, 1012,
  1022, 1078, 1158
Catholic Hospital Associ-
  ation (CHA), 292

Catholic League for
 Religious and Civil
 Rights (CCRCR), 286
Catholic Peace Fellow-
 ship (CPF), 287
Catholics for a Free
 Choice (CFC), 433,
 443
Cheaney v. State of
 Indiana, 1017
Children's rights:
 United States, 1463
Christian Action Council
 (CAC), 93
Christian ethics, 508,
 951
Church and social prob-
 lems: Catholic church,
 493, 819; United States,
 819
City of Akron v. Akron
 Center for Reproductive
 Health, Inc., 559, 584,
 764, 783, 1101, 1134,
 1213
Commonwealth of Massach-
 usetts v. Pierre Victor
 Brunelle, 1074
Constitutional law:
 United States, 450, 698,
 699, 751, 929, 930, 940,
 1251
Contraception (general),
 43, 75, 145, 195, 227,
 405, 436, 549, 668, 758,
 837, 852, 877, 932, 980,
 1160, 1173, 1197, 1210,
 1312, 1353, 1362, 1364,
 1377, 1450, 1495, 1500,
 1538, 1596, 1616, 1626,
 1653; developing coun-
 tries, 68; United
 States, 241, 810, 813,
 1064, 1294
-bibliography, 1449
-case studies, 112, 194,
 341, 700, 1051, 1231,
 1283
-congresses, 743
-history (general), 78,
 668, 917, 1408; United
 States, 534, 1252
-moral and ethical as-

pects, 199, 852, 1642,
 1653; Catholic church,
 342, 691
-psychological aspects, 944
-religious aspects: Catholic
 church, 557, 989, 1227,
 1238, 1316; history of
 doctrines, 1123
-research, 436, 561, 587,
 669, 738, 1165, 1318,
 1655, 1656; history,
 378, 1612
Contraceptives, 148, 201,
 305, 384, 437, 465, 487,
 541, 554, 564, 641, 787,
 789, 812, 861
Cooke, Terence Cardinal,
 27, 114, 170
Cuomo, Gov. Mario M., 255
 368, 369, 370, 649, 1478,
 1599

Diamond v. Charles, 445
Doe, Mary: trials, litiga-
 tions, etc., 788
Doe v. Bolton, 210, 240,
 663, 864, 865, 999, 1015,
 1407, 1479
Doe v. Brighton Hospital
 Association, 1015
Dooling, John Francis, Jr., 9
Dred Scott case, 392, 1117

East Medical Group (White
 Plains, New York), 757
Edelin, Kenneth Carlton, 31,
 152, 306, 361, 363, 364,
 365, 482, 483, 484, 914,
 1080, 1115, 1137, 1354,
 1358
Equal Rights Amendment
 (ERA), 123, 489, 796,
 934, 983
Ethics, 154, 157, 644,
 880, 1062, 1098, 1565,
 1632
Euthanasia, religious as-
 pects of: Christianity,
 106, 915

Family planning (general),
 2, 76, 151, 158, 198,
 212, 223, 270, 291, 428,

520, 521, 580, 615, 668,
729, 753, 799, 938, 945,
1009, 1025, 1160, 1448,
1543, 1575, 1650, 1654,
1655, 1656; developing
countries, 560, 754,
1516; United States,
469, 526, 538, 539, 773,
811, 1191
-bibliography, 1371
-handbooks, manuals,
etc., 1125, 1465
-history: France, 1018;
United States: ab-
stracts, 1066
Family planning amend-
ments: of 1986, 1527; of
1987, 1534
Feminism, religious as-
pects of: Christianity,
563; United States, 505,
601, 1095
Ferraro, Geraldine, 288,
952
Fertility, human, 669

Gamble, Clarence James,
1612
Genocide, 359, 1584

Harris v. McRae, 357,
613, 1646
Hatch Amendment, 219, 297
Hellegers, Dr. Andre, 706
Helms-Hyde Bill (Human
Life Statute), 548
Human life amendments,
132, 134, 187, 267, 268,
274, 328, 377, 421, 431,
496, 627, 737, 746, 747,
902, 1106, 1116, 1120,
1147, 1269, 1285, 1517,
1531, 1572
Human Life Bill, 769,
863, 1118, 1314, 1518,
1529
Human reproduction: law
and legislation (United
States), 315; research,
669
Humanae Vitae (papal
encyclical), 20, 163,
245, 291, 373, 473, 492,

676, 719, 843, 847, 1000,
1001, 1053, 1133, 1163,
1166, 1235, 1273, 1274,
1376, 1402, 1422, 1433,
1539, 1636, 1642
Hyde Amendment, 7, 45, 316,
357, 460, 486, 768, 840,
1104, 1511

International Planned Parenthood Federation (IPPF):
history, 416, 736

John Paul I, Pope, 1630
John Paul II, Pope, 280,
994, 1157

Kemp-Hatch Bill, 80
Krol, John Cardinal, 485

Law and ethics, 672

McCormick, Katherine Dexter
(Mrs. Stanley), 384
McCorvey, Norma, 1295
McKinnon, Edna Rankin, 477
McLeod, Mary Alice, 1020
McRae v. Califano, 438,
481
Madeiros, Humberto Cardinal,
301
Malthusian League, 900, 901
Massachusetts v. Edelin, 59,
77, 1547
Medicaid: funding of, 56, 62,
91, 566, 1470
Medicaid v. Health
Insurance Coverage, 24
Meese, Edwin, 1438
Morreale case, 126

Nathanson, Bernard N., 850,
1088, 1261
National Abortion Rights
League (NARL), 652, 1436,
1489, 1621
National Association for
Christian Political Action
(NACPA), 1082
National Opinion Research
Center (NORC), 1326,
1636
National Organization for

Women (NOW), 113, 958, 1338
National Research Council (NRC), 169
National Right-to-Life Committee (NRLC), 92, 652, 1471, 1621
Natural family planning, 344, 379, 429, 474, 502, 503, 593, 595, 694, 724, 741, 806, 842, 848, 942, 975, 981, 1023, 1024, 1070, 1093, 1111, 1169, 1215, 1380, 1381
Nixon, Pres. Richard M., 27, 775
NOW. See National Organization for Women

O'Connor, John J. Cardinal, 649, 849, 868
Operation Rescue, 337, 517, 898, 1086, 1461, 1625

Papal encyclical. See Humanae Vitae
Paul VI, Pope, 414
Pennsylvania: Abortion Control Act, 19, 621
Pincus, Gregory Goodwin, 384
Planned Parenthood Association of Nashville, 100
Planned Parenthood Association v. Ashcroft, 559
Planned Parenthood Federation of America (PPFA), 102, 805, 809, 814, 1206, 1350, 1351, 1494, 1512, 1576, 1640
Planned Parenthood Foundation (PPF), 495, 1524
Planned Parenthood v. Danforth, 442
Plessy v. Ferguson, 256
Pro-choice movement (general), 15, 181, 222, 263, 490, 636, 720, 885, 886, 1007, 1054, 1266, 1326, 1328, 1333, 1429, 1441, 1442, 1519, 1520, 1546, 1552, 1603, 1613,
1614, 1623; New Jersey, 1276; United States, 38, 121, 235, 246, 250, 299, 360, 451, 501, 620, 622, 662, 696, 793, 873, 933, 1014, 1031, 1041, 1216, 1229, 1276, 1476, 1482
-case studies: United States, 355, 629
Pro-Life Act of 1988, 1246
Pro-Life Action League (PLAL), 65
Pro-Life Incorporated (New York), 242
Pro-life movement (general), 15, 17, 86, 87, 129, 171, 181, 336, 504, 508, 512, 519, 531, 568, 569, 571, 588, 604, 614, 659, 671, 740, 815, 935, 936, 972, 1007, 1054, 1059, 1060, 1065, 1078, 1175, 1222, 1226, 1230, 1278, 1290, 1326, 1342, 1348, 1349, 1373, 1383, 1393, 1397, 1427, 1429, 1430, 1431, 1491, 1545, 1546, 1551, 1568, 1588, 1593, 1613, 1619, 1623; Chicago, 81; New York: (state), 1423; United States, 16, 64, 79, 218, 228, 246, 250, 258, 299, 326, 333, 350, 387, 522, 601, 620, 631, 662, 689, 714, 721, 819, 859, 866, 888, 889, 893, 894, 895, 913, 925, 933, 943, 968, 995, 1032, 1034, 1040, 1057, 1087, 1091, 1141, 1145, 1164, 1185, 1232, 1435, 1455, 1602, 1648
-case studies: United States, 355, 629
Public opinion: United States, 90, 97, 801, 965, 1063, 1365, 1399, 1457

Rehnquist, Justice William H., 1424
Religious Coalition for Abortion Rights (RCAR), 1454

250

Religious ethics, 1474
Respect for life, 338,
  790, 1073, 1131, 1247,
  1262
Restell, Madame, 215,
  825
Right to life movement,
  1, 48, 53, 83, 105, 175,
  187, 264, 271, 353, 366,
  374, 407, 422, 459, 476,
  524, 635, 637, 707, 739,
  827, 833, 857, 892, 906,
  931, 1067, 1096, 1114,
  1136, 1152, 1218, 1219,
  1277, 1343, 1426, 1452,
  1462, 1487, 1559, 1562,
  1590, 1617, 1645
Right to Life Party, 1423
Roach, Archbp. John R.,
  170
Robin, Paul, 1018
Rockfeller, Gov. Nelson
  A., 27, 114, 919, 920
Roe, Jane: trials, liti-
  gations, etc., 527, 743,
  788, 1295
Roe v. Wade, 12, 21, 22,
  23, 29, 35, 44, 88, 89,
  180, 207, 210, 220, 225,
  237, 240, 243, 249, 256,
  262, 319, 330, 331, 367,
  392, 399, 401, 466, 585,
  591, 623, 630, 633, 663,
  748, 864, 865, 874, 959,
  976, 999, 1015, 1075,
  1079, 1117, 1122, 1171,
  1172, 1174, 1265, 1270,
  1272, 1315, 1324, 1344,
  1360, 1389, 1395, 1407,
  1412, 1425, 1445, 1447,
  1451, 1459, 1469, 1473,
  1479, 1517, 1548, 1558,
  1600, 1628, 1659
Roncallo Amendment, 32
Ryan, John Augustine, 468

Sacred Congregation for
  Religious and Secular
  Institutes (SCRSI), 432
Sanger, Margaret, 71, 94,
  135, 376, 384, 456, 468,
  608, 666, 791, 917, 971,
  1056, 1066, 1243, 1284,

1504, 1570; bibliography,
  1066
Sexual ethics, 82, 426
Simopoulos v. Virginia,
  559
Social ethics, 504, 508
Social movements, 380, 985
Social problems, 985; public
  opinion, 782
Stanford, Susan, 1437
Stanton, Elizabeth Cady, 673
Stevens, John Paul, 743
Stopes, Marie Charlotte
  Carmichael, 684

Teenage pregnancy, 296, 772,
  992; United States, 75,
  103, 186, 197, 253, 281,
  491, 513, 556, 800, 1003,
  1084, 1151, 1359, 1363,
  1498, 1586
Teenagers: sexual behavior
  of (United States), 111,
  162, 168, 179, 279, 389,
  409, 488, 542, 638, 808,
  1168, 1207, 1242, 1292,
  1298, 1350, 1484, 1525
Thornburgh v. American
  College of Obstetricians
  and Gynecologists, 445,
  1161
Timlin, Bp. James C., 142

Unborn children (general),
  155, 203, 247, 312, 406,
  674, 802; law, 238, 586,
  675, 1135, 1255; United
  States, 229, 425, 639, 1016,
  1526, 1528
United States: moral conditions, 96
United States v. Vuitch,
  887

Voluntary Family Limitation
  Act, 500

Wade, Henry: trials, liti-
  gations, etc., 527, 743
Wattleton, Faye, 28, 269,
  665, 1139, 1574, 1577
Webster v. Reproductive
  Health Services, 30, 89,

348, 402, 448, 490, 558,
642, 829, 884, 978,
1021, 1330, 1389, 1493,
1514
White, Justice Byron R.,
499, 743
Williams v. Zbaraz, 613
Women: United States,
551; history, 910;
social conditions, 910,
1307
Women's rights, 304, 671,
1305; history, 125, 673,
1299; United States, 61,
173, 310, 332, 347, 445,
551, 579, 592, 688, 760,
870, 956, 1102, 1193,
1250
Women's studies: ad-
dresses, essays, lec-
tures, 1282
Woodland Hills tragedy,
298

Youth: sexual behavior
of, 491, 924; addresses,
essays, lectures, 547

About the Compilers

RICHARD FITZSIMMONS is Director of the Library at the Penn State Worthington Scranton Campus. He is the author of the *Library Resources Book* and his writings have been published by the American Library Association, XEROX Educational Corporation, and the Scranton (PA) School District. He has been a presenter at the International Adult Literacy and Technology Conference and at conferences of the American Library Association. He is a past president of the Pennsylvania Library Association and has been elected a County Commissioner in Pennsylvania.

JOAN P. DIANA is Director of the Library at the Penn State Wilkes-Barre Campus. She is a former director of the School Library Media Division, Pennsylvania Department of Education. Her publications are included in the *Encyclopedia of Library and Information Science* and the Pennsylvania Historical and Museum Commission's *Legislative Biography Project*. In addition, she is a regular contributor to in-house and professional publications related to the library profession. She has been a presenter at and active on committees of the American Library Association and is a past president of the Pennsylvania Library Association.